EL CID

EL CID

The Life and Afterlife of a Medieval Mercenary

Nora Berend

PEGASUS BOOKS
NEW YORK LONDON

EL CID

Pegasus Books, Ltd.
148 West 37th Street, 12th Floor
New York, NY 10018

First Pegasus Books paperback edition July 2026
First Pegasus Books cloth edition edition January 2025

Library of Congress Cataloging-in-Publication Data is available.

Paperback ISBN: 979-8-89710-180-1
Hardcover ISBN: 978-1-63936-646-0

10 9 8 7 6 5 4 3 2 1

Printed in the United States of America
Distributed by Simon & Schuster
www.pegasusbooks.com

para mis hijas maravillosas

Contents

Al-Andalus and the Christian kingdoms from the eighth to the mid-thirteenth centuries

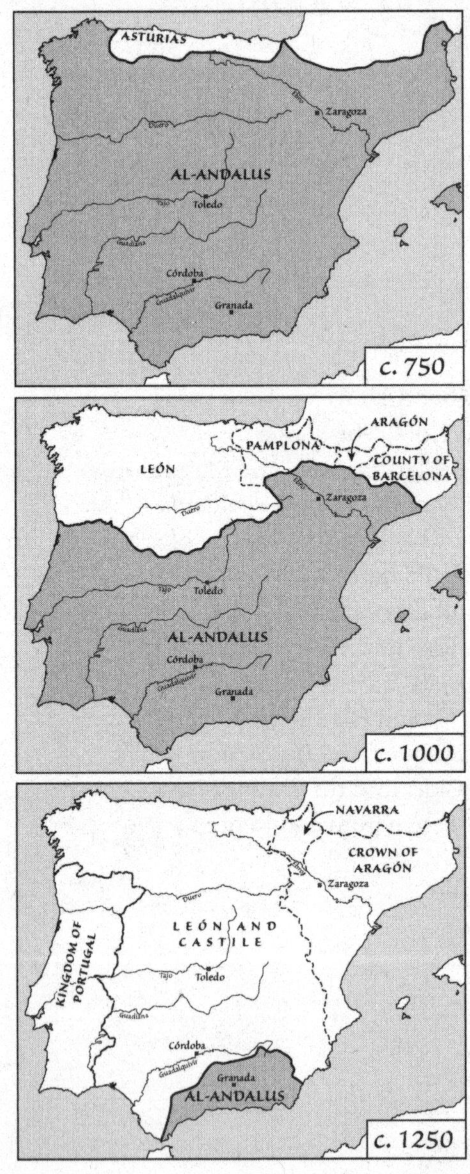

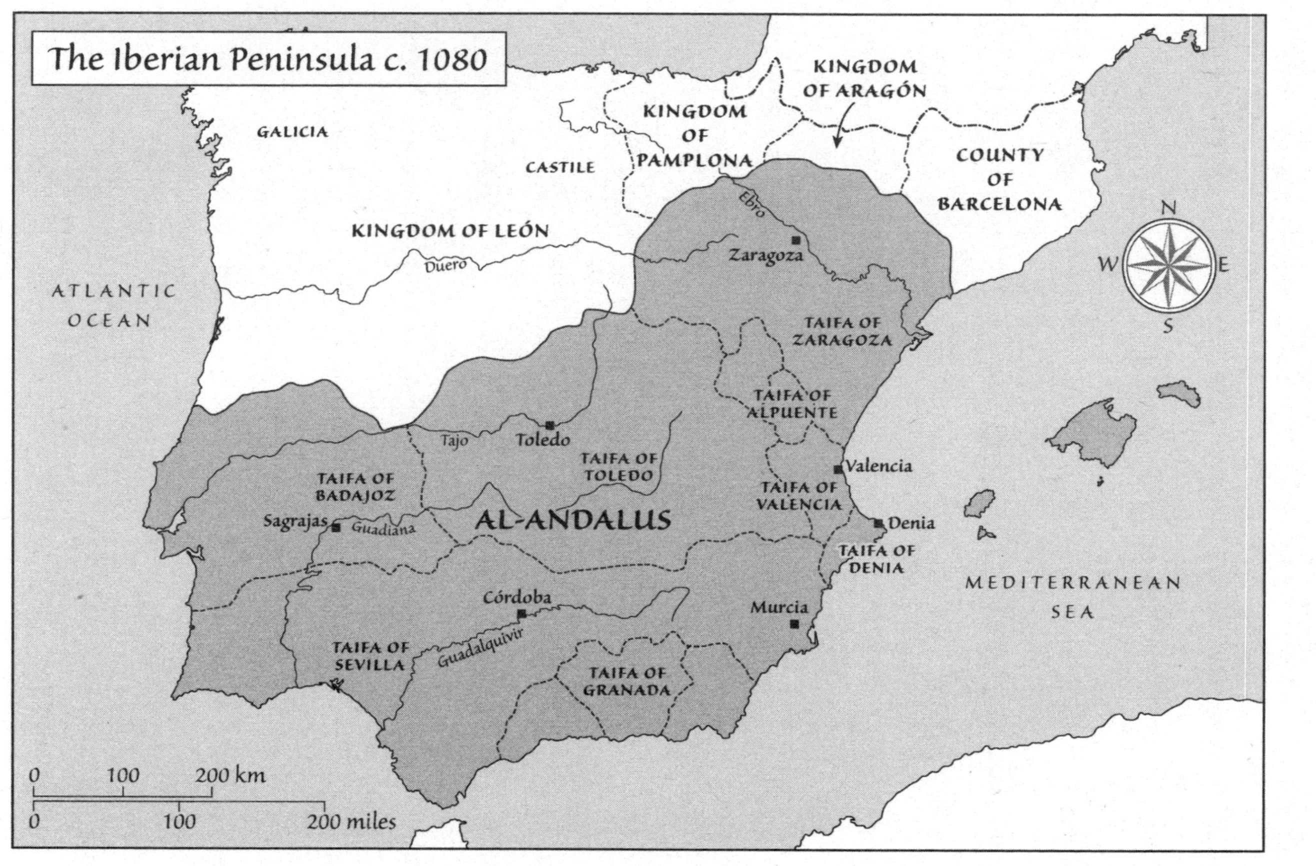
The Iberian Peninsula c. 1080
GALICIA
CASTILE
KINGDOM OF PAMPLONA
KINGDOM OF ARAGÓN
COUNTY OF BARCELONA
KINGDOM OF LEÓN
Duero
Ebro
Zaragoza
ATLANTIC OCEAN
N
W
E
S
TAIFA OF ZARAGOZA
TAIFA OF ALPUENTE
Tajo
Toledo
TAIFA OF TOLEDO
Valencia
TAIFA OF BADAJOZ
TAIFA OF VALENCIA
Sagrajas
Guadiana
AL-ANDALUS
Denia
TAIFA OF DENIA
MEDITERRANEAN SEA
Córdoba
Murcia
TAIFA OF SEVILLA
Guadalquivir
TAIFA OF GRANADA
0
100
200 km
0
100
200 miles

List of Illustrations

A Note on Names

During the medieval period itself, there was no consistency in the use of names across diverse sources. Over the following centuries, names were often changed further, and texts in different languages also used local forms of the same names. Therefore, the names of Rodrigo and Jimena, and even of Rodrigo's horse, occur in multiple variations in this book. I have kept the version of the name used in the sources that I cite.

Introduction: A Hero for All Seasons

A group of warriors on horseback rode swiftly north to Logroño, a town at the heart of the sparsely inhabited Rioja region in the northern part of the Iberian peninsula. They could cover a great distance without encountering any opposition. On reaching the town, they overpowered its defenders, who were no match for them, and they proceeded to pillage it. The warriors burned and looted, shedding blood as they swept through the streets and houses, destroying the town. They then devastated the rest of the region of La Rioja. These lands belonged to the Christian king Alfonso VI of Castile, who at the time (1092) was occupied waging war against the Muslims of Valencia. The army destroying King Alfonso's lands was commanded by one of the most successful mercenaries of the age, Rodrigo (or, in the parlance of the times, Ruy) Díaz, better known to posterity as el Cid. While raiding was a common occurrence, this particular raid elicited angry condemnation from a somewhat later chronicler, the author of the twelfth-century *Historia Roderici* (translated by Simon Barton and Richard Fletcher): 'Most savagely and mercilessly through all those regions did he lay waste with relentless, destructive, irreligious fire. He took huge booty, yet it was saddening even to tears. With harsh and impious devastation did he lay waste and destroy all the land aforesaid. He altogether stripped it of all its goods and wealth and riches, and took these for himself.'

What is remarkable is not that some condemned him, but that the memory of his military feats against Christians was quickly effaced and replaced by Christian adulation. Nobody could have predicted such an outcome when Rodrigo and his men ravaged La Rioja. From a modern perspective, one could easily characterize Rodrigo as a turncoat or traitor: he switched sides, from a Christian king to the Muslim ruler of Zaragoza. For he had once been in the service of the former: he had started his military career at the court of King Sancho II of Castile, where he was the head of the king's personal military retinue; after Sancho's death, he served the dead king's brother, King Alfonso VI of León-Castile. His ambition and independent actions led to clashes with the king and finally to exile. He was then employed as a mercenary by successive Muslim rulers of Zaragoza. In their service, he fought against Christian princes of the peninsula. It was during this period that he led his army of warriors, consisting of Christians and Muslims from the Iberian peninsula, against the king's lands. He took particular care to ravage those areas that were in the hands of the king's faithful vassal García Ordóñez, because of a long-standing enmity between the two men. From his successful campaign, Rodrigo returned to the Muslim court of Zaragoza, where he was welcomed and honoured. Yet six years later, shortly before Rodrigo died, a churchman had already described him as a warrior sent by God to fight against the Muslims, and over the next two centuries he was transformed into the perfect Christian knight, and a saintly figure, celebrated as a Christian hero fighting for the faith.

Rodrigo Díaz lived in the second half of the eleventh century, at a time when the Christians of the northern part of the Iberian peninsula began to make the first inroads against the south, Muslim al-Andalus. In the final years of his life, he struck out on his own and carved out an independent principality for himself deep in Muslim al-Andalus, which after his death quickly fell to the Muslims again and had to be evacuated. Already in these last years, his legend germinated. Cluniac monks (members of a reformed Benedictine monasticism), benefiting from Rodrigo's donations, started to transform their benefactor into a hero sent by divine providence. In subsequent centuries, the legend grew and the mythic hero el Cid – a sobriquet combining the Spanish definite article with a word derived from the Arabic *sayyid*, meaning 'lord', that he may or may not have borne in life – replaced the historical figure. The man Rodrigo died well over 900 years ago. El Cid, though many would gladly slay him, not only refuses to die but, similar to shape-shifters of ancient legend, takes new forms to satisfy the needs of every age.

How could a medieval mercenary become a hero for all seasons?

Celebrated or condemned for his brutal actions in his life, he was acknowledged as a very successful warrior leader, who could reward his followers with booty. Perhaps, had he not died without a male heir, his incipient principality of Valencia even would have become a kingdom. His military achievements were certainly remarkable, yet they do not explain his many transformations in legend. How could a man fighting indiscriminately against Muslims and Christians be depicted as a Christian saviour sent by God within his own lifetime? And how could he, whose insubordination to royal commands in life led to a complete break with the king, be posthumously transformed not merely into a devout Christian motivated by his religious beliefs, but also a steadfast vassal who fought for his lord the king? In the thirteenth century, an epic poem was written about his deeds, and the Cid of the poem was a superhero: never defeated in battle, he accomplished stupendous feats, yet remained loyal to his king despite having been unjustly exiled. Later in the same century, he became a quasi-saint thanks to the imagination of the monks of San Pedro de Cardeña: his dead body led the troops to victory over the Muslims, helped by a heavenly host, and his uncorrupted body even produced a miracle. Why would medieval monks venerate a brutal warrior?

Nor did his transformation stop there. A bid in the sixteenth century to have him officially recognized as a saint by the papacy failed, but he gained international literary recognition, becoming the protagonist of many pieces, notably a play by seventeenth-century French dramatist Pierre Corneille. Of all people, it was Rodrigo who was transformed into an almost Hamlet-like hero, agonizing over opposing moral commitments. Within Spain itself, the Cid was gaining the stature of a national hero, even as society became increasingly split, eventually leading to a civil war. How is it possible that a mild-mannered academic and a military dictator both found in the Cid a model and an inspiring example? Amid growing tensions in Spanish society in the early twentieth century, the historian Ramón Menéndez Pidal found in the Cid the hero who was to give hope to and unite Spaniards, an incarnation of Spain's special national character, whose example would mobilize the entire population. The Spanish military dictator Franco also saw him as the 'spirit of Spain' and himself as a modern-day Cid. He used his version of the Cid not just to divide, foisting his brand of Catholic Castilian supremacy on all, but to legitimize mass murder, waging what he saw as a crusade against Republicans. Emerging victorious from the civil war, Franco turned the Cid into an exemplar, part of compulsory education in schools and at the military academy. A statue of the Cid, sword drawn, beard flying, was erected in the Castilian city of Burgos. Projecting a legitimizing image to an international audience, the well-known film starring Charlton Heston was also produced in Franco's Spain.

It may seem logical that after this twentieth-century legacy the far right would carry on evoking the Cid in racist hate speech and hail him as their righteous precursor in the clash of civilizations. Yet it is much harder to explain why the very same legacy did not deter those who embrace multiculturalism from taking up the Cid as a representative of medieval Spanish *convivencia*, a leader who lived together with Muslims, an emblem of the peaceful coexistence of people of different faiths. The Cid became both a model for the far right and the symbol of multiculturalism. Children's books, including one by British author Geraldine McCaughrean, also retell the tale of the ideal knight. He is a hero to people from diverse backgrounds, who hold opposing values and ideologies; people from opposite ends of the political spectrum have lionized him. The 1961 movie *El Cid* appealed to Francoists, but also to President John F. Kennedy, who reportedly held multiple screenings of it in the White House.

This book will trace how an eleventh-century mercenary became a world-famous star. It will explore the apparent paradoxes in the story of a medieval warrior who came to be worshipped as a saint, the embodiment of virtues and patriotism, a moralist, and the very soul of the Spanish nation. When we peel away the legends of the greatest Spanish national hero and find a man who was a successful but opportunistic and brutal warrior, we must wonder how he could enjoy such a stupendous afterlife, how he can be a hero for people of all political persuasions.

Today, the Camino del Cid takes tourists to the supposed scenes of his exploits across Spain. Modelled on the famous pilgrimage route, the Camino del Santiago, this road of well over a thousand kilometres meanders to 365 places mentioned in the thirteenth-century epic poem about the Cid. We need to pursue a different, but no less meandering, route, if we seek to understand the Cid's real achievements and his afterlife. This road will take us through time, to the individuals and communities that created and fostered his cult. For legendary heroes do not emerge spontaneously: we need to understand the agency of those who created the hero from the man and continued to invest him with diverse meanings. People who participated in this process benefited in varied ways – from financial profit to gaining legitimacy – from the ascendence of the hero they helped make. As we follow this trail, we shall see how the historical figure was swathed in layers of legend; we shall encounter the many faces of el Cid; and discover who lionized him and why in the centuries after his death.

The source material on the Cid spans many centuries. While the greater the distance from Rodrigo's lifetime the less reliable narrative accounts become, none of them is fully trustworthy; all were composed for a reason, and that aim strongly determined how he would be portrayed. While none can be blindly followed to reconstruct the historical Rodrigo, all give valuable clues to how the Cid was constructed.

The story of el Cid is worthy of the pen of Tolkien, the stuff of legend and of men larger than life. There is thus a quiet irony in the fact that it is a woman who writes this account of the medieval superman; a successful military adventurer in life, and a paragon of supposed manly virtues in death. Women were largely written out of the Cid's life; present only as marginal characters, important only in so far as they were connected to him. Men composed his panegyric, men embraced his legend and marched in his name. Time, then, to redress the balance.

Why is this story still important in the twenty-first century? Through it, we can understand not merely significant aspects of Spain's history, but also the process of historical legend-making, from the Middle Ages to modern populist politics. These legends are much more pervasive in our lives than real historical knowledge, and have disproportionately influenced people, who often do not even realize how large the gap can be between history itself and the shifting, constantly changing legend that claims to be history. In the case of Rodrigo Díaz, when we scrape away the legends we find a man who lived in a period that cannot be encapsulated by easy judgements revolving around 'a clash of civilizations' or 'good' confronting 'bad'. We must understand the complexity of the times, when people fought against each other, then cooperated with their erstwhile enemies, to then turn against them once more; a period when people used arguments based on religion to justify warfare, but also ignored these arguments to just as easily wage war against co-religionists or ally with supposed religious foes. As with all good stories, moreover, that of the Cid's transformations makes us think about and question what it is that makes us human. What is it that appeals to us in military deeds, and why do we insist on transforming the most unsuitable individuals into heroes?

I

Blood and Gold: The Times

The historical Rodrigo can only be understood in the context of his own times. Cleansed of legends, the defining thread in his life was his military prowess. The precise nature of his abilities will be incomprehensible without reckoning with the era he lived in, a time of war and instability. Men won booty and land through warfare, but the fighting was opportunistic, and religious justifications of war between Christians and Muslims coexisted with pragmatic decisions that disregarded the religious divide. How did such a society come into being? At the time of Rodrigo's birth, the Iberian peninsula, which probably had no more than about four million inhabitants, was divided between a small and poor Christian north and a prosperous Muslim south. That situation was the outcome of a military conquest in the early eighth century: the Visigothic kingdom, which was one of the successor states of the Roman empire, was defeated and conquered between 711 and 715 by Arab-led Berber troops.

Although under Muslim leadership, many of the conquerors were only nominally Muslim at the time. A fully Islamicized society emerged in the Iberian peninsula after the conquest. Many of the local inhabitants converted to Islam or at least accommodated to living under Muslim rule. Muslim Iberia, called al-Andalus, was born. Initially, it was a part of the Umayyad Caliphate, an Islamic empire whose centre was in Syria. After the Umayyads – an Arab dynasty – were deprived of power in Damascus, one member of the dynasty, ʿAbd al-Rahman, managed to escape to the Iberian peninsula in 756 and turned al-Andalus into a politically independent emirate, with its capital in Córdoba. His dynasty ruled there for centuries, and his namesake ʿAbd al-Rahman III declared himself caliph (a term that designated the highest political authority) in 929. Over time, they fashioned a prosperous realm. This prosperity was based on agricultural and craft production and trade. A crucial commodity in this trade were slaves, including Slavic people traded from Eastern Europe, castrated in al-Andalus, and sold on as eunuchs in the Muslim world. At its inception, al-Andalus covered the peninsula with the exception of the northern fringe. That northern part was of no interest to the conquerors on account of its poor climate and terrain and was therefore quickly abandoned. Local populations started to organize there in the mountainous regions, eventually leading to the formation of the first Christian kingdom in Asturias.

The rulers of al-Andalus exercised the usual Islamic policy of the times towards Christians. 'People of the Book', including Christians and Jews, were not to be compelled to convert to Islam. They were able to continue their life as protected minorities, in exchange for the payment of a special tax, and constrained by certain rules, such as the prohibition against Christian men marrying Muslim women. *Dhimmi*, as such protected minorities were called, were not to display signs of their religion openly, nor wear clothing used by Muslims, bear arms or claim superiority over those who professed Islam. At the same time, these communities could be governed by their own laws, and enjoyed the protection that Islamic law provided for their property and person. Nonetheless, both Islam, as the religion of the victors, and socio-economic possibilities only available for Muslims exerted such strong attraction that conversion took off within a few generations. According to one hypothesis, only around 8 per cent of the population consisted of Muslims by 800, but this jumped to 50 per cent by 950 and to 75 per cent by 1000. Alarmed by the conversion of their fellow Christians, some ecclesiastics in the 850s mounted a dramatic public opposition to assimilation by seeking martyrdom. They openly blasphemed Islam, for example by stating publicly that Muhammad was languishing in hell for having misled the Arabs, in the knowledge that such a deed entailed the death penalty.

The ensuing movement of the so-called Martyrs of Córdoba resulted in the execution of at least forty-eight Christians, mostly ecclesiastics, within a decade. According to the account of their deaths, such executions involved the flogging of the victim, in some cases the cutting off of hands and feet, decapitation and the crucifixion of the body. Emulating early Christian martyrs, those voluntarily going to their death wanted to convince their co-religionists of the superiority of Christianity. Yet they could not turn back the tide. Although large numbers of Mozarabs (as the Christians of al-Andalus were called) emigrated to the northern, Christian regions, and not everyone converted to Islam, many did. Furthermore, the culture of the Christians who remained was not based on segregation, but, rather, was progressively arabicized. The local vernacular Romance languages incorporated Arabic words, thousands of which are still present in Spanish today, including *ajedrez* (chess), *azúcar* (sugar), *hazaña* (feat) and *berenjena* (aubergine). New technologies and crafts were introduced. So was Arabic-language science and literature, which included the translations of many works from classical antiquity, the Greek originals of which had been lost and were unknown by Europeans.

At the same time, however, the political development of the northern Christian fringe continued. In the ninth century, a king came to power in Pamplona, in an area that was contested between the emirate of Córdoba and the Frankish rulers. The kingdom of Pamplona eventually became an independent realm. During the ninth and tenth centuries, local populations, along with those who fled from the conquerors, created new Christian kingdoms that slowly incorporated lands – from which central authority had disappeared in the eighth and ninth centuries – up to the River Duero. By the eleventh century, the kingdoms of Aragón, Castile and León all appeared on the political scene. This process was anything but smooth: territories merged and divided, siblings jostled for power, rulers tried to impose their authority on weaker neighbours. Therefore the counties and kingdoms of the northern part of the peninsula were unstable and were continuously reshaped by the military might of Christian rulers as well as by happenstance. For example, for a while in 914 the kingdom of Galicia ceased to exist as an independent realm because its ruler, Ordoño II, inherited the throne of the more prestigious León upon the death of his elder brother García, and integrated Galicia into the kingdom of León. When Ordoño himself died ten years later, his younger brother,

Fruela II, up to then king of Asturias, united Ordoño's domains and his own, and thus the enlarged kingdom of León gobbled up these formerly independent realms. Yet kingdoms were just as easily broken apart again.

Until the early eleventh century, the key determinant of the fortunes of northern Christians, however, was the strength of Muslim al-Andalus. The instability caused by Andalusi rebellions sporadically allowed for some expansion of the borders of Christian realms, but as long as al-Andalus remained under the rule of one caliph, the northern kingdoms were able to expand into marginal areas at best, rather than conquer significant territories from the Muslims. At worst, they suffered Muslim raids and were forced to become client states: for example, King Vermudo II of León paid annual tribute for protection by Muslim troops, and when he tried to break that arrangement in 987, several of his towns were sacked. The last decades of the tenth century were dominated by the feared al-Manṣūr ('the victorious'), known to the English-speaking world as Almanzor. He started life as Abu ʿĀmir Muḥammad ibn ʿAbdullāh ibn Abi ʿĀmir al-Maʿafiri, and became a leading figure at the caliph's court at Córdoba, holding several important positions and eventually securing de facto rulership. He was all-powerful as long as he lived and a permanent threat to the northern Christians: between 977 and 1002 he conducted fifty-six campaigns against the Christians in the north and reconquered the small gains they had made in previous generations. One of his notable deeds was the sacking of Santiago de Compostela in 997, carrying off the church doors and bells to Córdoba. A later Christian chronicler was keen to reassure his readers that such an enemy reaped everlasting punishment: 'after many dreadful defeats of the Christians, Almanzor was snatched away by the Devil (who had taken possession of him during his lifetime) . . . and buried in Hell.'

The balance of power between al-Andalus and the northern kingdoms, however, began to shift in the first half of the eleventh century. Al-Manṣūr had sidelined the caliph, turning him into a figurehead, which soon destabilized al-Andalus. Al-Manṣūr's older son inherited his father's position and power, but when he died, his heir – his younger brother – was soon murdered. Political instability grew, with army leaders, administrators and local strongmen undermining central authority in order to carve out power for themselves. The Christians of the north were beginning to awaken to the new possibilities to acquire riches and land. Already in 1009, when a Berber revolt broke out in Córdoba, the Castilian count Sancho Garcés briefly allied with the rebels to regain forts in the Duero valley that he had previously lost to al-Manṣūr.

In 1031, Hisham III, the last Umayyad caliph of al-Andalus, was overthrown: he had attempted to buttress the caliph's already weakened central power by raising taxes, which proved to be his undoing. Conspirators from the elite unseated Hisham and murdered his military chief (vizier). Hisham managed to escape from his prison, but had to flee and was never able to regain power. The Muslim south fragmented into small kingdoms, called the taifas, a term that comes from the Arabic *ṭā'ifa*, meaning party or faction. Often, the term 'petty kings' is used in English to describe the result of the shattering of central power. After 1031, thirty-three taifas emerged; they were to all intents and purposes city-states under their own rulers, with their own hinterlands. Army generals and provincial governors of the former caliphate, as well as members of the local elites, were among these new taifa rulers. Many of the smaller and weaker ones were eventually conquered by a stronger nearby leader; thus the taifa of Sevilla incorporated a dozen of its less fortunate neighbours in the 1040s and 1050s.

Although politically fragmented, economically al-Andalus still represented a reservoir of riches and prestige objects – such as luxury textiles, ceramics and ivory caskets – to the Christians of the north. The new inhabitants of the south had turned even arid wasteland into a cultivated paradise by constructing irrigation systems with canals and waterwheels, the *noria*, that lift water into aqueducts. Those on rivers were very large, 15–20 m in diameter; the remains of a few can still be seen in Spain to this day, such as the one in Córdoba on the Guadalquivir river. Watermills were also used; a small mill from the tenth century was found in Valencia. The Arab conquerors introduced the cultivation of diverse fruits and vegetables that had not been grown in the peninsula before, such as orange and lemon, fig and watermelon, pomegranate and almond, rice, aubergine and artichoke, and spices such as nutmeg, cloves and cinnamon. Craftsmen produced fabled metalwork, such as Toledo steel, ivories, textiles, including silk garments, leatherwork, such as cordovan, and glass. A renowned maker of astrolabes, astronomical instruments used to calculate the position of celestial bodies, was active in Toledo in 1067. The only place to manufacture paper in Europe at the time was also in al-Andalus: there is evidence of a papermill at Xàtiva at least from the middle of the twelfth century. The towns of al-Andalus far surpassed those found in western Christendom: Córdoba's population reached approximately 100,000 in the tenth century, a size only matched by cities such as Venice or Florence in Catholic Europe around 1300. Even then, 20,000 inhabitants denoted a large city in Latin Christendom. These Muslim cities were not only distinguished by their size from those in Christian realms; a rich urban culture also flourished in al-Andalus, with communities of scholars and physicians, a varied population and a spectacular built environment that included baths and mosques. These towns were linked by trade to places as far away as Baghdad, Cairo and India.

After its fall, al-Andalus was remembered as an earthly paradise. Indeed, a holiday in the region today – seeing the remnants of once sumptuous palaces, hearing the soothing trickle of water fountains and smelling the sweet orange blossoms – produces a similar impression on modern visitors. So it must also have seemed to the northerners when they came face to face with a material civilization so much richer than their own. This is evident in the flow of Andalusi goods to the north. Moreover, cultural borrowing did not merely affect those local inhabitants who stayed in al-Andalus after the conquest. Some innovations reached the north, where, in the late tenth century, we find the first evidence of Europeans adapting Arabic numbers. The scribe of the so-called *Codex Vigilanus* at the monastery of San Martín de Albelda in the kingdom of Pamplona carefully traced the numbers from one to nine, copying them right to left in the fashion of Arabic script, praising the ingenuity of the inhabitants of India who invented them. The northerners, however, were primarily interested in plundering the earthly paradise of al-Andalus.

While political fragmentation weakened Muslim al-Andalus, the Christian north was in flux, too. Instability there was driven by a hunger for riches, its rulers eyeing any land in their vicinity, be it

Christian or Muslim, for potential plunder or conquest. The most successful Christian kings now started to exploit their weaker Muslim counterparts more systematically, while their warriors were eager for easy booty. This political mosaic provided the perfect backdrop to what the historian Angus MacKay called a protection racket. Warriors from the north were able to conduct lightning raids into the south, destroying the intricate irrigation system that kept the economy flourishing, burning trees and crops and taking animals and captives back north. Serious damage could be inflicted very rapidly, but to repair it, to replant trees and reconstruct canals, took a long time. Although in the tenth century the Córdoban caliphate had set up a line of round watchtowers, at about 40-km intervals – some of which, such as that at Atalaya de El Vellón, still survive – these were insufficient to protect the taifa territories. So were local castles and village fortifications that appeared in response to Christian raids starting in the eleventh century. To avoid such destruction, therefore, Muslim rulers soon placed themselves under the protection of Christian kings and paid them in gold to avoid raids. Initially, plunder and tribute payments from the taifas, rather than territorial gains, were in the sights of the Christian rulers. But by the second half of the eleventh century, gaining wealth and self-confidence, some began to conquer territories from the Muslims.

Around the time of our protagonist Rodrigo Díaz's birth, one ruler was particularly successful in imposing tribute and enlarging his realm. Fernando was initially count of Castile, a frontier region of the kingdom of León (hence its name, as an area protected by forts, from the same root that gave us 'castle'). He defeated the king of León in battle (1037) and appropriated his kingdom, styling himself King Fernando I. From the 1050s, Fernando conquered areas on the southern side of the Duero river, a region that is now part of Portugal: Lamego (1057), Viseu (1058), followed by Penalva, Travanca and encompassing the entire Beira Alta region with the conquest of Coímbra (1064). In this way, territorial expansion at the expense of al-Andalus began in earnest. Fernando also started to raid across the frontier into the rich neighbouring taifas, Toledo, Zaragoza and Badajoz, and in 1063 he even breached the territory of the taifa of Sevilla. As one text described it, King Fernando rode into Muslim territory, depopulated the lands of the barbarians and burned many farms. All these Muslim rulers agreed to pay him tribute, the so-called *parias*, to escape from such raids. Power relations between north and south, therefore, started to be reversed, with the northern Christian rulers gaining the upper hand.

According to the traditional view, this was part of an ideologically driven war to reconquer Christian lands. It has often been repeated that either directly after the Arab-Berber conquest (711–715), itself misleadingly designated as a 'Muslim' conquest, or sometime later, the Christian inhabitants of the peninsula rallied to regain all the lands taken from them, and, through a series of military campaigns called the Reconquest, or *Reconquista* in Spanish, finally achieved that aim in the thirteenth century, with the exception of Granada. The eleventh century is often seen as the true start of the Reconquest in practice. Because of some successes of northern Christian territorial expansion at the expense of al-Andalus, such an explanation of events may be tempting, yet it seriously distorts the historical processes. While it is true that Christian political power eventually replaced Muslim domination, the process that led to that change was complicated and haphazard; nor was a clear-cut ideology of 'Reconquest' motivating Christians during the lifetime of Rodrigo.

Eleventh-century Christian rulers of the peninsula were more likely to die as a result of hostilities with fellow Christians than fighting against Muslims. Vermudo III of León, for example, had to flee in 1034 when Sancho III of Pamplona occupied his throne, and after briefly returning to power he then died in battle in 1037, defending himself against his brother-in-law, Fernando of Castile. The same Fernando killed his own brother García Sánchez III of Pamplona (who had fought alongside him against Vermudo III) in battle in 1054, and extended the realm of León-Castile. Sancho IV, king of Pamplona, provides another example: he was assassinated in 1076, pushed off a cliff while hunting, allegedly due to a plot led by his brother Ramón and his sister Ermesinda. Warfare was clearly not restricted to hostilities against 'religious enemies'. Further, Christian kings were more than happy to take advantage of their co-religionists' weakness, even if the latter were fighting against Muslims. For example, Fernando I was forced to abandon his campaign against the Muslim taifa of Toledo when he was attacked by the Christian king Sancho Garcés IV of Pamplona in 1058. The opportunistic nature of territorial conquest is also revealed by the aftermath of Sancho IV's death: Sancho Ramírez I of Aragón and Alfonso VI of León-Castile invaded the kingdom of Pamplona and partitioned it.

Alliances cross-cutting the Christian–Muslim confessional divide sprung up as well. Each and every ruler wanted to gain territory and had reason to fear their neighbours, irrespective of their religious adhesion. Therefore allies were sought wherever they could be found, based on momentary common political interest rather than religion, and so Christians and Muslims frequently fought together against other Christian–Muslim confederacies. The death of Ramiro I of Aragón in 1063 is a case in point. He was killed in the Battle of Graus, which is often cited in traditional historical works as a battle of the Reconquest. Yet in fact he fought against a Castilian–Muslim coalition led by his nephew Sancho II of Castile, rather than against Muslims to reconquer land. Another of the many examples comes from the 1080s, when the Muslim ruler of Játiva, a tributary of the taifa of Valencia, refused to pay or recognize the newly installed al-Qādir of Valencia. This provided a welcome opportunity for the taifa king of Denia and Tortosa; with the help of Catalan warriors led by one Guirart el Romano, he protected Játiva from al-Qādir's retaliation, and brought it under his own control. There were many other cases when Christian warriors assisted one Muslim ruler against another, to expand or protect their realm.

Moreover, pillaging was both a frequent occurrence and a way of making a living. In these activities, Christian warriors did not confine themselves to al-Andalus. Saints' lives and chronicles detail stories of how livestock was seized by Christian raiders from Christian villages or monasteries and even sold off to the Muslims south of the border. Yet warriors who could direct their plundering activities against Muslims were saved from both the opprobrium of ecclesiastical writers and the possible revenge of the looted populations.

The more immediate events that set the scene for the story of the Cid unfolded in the wake of Fernando I's death in 1065. According to the king's testament, his lands were divided between his three sons, creating three kingdoms: the eldest, Sancho II, inherited

Castile; Alfonso VI, León; and García II, Galicia. They also inherited the right to collect *parias* (tribute) from various taifas: Sancho from Zaragoza, Alfonso from Toledo and García from Badajoz and Sevilla. However, war soon broke out between the brothers. While the accounts of the exact sequence of events vary, the outcome is well-attested. García, defeated by his brothers, was exiled to the taifa of Sevilla. Next, Sancho imprisoned Alfonso; however, he was released after one of their sisters, Urraca, interceded for him and he went into exile in the taifa of Toledo. Sancho II was not content with these conquests and besieged his sister Urraca's fortress of Zamora. After successfully defeating two kings, why would he have quailed before snatching a coveted fort from his sister? Yet, at the siege of Zamora, Sancho II was killed by an assassin. Writing some decades later, a chronicler attributed the deed to 'a knight of great courage' from Zamora, who transfixed the king with a spear from behind. Later legend has it that one of Urraca's nobles tricked Sancho. By claiming to have switched sides, not an uncommon occurrence in the period, and under the guise of showing him a weak spot to take the city, he lured Sancho away from his men and murdered the king while he was relieving himself. Alfonso VI returned from exile and stepped into his brother's shoes as king of León-Castile. Although we have no evidence of his complicity in the murder, legends from the thirteenth century onwards began to link his name with the event that he certainly benefited from. He definitely imprisoned his brother García to prevent him from reclaiming the kingdom of Galicia.

This enlarged kingdom of León-Castile was the most significant of the Christian kingdoms by the later eleventh century. Moreover, while indiscriminate fighting against both Muslims and Christians was ongoing, King Alfonso VI of León-Castile also nourished a desire to be emperor of all *Hispania*, a title he started to use in 1077. According to the *Historia silense*, written in the first third of the twelfth century, which chronicled the history of Alfonso VI's family, Alfonso was already bemoaning the fate of the Visigothic kingdom during the period of his exile in Muslim Toledo. The chronicle uses a range of words to denote Muslims, and claims that although Alfonso enjoyed the hospitality of the 'barbarians' and was held in the highest regard by the 'Saracens' so that he was able to walk around Toledo at will, he lamented how the once Christian city could be sacked by 'pagans'. Once in power, he increased the number of taifa rulers under his protection who had to pay him *parias*, even attacking Granada at the southern tip of the peninsula to bend its ruler to his will. He was helped in this endeavour by the military leader of the taifa of Sevilla.

The memoirs of the ruler of Granada, ʿAbd Allāh, which are full of colourful stories, describe how Alfonso VI became involved in extorting money from him. While we cannot determine these stories' exact veracity, they do give us a flavour of the times. Hearing of hostilities in al-Andalus, Alfonso VI sent his envoy to the taifa ruler, demanding tribute. ʿAbd Allāh refused, since he felt secure; Sevilla, another taifa state's territory, lay between him and Alfonso, which would serve as a buffer. He did not believe that a Muslim ruler could become an ally of Alfonso against another Muslim. However, Ibn ʾAmmār, vizier of the taifa of Sevilla, saw an opportunity, because he wanted to conquer Granada for himself. He promised Alfonso VI's envoy that the king would receive not merely the 20,000 dinars a year from Granada that he had asked for, but 50,000. Moreover, he offered help so that Alfonso could take Granada, in exchange for gold. Alfonso and Ibn ʾAmmār cooperated to build a fortress from which troops could harass Granada, and ʿAbd Allāh regretted not having accepted Alfonso's terms. Ibn ʾAmmār continued to intrigue against Granada with Alfonso, giving the latter significant amounts of gold coin and promising more. According to ʿAbd Allāh, this awakened Alfonso's greed as well as his cunning, but he had no intention of helping one Muslim ruler gain an important city from another, since either could use it as a base against Alfonso.

ʿAbd Allāh claimed in his memoirs that Alfonso knew he would not be able to conquer Granada outright: it would not surrender without a fight, and so he would have to spend large amounts of money and wage a long war to try to take it. Even then, were he able to conquer it, since the locals hated him he would not be able to hold the city without substantial numbers of troops stationed there. Therefore, he would be better off simply exploiting the hostilities between the Muslim rulers, drawing as much revenue as he possibly could from both sides: from one by the promise of an alliance, from the other by assurances of protection. This way, they would both lose their wealth and be exhausted by fighting each other, and their territories would ultimately fall into his lap. Alfonso proceeded to demand 50,000 mithqāls from ʿAbd Allāh, the equivalent of 212.5 kg of gold, in exchange for his protection. After prolonged and difficult negotiations, ʿAbd Allāh managed to reduce the amount to just over half of what had been demanded. In addition, he had precious carpets, textiles and vases collected, giving them to Alfonso as a gift. This was just the beginning, as ʿAbd Allāh also had to promise to pay 10,000 mithqāls a year in tribute to Alfonso.

Whether we want to believe that ʿAbd Allāh had a special insight into Alfonso's psychological make-up, or think he just attributed the meanest motives to an adversary, the benefits that Alfonso (and other Christian rulers) gained in this period are beyond any doubt. Immense riches flowed to them, in the form of gold coins and luxury items. A chronicler described how the taifa ruler of Toledo gave a vast amount of gold and silver and precious garments to Fernando I to stop him from attacking his lands. The payment of tribute is also described in detail in a treaty from 1073 between the taifa of Zaragoza and Sancho IV of Navarra. It specified the payment of a yearly tribute of 12,000 mancusos (gold dinars) by the taifa ruler, in exchange for military aid against Muslims and Christians alike. The Christian kings of the peninsula used these treasures to pay their troops, erect fortifications and purchase siege engines, pay for experts who provided military technology and reward members of their household and followers. They also endowed religious institutions such as monasteries and churches, hoping to secure the salvation of their soul. Reliquaries made of precious metal housed the remains of saints; caskets and crucifixes made of ivory and jewel-encrusted liturgical objects adorned the churches. One text refers to Fernando I furnishing a newly built church with silver, gold, gemstones and silk hangings. Some of the *parias* collected by Fernando I in the last years of his life, and after his death, by Alfonso VI, flowed to the monastery of Cluny in Burgundy, paying for masses for the king's soul; an annual gift of a thousand gold coins that surpassed in value all the other income of the monastery.

The Christian kings were frequently beneficiaries of Muslim infighting. Plotting to take territories from other Muslim rulers, taifa kings repeatedly included Christian monarchs in their schemes.

These dynamics led Yahya al-Qādir, grandson and heir of Yahya ibn Ismail al-Mamūn, taifa ruler of Toledo, to turn to Alfonso VI, a friend and ally of his grandfather, for help when faced with a revolt a few years after inheriting the throne. Al-Mamūn had welcomed Alfonso at the time of the king's exile when his brother Sancho had wrested power from him. Once on the throne, Alfonso became the protector of the taifa of Toledo in exchange for *parias*. Al-Qādir was only able to provide this tribute by squeezing his own subjects. Increasingly unpopular, al-Qādir faced revolts, which he countered by ceding yet more tribute as well as frontier forts to Alfonso, thereby descending into a vicious cycle that only benefited the Christian king. Moreover, Alfonso's troops, maintaining al-Qādir's rule, gained a permanent foothold within the taifa of Toledo. When, in 1084, al-Qādir once again requested his help, Alfonso intervened in a novel way. Whether at his own initiative, or in response to al-Qādir's request to be transferred to Valencia, Alfonso decided to take Toledo and attach it to his realm. This decision was doubtless prompted by the city's great symbolic significance as the capital of the former Visigothic kingdom. Those opposed to al-Qādir resisted a handover, but Alfonso surrounded the city, cutting off its food supply. Toledo tried to seek help from other taifas but ultimately surrendered in 1085. Alfonso transferred al-Qādir from Toledo to the taifa of Valencia and annexed the territory of Toledo to his own kingdom.

This unprecedented move sent shock waves through al-Andalus. According to ʿAbd Allāh, Alfonso had a plan to squeeze all the taifas in a similar manner until they fell into his hands. Ibn al-Kardabūs's history of al-Andalus, the *Kitāb al-Iktifā*, written in the last decades of the twelfth century, claimed that 'the tyrant Alfonso' was so consumed by pride that he found all who walked the earth contemptible, and in his delirium of grandeur called himself emperor. So Alfonso's posthumous press among Andalusi Muslim authors was certainly extremely negative. The other taifa rulers at the time undoubtedly shared the view that they were endangered by the expanding Christian kingdom, and those of Badajoz, Sevilla and Granada called on the aid of the Almoravids (*Al-Murābiṭūn*) from Morocco. The Almoravids were a Muslim dynasty originating from nomadic Berbers of Africa who had started to gain territories from the middle of the century. Their distinctive dress included a veil below the eyes for men, and they were followers of the Maliki school of law, a conservative and rigorist form of Islam.

The leader of the Almoravids, Yūsuf ibn Tāshfīn, answered the taifas' call and unleashed a new invasion to reverse Christian successes in 1086. His army landed at Algeciras, and the troops of the taifas joined him. Alfonso VI met these armies at Sagrajas on 23 October, where his forces initially seemed to be gaining the upper hand due to their surprise attack. Nonetheless, the initial surprise gone, and the combined taifa and Almoravid armies launching their assault, Alfonso's army was at a disadvantage, the warriors already tired from having had to cover a large distance to arrive at the battlefield, and without a plan for the battle itself. Writing a century later, Ibn Kardabūs gave much credit to the astrological knowledge of the taifa ruler of Sevilla, who, using an astrolabe, calculated Yūsuf's horoscope, and determined the ideal place for his camp. Whether we prefer to attribute the outcome to astrology or the well-trained and disciplined Almoravid army, Alfonso suffered a spectacular defeat. He managed to escape, wounded in the leg, and ride north to organize the defence of Toledo. A Muslim chronicler claimed that the victors cut off the heads of those 'polytheists' (as they called Christians) they found on the battlefield, and with these heads constructed minarets; for three days the muezzins issued the call to prayers from the tallest one.

The defeat reverberated across Christendom. Far away, in the French monastery of Cluny, monks were praying for Alfonso. In Rome, the pope began to be concerned about the fate of Iberia's Christians. In the peninsula itself, many tried to benefit from the upheaval and to snatch lands from Alfonso. For the defeat was not a stand-alone event. Although after the battle Yūsuf ibn Tāshfīn had to return to Morocco because of the sudden death of his son and heir, over the next decades the Almoravids were drawn ever more deeply into Iberian politics. Calls for help from Iberian Muslim rulers were repeated: the taifa ruler of Sevilla appealed to Yūsuf ibn Tāshfīn to return to the peninsula, to wrest the fort of Aledo from its Christian conqueror García Jiménez, who used it as a base for attacks against Muslim Murcia and Orihuela. In the spring of 1089, Yūsuf, and the taifas of Sevilla, Málaga, Almería, Granada and Murcia joined forces and besieged Aledo. The defenders appealed for help to

Alfonso VI, and, as his troops approached, the siege was lifted. The eyewitness testimony of ʿAbd Allāh, ruler of Granada, suggests that the main reason for abandoning the siege was Yūsuf's realization that the conflicts among the taifas, and an open revolt in Murcia that aided the Christians, doomed his efforts to failure. This was one of the reasons that led to a hardening of Almoravid attitudes towards not just the Christians of Iberia, but the taifa rulers as well.

Many local Muslims started to complain to Yūsuf about their rulers, and the taifa king of Granada, ʿAbd Allāh, recounts how he began to fear Almoravid intervention, as he was threatened for being mendacious and for negotiating with Alfonso VI. Yūsuf returned to the Iberian peninsula once again the following year, in June 1090. He besieged Toledo, but failed to take it, and the taifa rulers did not join in his campaign. Yūsuf then started to move against the taifa rulers themselves. Some of their critics had already defected to the Almoravids. Religious scholars at the Almoravid court also objected to the lax lifestyle of Iberian Muslim elites, their wine-drinking and allegedly heterodox faith, which provided justification for their deposition. Yūsuf deposed ʿAbd Allāh of Granada and his brother, the ruler of Málaga, and exiled them to Morocco before the end of 1090. Many other taifa rulers came to share the same fate. Baza, Almería and Córdoba were taken over by the Almoravids, who then successfully besieged Sevilla in 1091. One of Yūsuf's nephews led the campaign in 1092, taking Murcia, Aledo, Denia, Játiva and Alcira. In 1093–4, the Almoravids were conquering the western part of the peninsula, with Badajoz falling to them in early 1094. Almoravid armies thereafter returned regularly to the peninsula, and defeated Alfonso VI again in 1097. By the end of the eleventh century only the taifas of Zaragoza and Albarracín were not under Almoravid lordship. By the early twelfth century, the Almoravids ended up conquering all of the taifas, and reconquering some of the areas that had been taken by the Christian kings, although they were unable to retake Toledo.

The eleventh century was thus a time of great instability in the Iberian peninsula, a period when life revolved around warfare and warriors constituted the elite of society. In the northern realms, these mounted knights held landed estates or were maintained by money granted by the king. They trained from early adolescence in horsemanship and the use of weapons. Sword, spear, spurs, mail-coat and helmet was their standard equipment. They practised violence as a way of life. The Muslim contemporary ʿAbd Allāh wrote of an attack by Alfonso VI against the taifa of Badajoz, which resulted in a large number of dead on both sides:

> The Christian's troops then made a surprise attack on the Muslims who were not yet ready . . . many who were unable to defend themselves perished. No sooner was the battle cry given to the [Muslim] army than the men mounted in pursuit of the Christians who laboured under the weight of their arms and the long distance they had covered. The Muslims set off in pursuit and were hot on their heels. A large part of the Christian army perished and were left scattered along the road: some of them had been slain, while others had died beneath the weight of their arms.

The violence of the battles is also attested to by recent archaeological excavations. The skeleton of Vermudo III, who died in battle against his brother-in-law Fernando, indicates the manner of his death at the age of nineteen. The enemy's spear entered his right eye, bursting the eye socket and ripping off his upper jaw. Additionally, more than a dozen sword wounds pierced his lower abdomen, femur, hip and cheek. According to a narrative account, he rode a faster horse than the rest of his host, and therefore met the enemy alone, exposing him to the unequal fight. Gruesome details abound in the written sources as well. According to a later chronicler, when Fernando I conquered Viseu, he wanted to revenge his father-in-law Alfonso V of León who had fallen there three decades earlier while besieging the town; when his men found the archer who had killed Alfonso, he ordered that both his hands be cut off. While the story may well be invented, the spirit behind it is telling.

Violence was not merely practised, it was glorified in war. This was true more generally in Europe. Thietmar, bishop of Merseburg (1009–18), in his chronicle had no qualms about depicting the future Henry I as 'a warrior of good character', when, sent to Slavic lands by his father, 'after much destruction and burning, he returned victorious'. The protagonist of the *Song of Roland* (written largely during the eleventh century) is celebrated for fighting to the death, along with an archbishop accompanying the army, while 'pagans [that is, Muslims] are slain by hundred, by thousand', heads are sliced off and Roland kills an enemy warrior and his horse with one stroke. Roland dies a martyr in battle and angels take his soul to heaven. By the end of the century, the idea that knights could kill enemies and thereby gain their salvation triggered the crusades. In the Iberian peninsula itself, chroniclers noted with approval numerous instances of laying waste to the enemy's lands. An early twelfth-century chronicle celebrated a Christian king who was 'a devout vindicator of the Christian faith with the strength of his army', because the enemy was 'cut down like cattle'. Another narrative, the *Chronicle of the kings of León* (*Chronicon regum Legionensium*, c. 1120s), applauded Fernando I, 'a good and God-fearing man' who 'made a great slaughter of the Saracens'. Many illustrated manuscripts of the monk Beatus of Liébana's commentary on the Apocalypse show the eschatological combat at the end of times, where violence by the divinely supported side is clearly something to be celebrated; for example, divine minions wielding prominent swords defeat the Beast and evil figures, while birds peck at dead bodies. The twelfth-century Bible of San Isidoro of León illustrates biblical battles with figures clad in chain mail, making them seem contemporary, and the scene of an Israelite victory includes a decapitated head and mutilated body parts strewn on the ground.

The martial characteristics of the eleventh century in the Iberian peninsula dictated the sphere of action for many rulers and nobles. The ever-changing political landscape and possibilities for plunder, and, increasingly, territorial conquest, made warfare central to life. It was a time when talented warriors were able to prosper: a time propitious for Rodrigo.

2

Through a Glass Darkly: The Man Rodrigo

Rodrigo, or, as he appears in the medieval texts, Ruy Díaz, was probably born in the mid- to late 1040s to an aristocratic Castilian family. His father, Diego Laínez, according to one modern theory, was even related to the kings of León, although this genealogical reconstruction is disputed. Of his mother, and possible siblings, we know nothing. The date of his birth is unknown, too, and modern scholars have put it as early as 1043 and as late as 1057; these calculations derive from his first appearance as an active warrior. Traditionally, his birthplace has been named as Vivar, near Burgos in Castile. However, the earliest text to mention this is a thirteenth-century epic, the *Poema de Mio Cid*, which may or may not be accurate on this point. He and his family owned land in the area, so although Vivar cannot be ascertained as his birthplace, the family certainly had connections to the region.

No explicit information remains about Rodrigo's upbringing. A rare near-contemporary snippet refers to the education of the sons of King Fernando: 'first, they should be instructed in the liberal disciplines to which he himself had given study. Then, when they were of the right age, he had his sons learn to ride . . . to practise the use of weapons and to hunt.' Alas, the passage was lifted from Einhard's *Life of Charlemagne*, written in the first half of the ninth century, although perhaps not very much changed in how the elites grew up between then and the eleventh century. Very little is known generally about the upbringing of aristocratic boys in Rodrigo's lifetime. At least some were taught rudimentary reading and writing at home, and both hunting and military training in equestrian skills and the use of weapons prepared them to become warriors. Like all aristocratic men, Rodrigo must have been taught military skills, and he was also able to sign his name in Latin, in what has been described as rather coarse lettering. Whether he could read remains a mystery. He may well have spent some of his formative years at the royal court of Castile, as one of the sources, the *Historia Roderici* – written according to some historians in the first half of the twelfth century, to others in the 1180s – claims that Sancho II raised Rodrigo and 'girded him with the belt of knighthood'. Some aristocratic youth certainly spent time at the royal court, others at the court of magnates, as a kind of military apprenticeship; this involved further training in the use of arms as well as learning about tactics and strategy. At least from the twelfth century they then underwent a knighting ceremony. Military service to one's lord and bravery in battle were the hallmarks of their life from then on, as well as the way to riches and glory. There is evidence of some boys as young as fourteen participating in battle.

When he emerged on the historical stage, Rodrigo was already a successful warrior, since he was entrusted by King Sancho II of Castile (1065–72) to lead his personal military retinue, including in battles against the king's brother Alfonso. Allegedly, as an 'adolescent' (which in medieval texts could cover any age between fourteen and twenty-five), Rodrigo also defeated a Navarrese champion in a duel that took place in order to decide the fate of a frontier fortress claimed by both the Castilian and Navarrese monarchs. When Sancho II died while he was busy conquering his younger siblings' share of their father's inheritance, his brother Alfonso VI (1065/72–1109) reunited León-Castile under his own rule, and Rodrigo transferred his loyalty to Alfonso, entering his service. Here, another decisive event of his life occurred: his marriage to Jimena. According to one text, Alfonso appreciated him so much that he gave his niece in marriage to Rodrigo. Jimena's precise descent has been disputed, but she was certainly connected to the ruling family.

The marriage probably took place in 1074, because a charter detailing the properties given by Rodrigo to Jimena was drawn up, dated to that year. The extant document displays certain inconsistencies, notably in the official titles of some of the witnesses, who had not yet obtained these titles in 1074, which prompted suggestions that the dating may be incorrect or even that the charter is a forgery. Another explanation suggests that the charter had to be drawn up again at a later date, in 1079, because Rodrigo no longer owned some of the properties he had originally conferred on Jimena, and therefore a new list of properties had to be established. Nonetheless, this newly written charter conserved the date of the original corresponding to that of the marriage. Rodrigo's charter to Jimena followed Leonese custom, where the groom gave properties constituting up to half of his estate to his new bride. This document is a rich source, attesting to the extensive landholdings of Rodrigo by this time, as well as their scattered pattern: he gave her parts of thirty-four villages, and three entire ones, as well as a monastery, in different parts of Castile. The spouses named each other as the only heir of the surviving partner, and their property was to pass to their children after the death of both. The charter also demonstrates what the earliest sources explicitly confirmed, that Rodrigo was a member of the highest social circles (rather than a scion of the lesser nobility, as later texts claimed): the two guarantors who signed the charter were the Leonese counts Pedro Ansúrez, count of Zamora, and García Ordóñez, count of Nájera, and the witnesses included not only the highest echelons of the court but King Alfonso VI himself, together with his sisters. Rodrigo did not have to fight his way to the top from obscurity; rather, he was born into the aristocracy that held lands and power, and constituted the elite, with access to the king. Whether or not they married in 1074, by 1076 Rodrigo and Jimena were definitely man and wife, as together they gave donations to a monastery, a normal aristocratic practice of patronage, to ensure the monks' prayers for their salvation.

Rodrigo acted for Alfonso VI in a variety of ways. The late thirteenth-century *Legend of Cardeña* paints vivid scenes of Rodrigo's activities in the service of Alfonso, collecting *parias* from southern taifas and defeating in battle those unwilling to pay. While this was, of course, an important part of his duties, they were far more varied, as the elite not only provided military service but also enabled royal administration. Along with other members of the court, he witnessed royal charters that listed donations of rights and land. He acted, together with other royal appointees, in adjudicating litigations, including one over grazing rights and another involving contested rights to a monastery. He was also present at the council in Burgos in 1080, where the decision was made to switch from the local Mozarabic to the Roman liturgy that was promoted by the pope. This meant giving up local traditions and aligning more closely with the papacy. It is often repeated that in 1075 he was present at the opening of the Holy Ark of Oviedo, a reliquary containing a range of relics, including, supposedly, a part of the True Cross, a cloth that had been wrapped around Christ's head at the crucifixion, bread from the Last Supper and some of the Virgin's milk. However, the document that lists Rodrigo Díaz as a witness at the opening of the ark was written in the thirteenth century and may merely reflect his already legendary status at the time. In any case, he was not just a warrior, but also a figure at court, who had to assess legal claims and make judgements.

In 1079, Rodrigo was sent by the king as an envoy to the taifa of Sevilla, to collect the *parias*. While there, troops from the taifa of Granada, along with their Christian allies, attacked, and Rodrigo became involved on the Sevillan side, protecting his king's Muslim tributary against some of Alfonso's own nobles and their Granadan allies. The clash was therefore not between Christians and Muslims, but between two groups of Muslims with Christian allies on both sides. The attackers were defeated; moreover, Rodrigo captured García Ordóñez and other Christian nobles; looting their belongings, he then freed them. This humiliation was not something people at the time would easily forget, and Rodrigo made high-ranking enemies, not just of García, but also of family members of the others he had captured, all eminent courtiers of Alfonso VI.

Alfonso does not seem to have objected to Rodrigo's actions in 1079, but as the latter became increasingly independent, the king's ire was aroused; and at that point, having powerful enemies at court ensured that the king would not be merciful. In 1081, Muslim raiders entered Castile and after a surprise attack on the castle of Gormaz carried off substantial booty. In revenge, Rodrigo and his army struck out without royal mandate against Toledo, taking captives and plunder. It was not raiding itself that led to royal censure – raids and pillaging were regular features of life in Iberia – but such an unauthorized military raid against a Muslim ruler under Alfonso's protection harmed the king's interests. It destabilized the precarious system reliant on tribute payments in exchange for security; Alfonso had been collecting such payments from Toledo, and so he had guaranteed the taifa freedom from raids. He could not tolerate one of his own high-ranking warriors breaching that guarantee. Therefore, Alfonso VI exiled Rodrigo from Castile. Exile in the Middle Ages was a punishment for crime, but also frequently meted out for political reasons. It was often temporary. Having to leave their lands, friends and family behind deprived those exiled from their normal social networks. Exile, however, could also open up new possibilities for making connections. In Iberia, those exiled could find a new home in some other part of the peninsula.

Rodrigo probably left Jimena and his children behind in Castile. One document suggests she may have returned to her family together with her children; later, the thirteenth-century *Poema* claimed Rodrigo left his wife and children at the monastery of Cardeña. While we have no reliable information, the first version is more likely, as the *Poema* is already interlinked with the growing cult of the Cid, of which the monastery of Cardeña was an important driver. Rodrigo himself first went to Barcelona, offering his services to the count, who was not interested. Then he continued to the taifa of Zaragoza.

In exile, Rodrigo had one asset: his skills as a warrior, which enabled him to live off his military success. Calling on these skills, he entered the service of the Muslim ruler of Zaragoza, al-Muqtadir, as a mercenary commander, continuing for five years in the employ of a series of rulers. Some Spanish scholars now prefer to use the term 'salaried vassal', suggesting it is more precise than 'mercenary', which has sometimes been interpreted as a condemnatory moralizing term, and is now used in contemporary parlance to describe private military forces operating separately to national armies. In its original meaning, 'mercenary' designates precisely Rodrigo's role at Zaragoza: military service in exchange for material recompense. Al-Muqtadir was already a seasoned ruler: he had been on the throne since 1046, when Rodrigo must have been a small child or perhaps not even born yet. He was well aware of the threats to Zaragoza, not least the kingdom of Aragón, a dangerous enemy on the rise; so al-Muqtadir welcomed warriors who would secure his realm.

What did Rodrigo think and feel, surrounded by the splendour of the court? One of al-Muqtadir's palaces, the Aljafería, partly survives, giving us a glimpse, even in its decay, of the beauty that was once the everyday setting for court life. It was a fortified complex with walls and towers, that contained a courtyard with a garden, halls and a mosque. The famed Golden Hall, with its multifoil arches, alabaster pillars and wooden ceiling decorated with stars, still beguiles visitors today. Al-Muqtadir also had a reputation for being learned in mathematics and astronomy, and his court was home to many scholars. Yet medieval sources convey none of Rodrigo's reactions to his changed surroundings; nor do they reflect on the interactions he had during those years. Instead, they focus only on his military deeds.

Al-Muqtadir died not long after Rodrigo's arrival. Before his death, he divided his realm between his two sons. Yūsuf al-Muʾtamin received the city of Zaragoza itself and the western half of the taifa, while Mundir al-Hayib received the cities of Lérida, Tortosa and Denia, with the eastern part of the realm. The brothers' mutual hostility soon led to war. Al-Hayib made an alliance with, and paid *parias* to, King Sancho Ramírez of Aragón and Count Berenguer Ramón II of Barcelona, relying on their help against his brother. These Christian rulers had their own territorial ambitions, looking to push their frontiers further whenever a possibility presented itself, for example by purchasing a castle, and, of course, never shying away from opportunistic gain. Thus Rodrigo's services were very much needed, and he remained in the employ of al-Muʾtamin. Some frontier fortresses were particularly coveted prizes in the hostilities, and in the summer of 1082 Rodrigo defended one of them, Monzón; he was sent there by al-Muʾtamin with troops. He captured another fort, Escarp, from Lérida. His military skills continued to serve him well not merely in the fortification, defence and capture of some other frontier forts, but also in battle during the same summer.

One of the frontier forts that were fortified under Rodrigo's supervision, Almenar, was shortly afterwards attacked by al-Hayib and his Christian allies, the counts of Barcelona, Cerdaña and Urgel, as well as nobles from Besalú, Ampurdán and other Catalan regions. A later account, which may not be correct in all the details, relates that Rodrigo, having heard of the imminent danger to Almenar, which was encircled by the enemy and had run out of water, called on al-Mu'tamin for help. Together, with their troops, they headed to a nearby fort, Tamarite. Rodrigo suggested that it would be better to pay off al-Hayib so he would lift the siege, as he had a great multitude of warriors. Al-Mu'tamin took this advice and tried to negotiate with his brother. Certain of victory, however, al-Hayib refused. Then Rodrigo ordered his troops to take up their arms and both sides threw themselves into the fight with gusto. Soon, al-Hayib and the counts were defeated. Many were killed, and others taken captive, including the count of Barcelona. Rodrigo took plenty of booty from the enemy camp, but transferred the captives to al-Mu'tamin, who freed them after five days. According to modern historians, they gained their freedom in exchange for a ransom or an oath, undertaking not to return to support al-Hayib. In any case, Count Berenguer Ramón II certainly refrained from new military ventures alongside al-Hayib for a while. Some of the details provided by this narrative source, the *Historia Roderici*, are definitely literary inventions rather than accurate accounts, but we can only identify these when there are other sources on a particular event. For example, in its account of Alfonso VI's taking of Toledo, the author claimed that the king had besieged Toledo for a very long time, and took it by assault after seven years. In reality, however, Toledo was not taken by assault. The siege consisted mostly of cutting off the city's food supply; above all, Alfonso VI exploited his position as the protector of the taifa ruler, and took advantage of the internal difficulties al-Qādir faced. Whether or not the narrative of the war between al-Hayib and al-Mu'tamin exaggerated the difficulties and invented Rodrigo's initially cautious approach in order to magnify the victory one cannot tell. Yet one part of the story certainly rings true: Rodrigo rose in al-Mu'tamin's estimation as a result of his victory, and the ruler showered him with gifts and gold and silver.

Rodrigo continued to fight successfully against the ruler's enemies, including Christian princes from the north. In 1084, King Sancho Ramírez of Aragón, whose lands were adjacent to Zaragoza, began to conquer some of the frontier forts of the taifa, so al-Mu'tamin and Rodrigo launched a raid against Sancho's lands; the destructive cavalcade lasted five days, bringing booty and prisoners to Zaragoza. Al-Muʾtamin, encouraged by these military successes, sent Rodrigo with his army to devastate some of the neighbouring lands of his brother al-Hayib. In the mountainous region near Morella, in the north of the province of Castellón, Rodrigo 'left no house undestroyed, no estate that was not sacked', and attacked the fort of Morella itself, causing damage to it. Al-Muʾtamin then had a fortress near Morella, Olocau, reconstructed and fortified, in order to serve as a base of operations against al-Hayib. These attacks brought al-Hayib and Sancho Ramírez into an alliance against Rodrigo, which resulted in an open battle. Rodrigo was once again victorious, taking not only booty, but also a very large number of captives, including leading magnates at the court of Sancho Ramírez and one of the Aragonese bishops. Again, presumably through negotiations, Rodrigo also managed to neutralize future threats from Sancho. Rodrigo was feted on his return to Zaragoza; his fame as a warrior was firmly established, while the booty he had collected from his enemies and the gifts from al-Muʾtamin enriched him. When al-Muʾtamin died in 1085, his son, Aḥmad al-Mustaʿīn II, retained Rodrigo's services.

Rodrigo clearly did not distinguish friend from foe based on their faith. He, like most men at the time, was not driven by religious allegiance. Again, according to a story that cannot be verified, while in the service of the taifa ruler of Zaragoza, Rodrigo once met Alfonso VI during the latter's failed attempt to take a frontier fortress. Apparently, Alfonso initially invited Rodrigo to return to Castile but then changed his mind. This episode is probably literary fiction; but a little later, after his defeat by the Almoravids at Sagrajas in October 1086, King Alfonso was indeed in grave need of warriors, and Rodrigo returned to his service. Alfonso recruited warriors from wherever he could, including north of the Pyrenees, so his decision to welcome back a famous and proven warrior, whatever disagreements they had had in the past, is not surprising. We don't know who initiated this reconciliation, whether Alfonso recalled Rodrigo, or Rodrigo decided to seek out the king. In any case, the king pardoned Rodrigo and gave him several forts and the right to keep as his own property, with hereditary rights, the lands and fortresses he would take in future from the Muslims. This reconciliation also meant that Rodrigo was reunited with his wife and children who had remained behind in Castile while he was in exile.

What a modern reader may want to know most is shrouded in silence. After five years, what did the spouses feel upon being reunited? Did the father feel overpowering emotions upon seeing his children again? Were the children glad to see him, or did they find this stranger they could barely remember unsettling and a little frightening? And how did those five years in Muslim lands change Rodrigo? We cannot know but perhaps already, by the end of 1086, Rodrigo returned to being an active member of King Alfonso's court. During both the summer of 1087 and spring of 1088, he witnessed documents issued by the chancery. Alfonso also appointed Rodrigo to replace Álvar Fáñez (who went on to act in a similar manner in Granada) as the representative of the king in charge of protecting al-Qādir in Valencia, and collecting his tribute from the second half of 1087. On occasion, he conducted negotiations with other taifa rulers. When al-Hayib of Lérida, Denia and Tortosa, along with his Catalan allies, besieged Valencia, hoping to conquer it, Rodrigo turned to al-Mustaʿīn of Zaragoza for reinforcements, and their combined troops went to al-Qādir's aid, protecting him in order to maintain Alfonso's overlordship of Valencia; their approach was sufficient to prompt al-Hayib's retreat.

Once again, the extraordinary fluidity of political alliances across the religious divide is apparent: we find Muslims and Christians cooperating on both sides, and Rodrigo himself effortlessly navigating his changing loyalties, from King Alfonso to the Muslim rulers of Zaragoza, then back again, while retaining Zaragoza as an ally. Alliances, however, could be ephemeral. Taking advantage of Rodrigo's absence, when he returned to Alfonso's court in Toledo, al-Mustaʿīn of Zaragoza allied with Count Berenguer Ramón II of Barcelona in the spring of 1088 to attack and take Valencia. Rodrigo returned in time, however, and while differing accounts exist on what exactly happened, it seems that he successfully negotiated with the count, who withdrew without battle and returned to his lands. Rodrigo also conducted campaigns against forts in neighbouring territories that could be used as bases for attacks against Valencia, and led raids to pressure local governors into paying tribute. In this respect, he was no mere agent of the king, but was enriching himself, collecting and keeping the payments. In modern parlance, he exploited the possibilities of being a local 'strongman' and built a side hustle. The governor of Murviedro and the ruler of the small taifa of Alpuente both became tribute payers to Rodrigo in this way.

Acquiring ever more riches from raids and tribute he collected from Muslims over the years, Rodrigo could reward his followers lavishly, and so he assembled and maintained a host of loyal warriors. He was not alone in leading such a band of warriors. By the early twelfth century, sources gave the name 'caballeros pardos', brown knights, to the bands of commoners, mercenaries and bandits who lived off raids and plunder. Religious allegiance was not among their concerns, as such groups included Christians and Muslims indiscriminately. According to the testimony of visual sources, such warriors rode on horseback, armed with powerful composite bows and swords, protected by chain mail and gambesons, thick padded jackets that provided some protection. The troops of Rodrigo probably included such warriors, and many entered his service permanently; the personal army he built up became a powerful force on the local scene. He was thus able to conduct raids against all those not paying tribute to him. Storehouses in Valencia were filled with the booty he collected. A growing network of local lords depended on his protection, in exchange for payments. Soon, al-Qādir himself was paying tribute directly to Rodrigo.

After a few years, in 1089 Rodrigo fell out once again with King Alfonso. The trigger for the second break and renewed exile came with the siege of Aledo by a combined troop of the Almoravids and taifa armies. After the defenders called on King Alfonso VI for help, he ordered Rodrigo, then staying in Requena, to join the royal army en route to lifting the siege. The author of the later *Historia Roderici*, sympathetic to his hero, details a rather unbelievable sequence of events, suggesting that Rodrigo missed the royal army by accident. According to this, Rodrigo set out with his troops in obedience to the king's command, going south in the direction of Aledo, but then stopping at Onteniente, still a long distance from Aledo and not on the route of Alfonso's army. From there, he sent out envoys further south to spot the royal troops and alert him to their arrival, so that he could march and join them with his warriors. These envoys failed to notice the approach of the royal army, and Rodrigo only found out about their presence when they had already passed on towards Aledo. Trying to reach them with his own troops, he was still more than 40 km away when Alfonso's advance convinced the army besieging Aledo to withdraw without engaging in battle. Alfonso immediately took the road to return to Toledo.

The *Historia Roderici* claims that Rodrigo returned north greatly saddened that he had missed the king. Alfonso, on the other hand, saw him as an unfaithful vassal who had failed in his duties. Rodrigo's jealous enemies at court fomented the royal anger, insinuating that he was a traitor who had decided not to go to Alfonso's aid, hoping that the Saracens would kill him and all with him. The king listened to their false accusations and ordered the confiscation of all the lands Rodrigo had earlier received from him; of all his hereditary patrimony; and of all the gold, silver and other riches he had accumulated. In addition, his wife and children were captured and imprisoned. Whether this new break with Alfonso was due to an unfortunate coincidence, or to Rodrigo's inability to show the loyalty required of him, can be debated. However, the fact that the king was quick to condemn him; that Rodrigo had already built up structures enabling his independence; and the decision of some of his warriors to 'return home' to Castile even before Alfonso's judgement suggest that not all the blame lies with the king.

Rodrigo did send one of his faithful knights to Alfonso to clear his name. The message the knight relayed to the king rejected the accusations as false, and offered a judicial duel: Rodrigo himself, or one of his knights, would fight a champion designated by the king. Such trial by combat was a normal part of judicial proceedings in Europe at the time; it was supposed to demonstrate divine judgement, as it was believed that the guilty party would be defeated. While Alfonso rejected this proposal, he did allow Jimena and her children to leave and join Rodrigo. Allegedly, Rodrigo then offered to prove his innocence in four different ways, through four oaths; he wrote down his pleas of defence and sent them to the king. He swore that the sole reason he had not met Alfonso to lift the siege of Aledo was because he had no information about the king's route, nor any way of getting that information in time. He reiterated that he was always faithful to Alfonso and had never betrayed him or committed treason. The first oath according to the *Historia* is as follows:

> I Rodrigo swear to you . . . who accuses me in connection with that expedition which King Alfonso made to Aledo to fight the Saracens, that the fact that I was not with him sprang from no other cause but this, that I did not know of his route . . . I was guilty of no lie . . . I was guilty of no deceit towards him, no conspiracy, emphatically no treachery, and no evil . . . If I lie, may God deliver me into your hands to do your will upon me.

The second oath reads:

> I Rodrigo swear to you, the knight who wishes to fight with me, who accuses me concerning the king's arrival at Aledo, that I had no reliable information about the king's arrival . . . until I heard reports that he was already on his way back to Toledo. If I had known . . . I tell you in truth that unless I had been ill or a captive or dead I would have presented myself before the king at Molina and accompanied him to Aledo and been at his side in any engagement he might have had with the Saracens, in good faith and truly without any evil intent.

This is followed by the clause on God's punishment should he be lying.

The third oath concerns letters Rodrigo had sent to the king; again he asserts he had no evil intent. The fourth and final oath sets out that until he discovered that the king had 'unreasonably and cruelly' imprisoned his wife and stripped him of his property, he 'spoke no evil of him, thought no evil, neither did anything against him'. Another obligatory clause on God's judgement ends the text. Rodrigo then gave the king the option of choosing any of the four written oaths, or allowing him to undertake a judicial combat to prove his innocence, with the king's chosen champion. Moreover, if anybody were able to suggest a better, fairer, more just manner in which Rodrigo could disculpate himself, he promised that he would undertake to clear his name in that way. As so often, we lack independent verification to assess how much of this was true, and how much is literary fiction. Yet the four oaths had a long afterlife even if in a very different way.

If Rodrigo did offer these, or other, ways of clearing his name, Alfonso was having none of it. So Rodrigo found himself in exile for the second time. However, the circumstances were very different. Rodrigo had a well-tried band of warriors; although some left him and returned to Castile after his failure to meet the royal army, plenty of them remained. He also knew Valencia and the neighbourhood well. His prowess and military renown made him a formidable independent military leader in south-eastern Iberia, with warriors from Castile, Aragón and the county of Portugal willing to serve under him – all he needed to offer were victories, booty and *parias*. As an independent leader of such a warrior band, who owed allegiance to nobody, he was able to collect the tribute from some of the taifa rulers, not in the name of a king, but for himself, and bolster his fortunes.

For several years, Rodrigo moved around with his band of warriors within the territories of the taifas of Denia, Valencia, Alpuente, Albarracín and Tortosa. He arranged for some abandoned forts to be refortified and took over others, places where he stayed for weeks or months. They were his bases of operation, usually in mountainous or other, naturally well-protected locations, within easy reach of water and food. Such freelancing was possible in sparsely inhabited areas where the notional power of rulers could not be effectively enforced. Rodrigo had already started to build up such bases before his exile; now he relied on them completely. In permanent need of booty and tribute to reward and retain his military following, he led cavalry raids. He targeted places where wealth was accumulated, such as a cave filled with gold, silver and precious fabrics at Polop that belonged to Mundir al-Hayib of Lérida, Tortosa and Denia, defeating the defenders after a siege that lasted a few days. Al-Hayib then sent an embassy to Rodrigo, the old and well-known enemy from the times when he had been in the service of al-Hayib's brother, to negotiate a peace treaty with him. How he achieved this, whether he paid in exchange for peace, is not recorded, but it is the most likely scenario. From then on, Rodrigo focused his activities on Valencia. He received tribute and gifts from the ruler al-Qādir, as well as separately from the commanders of various forts, including those who rebelled against al-Qādir.

Due to his military campaigns there securing his hold, Rodrigo also already had de facto control of a large region around Valencia. Al-Hayib, although he managed to secure peace, knew well that Rodrigo continued to be a danger, and would have preferred a more permanent solution. In the summer of 1090, he found an ally in Berenguer Ramón II, the count of Barcelona, who was the protector of al-Hayib's taifa principality in exchange for tribute. He did not want the flow of tribute diminished due to Rodrigo's extortions, and was therefore motivated to put an end to his activities. However, many other potential supporters, King Sancho Ramírez of Aragón and several Catalan counts, who had experienced military defeat by Rodrigo, were wary of crossing him again and refused to join the alliance. The planned attack started badly, as the allies were deprived of the element of surprise. Al-Mustaʿīn of Zaragoza alerted Rodrigo to the designs against him. Outwitting his enemies, Rodrigo took up his position in a gorge in the mountainous region near Morella. According to Alberto Montaner, this was most probably at the foot of Puerto de Torre Miró. Berenguer Ramón II pursued Rodrigo and set up his camp nearby, but he was at a disadvantage, being on lower, flat ground.

The *Historia Roderici* claims that at this point the two leaders exchanged a series of letters and provides the full text of two, one allegedly sent by the count of Barcelona and the response sent by Rodrigo. While historians used to think these were verbatim copies of real letters, more recent research has persuasively demonstrated their fictional, literary quality. The letters trade choice insults. Count Berenguer of Barcelona refers to a previous letter of Rodrigo transmitted through al-Mustaʿīn of Zaragoza, the text of which is not included in the *Historia*, 'which scorned and gravely insulted and moved us to great frenzy', and 'likened us to our wives'. The count accused Rodrigo of treachery, of destroying and profaning churches and putting his faith in auguries, by trying to predict the future by the flight of birds: 'your gods are . . . ravens, crows, hawks, eagles . . . you trust more in their auguries than in God.' He called on Rodrigo to descend from the mountain to meet him in battle, otherwise he would not be called Campeador (roughly 'battler'), but a *fraudator*, a deceiver. The count repeatedly expressed his conviction that God would avenge the insults Rodrigo had inflicted on him, as well as retaliate for all Rodrigo's other misdeeds against God. Rodrigo responded by berating the count for his 'womanly courage' and hinted that he had killed his own brother. He goaded the count to attack, insinuating that he was too afraid to do so, merely finding excuses to avoid a battle. 'Now you can make no excuse for not doing battle with me – if you dare to fight . . . If you daren't fight with me, I shall tell [King Alfonso] that what you promised to do with boasting and arrogance, you could not perform for fear of me.' He reminded the count that he had already taken him captive once before, and had only released him for ransom.

Honour was a crucial asset in medieval warrior society, and insulting the enemy brought them dishonour. Keeping and regaining honour through appropriate behaviour – for example, bravery and revenging insults – was essential for maintaining one's status. Honour and dishonour played a key role in the *Historia*, and the author may have wanted to create a story in which the count tried to dishonour Rodrigo, only to suffer dishonour himself at the outcome of the confrontation. With Rodrigo refusing to descend from the mountain, Berenguer Ramón II sent part of his troops at night to take up a position even further up the mountain from Rodrigo's hideout. The next day, taking Rodrigo by surprise, the count's troops attacked from both below and above. One account incorporated in a later chronicle suggested that Rodrigo had a counter-ruse up his sleeve, misleading Count Berenguer Ramón II about his intentions, so that the count divided his troops into four units and positioned them in different locations, thus weakening his army. According to this narrative, Muslims in Rodrigo's army played a key role in transmitting the false information. In the ensuing battle, Rodrigo was wounded, but his troops were nonetheless victorious. Moreover, the count of Barcelona and several of his leading men were again captured. Plunder from the enemy camp, which included golden and silver vessels, luxury textiles, mules, horses and arms, boosted Rodrigo's fortunes. So would the ransom for the captured leaders, although the *Historia* states that after initially demanding an enormous ransom, in the end Rodrigo did not collect it, but, instead, it seems, the count and his magnates took oaths that they would serve him. After repeated negotiations, Count Berenguer Ramón II also ceded control over some of the 'lands of the Moors' that had been under his power; in other words, the area south of Tortosa, around Burriana, could now be exploited by Rodrigo for tribute. Rodrigo neutralized an important enemy and extended the geographical scope of his dominion.

After recovering from his wound, Rodrigo continued to move around the territories he exploited and spent time in various forts where he and his entourage could count on having enough food. He stayed in the taifa of Zaragoza whose ruler was his ally. Most importantly, he led his warriors on successful raids and tribute-taking. He targeted local lords in the territory of the taifa of Valencia, perfecting the system whereby he exacted tribute in exchange for renouncing destructive raids. Al-Hayib's death, leaving an underage heir, also benefited Rodrigo, who could strengthen his de facto hold over the region. The regents who governed in the name of the child contacted Rodrigo for protection. In exchange for 50,000 gold maravedís a year, Rodrigo graciously acquiesced. His control firmly established in the areas north of Valencia as well as over the taifa of Valencia itself, Rodrigo was raking in gold in enormous quantities. Although he had no official title, he was already effectively the lord of the region. Yet in a world that was constantly in flux, new dangers arose and no one was safe. While Rodrigo was consolidating his power over the area, the Almoravids were beginning to take over the taifas in the south of al-Andalus in 1090–91.

This posed a danger to King Alfonso VI, who attempted to stop them. According to the *Historia Roderici*, he even accepted the assistance Rodrigo offered after the queen and his friends at court alerted him to the situation, exhorting him to join the king with all his troops and help him against the Almoravids. This was no magnanimous act of loyalty to Alfonso; Rodrigo was affected by the same danger, and a joint response made strategic sense. So the king and Rodrigo embarked once again on a military campaign together, moving towards Granada. According to the story, the king chose a site for his camp in the mountains, while Rodrigo erected his camp on the plain in front of the royal host. Rodrigo's enemies at court and Alfonso interpreted this as Rodrigo's audacious arrogance, failing to give precedence to the king, while Rodrigo claimed he wanted to protect Alfonso's encampment. In the end, the Almoravids decided not to engage in battle, and finally Alfonso started to withdraw towards Toledo. En route, Alfonso had more angry confrontations with Rodrigo, and some of Rodrigo's warriors left him to join the king, an echo of the events leading to his second exile. It seems that some of Rodrigo's men thought he was finished.

Undoubtedly, whatever the specific triggers this time, the king must have objected to Rodrigo's growing independent power. After all, although Alfonso was still nominally the protector of the taifa of Valencia, Rodrigo was reaping the benefits from squeezing the Valencian ruler, not to mention the other areas now effectively under his control. It is quite plausible that Alfonso started to see Rodrigo as an immediate threat to him, intent on developing his own power at the expense of the king. Alfonso became so enraged that he wanted to have Rodrigo captured, but the latter managed to escape. And while Rodrigo once again maintained his innocence, the king refused any further reconciliation. Alfonso returned to Toledo, and Rodrigo, to the region of Valencia.

Rodrigo fortified Peña Cadiella, a strategic location in the province of Valencia in the south against the advancing Almoravids, but he was especially mindful of the potential danger from Alfonso VI. In 1092, both sides were preparing for a possible confrontation. Rodrigo not only renewed his alliance with Zaragoza's ruler al-Mustaʿīn but also allied himself with King Sancho Ramírez of Aragón and mediated a peace between his two allies. In the meantime, King Alfonso VI gained the agreement of Genoa and Pisa (maritime republics that had earlier sent fleets to attack Mahdia in North Africa, and were interested in controlling the western Mediterranean) to provide ships for an attack on Valencia; this would have allowed an assault from the sea. Alfonso wanted to eradicate once and for all the bases of Rodrigo's independent authority. However, barely had the siege of Valencia begun when Alfonso had to return in haste to his own lands to defend them, because, in a daring counter-move, Rodrigo, instead of trying to defend the region from which he had been extracting so much revenue, launched an attack against the king's lands in Nájera and Rioja. We found him in Rioja at the start of this book. The lands he targeted here were held by Count García Ordóñez, one of King Alfonso's men, who, according to the *Historia*, was responsible for various insults and enmity towards Rodrigo. After devastating the lands and setting fire to buildings 'cruelly and without mercy', Rodrigo returned, victorious, with a large quantity of treasure and plundered riches to Zaragoza. This checkmated Alfonso VI for the time being.

Then Rodrigo's big chance came, allowing him to consolidate his power through territorial conquest and turn Valencia into a principality under his own rule. The Almoravids were already steadily advancing towards Valencia in 1092, conquering the various taifas. Al-Qādir had been utterly unpopular in Valencia, and in the autumn of 1092 an uprising led by Ibn Jahhāf, the city's judge (qāḍī), broke out. The rebels called on Almoravid help, which resulted in a small group of warriors arriving and gaining entry to the town. Of those who had been left in charge by Rodrigo, his Muslim appointee, Ibn al-Faray, who oversaw the collection of tribute, was captured by the rebels; some others were able to flee. Al-Qādir tried to escape, but was captured and executed, and Ibn Jahhāf became the de facto ruler of Valencia, behaving like a king. The news reached Rodrigo via some of his men and those faithful to al-Qādir who managed to flee. He decided to intervene, to retain control over the area that had been such a lucrative source of booty and tribute. He first conquered a nearby fort, Juballa (Cebolla), to use as his base of operations against Valencia. He also reached an agreement with ʿAbd al-Mālik ibn Razīn, the taifa ruler of Albarracín, a tiny neighbouring territory, who promised to deliver supplies and also to allow Rodrigo to buy and sell in his forts, in exchange for peace. It is clear that Rodrigo was not only a mighty warrior but also an excellent strategic thinker with the ability to make arrangements that supported his military undertakings. His skill in negotiating favourable outcomes can be inferred on many occasions.

In the summer of 1093 Rodrigo besieged Valencia itself. Despite some direct attacks against the city, most of the warfare consisted of drawn-out systematic raiding, including seizing livestock and crops, and burning and ravaging the hinterlands. During these raids, Rodrigo also took captives for ransom, such as the *alcaide*, governor, of Alcalá, extorting 10,000 maravedís for his release. He also attacked and destroyed various suburbs of Valencia, killing people and causing destruction, taking the wood from the destroyed houses to Juballa to be used in the fortifications there. Direct attacks against Valencia were repulsed by its defenders, but two suburbs, on the other side of the Turia river, surrendered. Rodrigo forbade his troops to do any more damage there, and guaranteed the inhabitants' right to carry on with their lives in exchange for paying taxes. Ibn Jahhāf negotiated with Rodrigo, whose demands that the Almoravid contingent leave Valencia and the city pay tribute to him were accepted, and Rodrigo withdrew – for a time. He also kept one of the suburbs and Juballa as bases. He continued to raid the lands of the commanders of castles who favoured the Almoravids and could pose a danger, as well as the territories of anyone he suspected would oppose him. During such rapid cavalry attacks, Rodrigo's troops would take valuable objects, cows, sheep, horses, crops, as well as men and women, and transfer all the riches to Juballa to use or sell. He participated personally in some of the battles and was wounded on at least one occasion.

Ibn Jahhāf played his cards in different ways depending on the immediate circumstances; while he made a pact with Rodrigo when the latter had the upper hand, he was more than willing to back out of it and turn again to the Almoravids when the circumstances seemed propitious in the winter of 1093. At the Almoravid approach, Rodrigo had the dams of the River Turia destroyed in order to flood the plain between his own and the Almoravid army. That night torrential rain also fell; by the morning, the Almoravids had withdrawn without engaging in battle. Very likely the Almoravid commander decided he could not win, but it is impossible to know if this was due to the inability of the Almoravids to spare a large enough army, since they were still fully engaged in conquering the taifas, or whether they had underestimated Rodrigo. In any case, Rodrigo decided not to wait for a new onslaught, and besieged Valencia again, to conquer the town before the Almoravids returned.

What ultimately led to conquest was not a heroic battle, but, rather, starving the defenders of Valencia by cutting off their food supplies. One Muslim author refers to a book written by Ibn ʿAlqāmā about the siege: 'whoever reads it, weeps, and the judicious man is stunned.' In January 1094, Valencia was completely encircled, and no one could either leave or enter the city. The suburbs around the city, apart from the one already in the possession of Rodrigo, were sacked and destroyed, with many of the inhabitants having taken refuge in the city. Ibn Jahhāf started further negotiations, but these broke down. According to one account, the inhabitants turned to eating rats, dogs and even cadavers. Even so, Rodrigo was unable to take the city by direct assaults. Therefore, he not only continued to starve the inhabitants of Valencia but according to one account even ordered all those who left the city in search of food to be burned alive. An Aragonese military campaign was devastating the northern part of the taifa of Valencia at the same time; whether or not this was coordinated with Rodrigo, it certainly helped him. Ibn Jahhāf sent to al-Mustaʿīn of Zaragoza for help, ready to submit to him; the taifa ruler, however, refused to send assistance. Ibn Jahhāf also tried to appeal again to Yūsuf, ruler of the Almoravids, but no immediate relief was in sight. With the population dying of hunger, and no prospect of external help that could reach him in time, Ibn Jahhāf finally negotiated the surrender of Valencia. On 17 June 1094, the gates of the city were opened, and Rodrigo entered with his army, as the starving inhabitants swarmed out to the fields to find food. We do not know exactly what Valencia looked like at the time, but it was certainly a walled city, for archaeological excavations reveal the remains of an eleventh-century 2.25-m-thick wall with D-shaped towers every 25 m. The city contained a mosque and the palace of the taifa kings with a tower. Its splendour was celebrated by Muslim authors even as they bewailed its fall. Valencia's opulence was renowned: it was rich in goods and people. The countryside around Valencia consisted of irrigated fields (*huerta*), producing fruit, vegetables and olives, as well as of vineyards. Trade, including that in silk, also contributed to the revenues that made the city rich.

The later chronicles of Alfonso X claimed Rodrigo had stated before this conquest that he would reign as the second King Rodrigo, just as the first Rodrigo (Roderic, the last Visigothic king of Spain, who died in the invasion of 711) had, who was not born from a line of kings. Ibn Bassām of Santarém, an Andalusi Muslim historian who wrote his chronicle at the very beginning of the twelfth century, not long after the events, offered a slightly different version of the story: Rodrigo allegedly said that the peninsula had been conquered under a Rodrigo (that is, in 711), and a Rodrigo would save it, meaning that he wanted to extend his rule to the whole of Iberia. Whether Rodrigo made any such statement cannot be verified, but that he meant to create his own principality, not as the vassal of King Alfonso VI but as an independent lord, is certain. In the fluid power structures of the times, this was a possibility open to some successful warriors. Perhaps he even aspired to turn the principality into a kingdom eventually.

He was not, however, fighting a religious war against Muslims or Islam. Not only had he served the taifa rulers of Zaragoza in the past, but there were also Muslims in his army, and Muslims served him in various capacities in Valencia. According to Ibn Bassām, Rodrigo also had books read to him, in particular Arabic biographies, and when the history of al-Muhallab was read out to him he went into raptures and was amazed by the story. What was so appealing about this warrior who had lived centuries earlier? Abū Saʿīd al-Muhallab ibn Abī Ṣufra al-Azdī, born in the early 630s, gained prestige through his military prowess. He fought successfully in many military campaigns serving Rashidun, Umayyad and Zubayrid rulers. He held the governorship of various provinces and died in 702. According to the historian Hugh Kennedy, al-Muhallab was 'a figure of almost legendary prowess on the battlefield and a man with a great reputation as a commander', so Rodrigo's fascination might have been because he saw him as a model. The story, if true, raises intriguing questions. Who decided on the reading material? Did Rodrigo know Arabic or was the text translated? There is no way of telling if the story is fictive or real. However, Rodrigo incorporating tactics learned from Muslims, whether from texts or from personal experiences, on the battlefield, is entirely plausible.

Once he took Valencia, Rodrigo had to consolidate his power, and become the ruler of the city and its attached territories, the entire taifa principality. During the negotiations for capitulation, he had reportedly promised Ibn Jahhāf that the latter could retain rulership over the city. It is hard to believe that Rodrigo ever meant to keep such a promise even if he made it. Indeed, Rodrigo soon accused Ibn Jahhāf of having stolen the treasures of al-Qādir, whom Ibn Jahhāf had sent to his death. In what can only come across as breathtaking hypocrisy, Rodrigo also accused Ibn Jahhāf of ordering the assassination of al-Qādir, and thus of treason. Ibn Jahhāf was arrested, transferred to Juballa and tortured. He was forced to list all his possessions in writing and swear to the veracity of the list in front of the elites of Valencia.

What happened next survives in two very different accounts. According to the first, Rodrigo then tasked the Muslim qāḍī he had just appointed, 'Alhuacaxi' (al-Waqqašī), together with the 'wise men' of Valencia to judge Ibn Jahhāf according to Islamic law, for killing his king. The Muslim notables maintained that the punishment for such a sin was death by stoning, and so Rodrigo had Ibn Jahhāf and thirty-five accomplices stoned to death. According to the second account, that of Ibn Bassām, Rodrigo was after al-Qādir's treasure, and he had Ibn Jahhāf swear before both Christian and Muslim worthies that he knew nothing about the location of the hidden cache. Yet Rodrigo soon discovered the treasure, claimed Ibn Jahhāf had misled him, and had him, his sons and his household tortured, and then condemned Ibn Jahhāf to be burned alive. Ibn Bassām claimed to base his account on an eyewitness testimony: a hole was dug, into which Ibn Jahhāf was placed up to his armpits, and a fire was lit around him. In order to shorten his horrible torment, Ibn Jahhāf reached out and pulled the burning wood closer to him so that he would die more quickly. Rodrigo intended to have Ibn Jahhāf's wife and children burned to death as well, but one of the Christians dissuaded him.

Ibn Bassām described Rodrigo as clever, but a tyrant, swollen with pride and greed, 'a man who made it his profession to chain prisoners, the scourge of the land', because 'there was no area he didn't pillage', but also as a skilful and fearless man, which allowed him to be victorious with a small group of warriors over much larger armies. Rodrigo indeed consolidated his power over the entire region of the taifa. He allowed Valencia's Muslims to retain their properties and laws; they also kept their mosques and Muslim officials, who were appointed by Rodrigo. They had to pay tax to Rodrigo and keep the peace. Those who wished could leave, but they had to do so without their possessions. Despite this very unfavourable condition, according to one account many Muslims chose to move elsewhere, and in their place Christians settled. Another

Muslim account, however, contradicts this, and claims that Rodrigo caused no harm to the city or its inhabitants, who were therefore pacified, and hope spread. Rodrigo forbade them to leave, and the author bemoaned the fact that Rodrigo possessed himself of the city's fortune, wellbeing and splendour. In addition to his conquest, Rodrigo also continued his lucrative raids into territories neighbouring Valencia's.

Al-Andalus reacted to the fall of Valencia to Rodrigo, as did the feared Almoravids. They had initially responded to their co-religionists' call for help to reverse Christian successes, but by this time they were sweeping through the peninsula to secure their own lordship there. Therefore, this challenge to their authority had to be met. According to the *Historia*, Yūsuf ibn Tāshfīn flew into a rage on hearing the news, and sent one of his nephews, ʿAbd Allāh Muḥammad, with a large army to retake Valencia, capture Rodrigo and bring him to Yūsuf in chains. A reinforcement of Andalusi Muslims from the taifa states also joined the army. As news of these preparations reached him, Rodrigo organized the defence. He had the walls of Valencia reinforced, provisions stocked, and summoned more troops, including both Christians and Muslims, from the areas under his lordship. According to Ibn ʿAlqāmā, a native of Valencia and contemporary chronicler, parts of whose text survive in Ibn ʿIdhārī al-Marrākushī's late thirteenth- early fourteenth-century chronicle, Rodrigo even turned for help to King Alfonso VI who sent some troops; these never reached Valencia. Rodrigo also demanded that the inhabitants of Valencia hand over any iron tools that could be turned into weapons, on pain of confiscation of property and death, in order to avoid a possible pro-Almoravid rebellion in the city. Further, he devised for rumours to be spread that an Almoravid takeover would mean the massacre of the entire population of the city. Ibn ʿIdhārī al-Marrākushī, relaying Ibn ʿAlqāmā, also claimed that Rodrigo tricked the men of Valencia into assembling on the seashore, and he then only allowed the weaklings to return, while exiling the valiant men. Their families believed, however, that the exiles had been killed, and the town was plunged into mourning. According to the same Muslim author, when the joint Almoravid–Andalusi army reached Valencia in the autumn of 1094, the defenders were terrified by the size of the attacking troops; all except Rodrigo, who had received auguries through the movement of birds that told him he would not be defeated. Rodrigo seeking omens in the flight of birds is mentioned in the *Historia Roderici* as well; various forms of divination are repeatedly mentioned in medieval sources, practices condemned by the church as superstition, but performed by lay people.

What exactly happened is narrated in varying accounts, with Muslim sources attributing Rodrigo's victory to a ruse. In one version, Rodrigo sent out a detachment with him apparently at its head; when the enemy gave chase he rode out with another group of warriors and devastated their camp, routing them. Another version has it that he sent a detachment under cover of darkness, that, undetected, took up a position on the other side of the enemy camp. Then, at daybreak, Rodrigo rode out of Valencia with the rest of his troops and attacked the enemy. As they hastily armed themselves and counterattacked, Rodrigo turned his troops around, pretending to flee back to the city. At that point, the rest of his warriors, until then hidden, attacked from the other side, confusing the enemy, who mistook them for reinforcements from outside. In the ensuing chaos, Rodrigo was victorious.

The *Historia Roderici*, however, avoids any suggestion of subterfuge and claims that Rodrigo was victorious after leading his troops out of the city and into battle. After their triumph, his men were more interested in looting than killing, enriching themselves with gold, silver, precious textiles, horses and mules, and various types of weaponry. This was the first defeat of an Almoravid army in the Iberian peninsula and its significance can be seen in the contemporary acknowledgement of Rodrigo's triumph: an archival document in Aragón was dated in the year that Rodrigo was victorious over the Almoravids.

Rodrigo had to defend Valencia one last time from an Almoravid attack, although he had an ally on this occasion. When Pedro I succeeded to the throne of Aragón after his father Sancho Ramírez was killed at the siege of Huesca in 1094, Rodrigo confirmed his alliance with the kingdom. In early 1097, as the Almoravid army, again under the leadership of Yūsuf's nephew ʿAbd Allāh Muḥammad, approached, the joint armies of Rodrigo and Pedro I met them near Bairén. They were disadvantaged on lower ground, and open to attack both from the Almoravid ships on the coast and from their cavalry on higher ground. Rodrigo, however, was able to raise the morale of the troops who ended up defeating the Almoravids.

One of the first things Rodrigo did after his conquest of Valencia was to extort more money from its richest citizens: he simply had them imprisoned until a ransom was paid. He was no more lenient in his methods when consolidating his power over the entire territory surrounding the city of Valencia. He led more military campaigns in the vicinity, for example occupying the fortress of Olocau about 30 km away. In 1097–8, Rodrigo besieged and conquered Almenar, where one of his enemies, the *alcaide* of Játiva, Abū-l-Faṭah, took refuge, and then Murviedro, north of Valencia. The *Historia Roderici* claimed that the defenders of Murviedro begged for help from Alfonso VI, al-Mustaʿīn of Zaragoza, ʿAbd al-Malik ibn Razīn of Albarracín, the Almoravids and the count of Barcelona. With the exception of the count of Barcelona, who conducted a short-lived and unsuccessful manoeuvre to draw Rodrigo away from the siege, all declined to help, with many expressing their fear of Rodrigo. Murviedro had no choice but to surrender.

Holding forts in the countryside was important not only for defence but also for squeezing the rural inhabitants for revenues and ensuring that they handed over the produce needed to feed Rodrigo and his men. For even after becoming lord of Valencia, Rodrigo's main endeavours were focused on acquiring riches. According to Muslim sources, he extorted significant amounts from the local Muslims under threat of death. The former taifa king Abū ʿAbd al-Raḥmān Muḥammad ibn Aḥmad ibn Isḥāq ibn Ṭāhir of Murcia, who had gone into exile to Valencia in 1078, was imprisoned by Rodrigo and wrote a letter in 1095 in which he both lamented his own fate, having to pay a ransom to be freed, and that of Valencia for the calamities that befell her. Rodrigo also continued to take booty from defeated enemies. Yet the government of the conquered city and its territories could not consist merely of extortion.

How did a warlord adapt to ruling over a principality? Tellingly, the *Historia Roderici* is utterly uninterested in this question apart from a few brief mentions of Rodrigo's ecclesiastical foundations, as if all that mattered were military victories and booty. It summarizes Rodrigo's last years thus: 'It would take too long . . . to narrate in order all the battles which Rodrigo and his companions fought and won, or to list all the lands and settlements which his strong right arm wasted and destroyed with the sword.'

One document throws more light on at least one aspect of Rodrigo's governance of Valencia – his donation charter to the newly established bishopric and its bishop, Jerome. It may also conserve the only authentic material trace left by the hand of Rodrigo, an autograph signature: 'Ego Ruderico simul cum coniuge mea afirmo oc quod superius scriptum est.' 'I, Ruderico, together with my wife, confirm what is written above.' The charter, dated 1098, is accepted by most scholars as an original document. While, as with many medieval charters, there is no absolute proof of its authenticity, it is unlikely to be a forgery, since within a few years of Rodrigo's death Valencia was in Muslim hands, and so no possible beneficiary could have had an interest in forging such a document. Further, it was stored in the cathedral of Salamanca, along with another charter from Valencia by Jimena, and it is logical that they were deposited there by Bishop Jerome, who after the fall of Valencia became bishop of Salamanca. He would have had an interest in conserving the documents that proved his rights to previously held possessions, in the hope that they would one day be restored to him.

This one line on the charter, written in Rodrigo's hand, is an intriguing glimpse into the world of a man we mostly know for his accomplishments as a warrior. It is a rough hand, but written in Latin, in the Visigothic script. It is certainly not the hand of someone used to writing often, yet it does suggest some education. This conforms to evidence from the twelfth century that shows other aristocrats' ability to sign charters either as donators or as witnesses. Therefore, Rodrigo may also have been more learned in the art of governing, despite the early sources' lack of interest. The charter also throws light on Jimena's role: she, too, confirmed the donation, because of her proprietary rights in the properties granted. She may have shared in some of the tasks of governing the city as well, which would have been within the capabilities of aristocratic women of those times.

The rest that we can glean on the topic of Rodrigo's governance of Valencia comes from Muslim sources. It seems Rodrigo was trying to find solutions on the hoof, and many of them did not last. This fluidity could not have facilitated his rule. Security continued to be a vital issue, and he employed some Aragonese warriors to guard the city. External attacks were not the only destabilizing factor: significant instability affected the local population as well. There were multiple waves of expulsion and emigration, both because Rodrigo was trying to exclude potential rebels and because people simply wanted to leave. Such population movements reduced the number of local inhabitants after the taking of Valencia, after the execution of Ibn Jahhāf, after the defeat of the Almoravids at Quart de Poblet, and again after the Battle of Bairén.

Yet the diverse sources are inconsistent. According to one story, Rodrigo distrusted the Muslims of Valencia to such an extent that he expelled brave men simply because he thought them potential rebels. But according to another, at first he appointed a Muslim qāḍī, al-Waqqašī, who served as a representative of the ruler in administering justice to the local Muslims; this position combined the functions of judge and magistrate. However, al-Waqqašī himself is another example of just how little stability there was: while he was among those who originally did not oppose the conquest by Rodrigo, in 1095 he fled to the taifa of Denia. He also composed a poem on the fall of Valencia, bemoaning the city's loss. Rodrigo had appointed a Jewish vizier by the autumn of 1094. Ibn 'Alqāmā accused this vizier, together with his other co-religionists, of oppressing the local Muslims. According to him, tax collectors, scribes and various administrative officers were selected from among Jews, while the vizier himself filled the role of city prefect who could order arrests and punishments. 'Each Muslim had at his heels a snooping agent who accompanied him every morning to ensure that he contributed something to the treasure chests of the master of Valencia. If he failed to do this he was killed or tortured.' It is quite incredible that Rodrigo would have been able to establish a regime that was more controlling than Stalinist Russia or the Stasi in East Germany. The one definite conclusion is that his governing of Valencia left a very negative impression on Muslims.

The 1098 donation charter of Rodrigo Díaz to Bishop Jerome and the cathedral of Valencia, with his autograph signature.

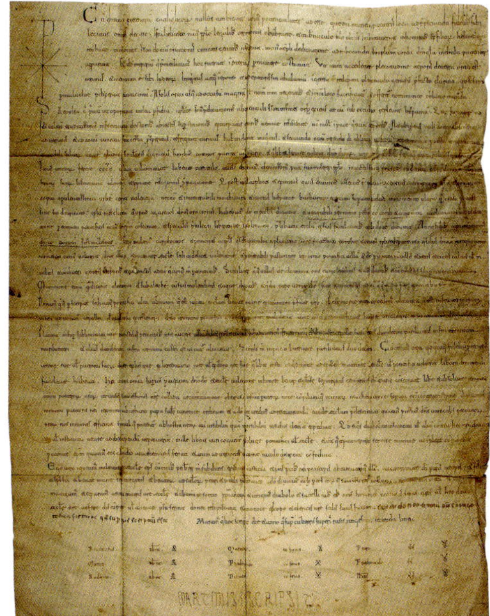

A representation of King Alfonso VI in the *Tumbo A* of the cathedral of Santiago de Compostela, from the twelfth century.

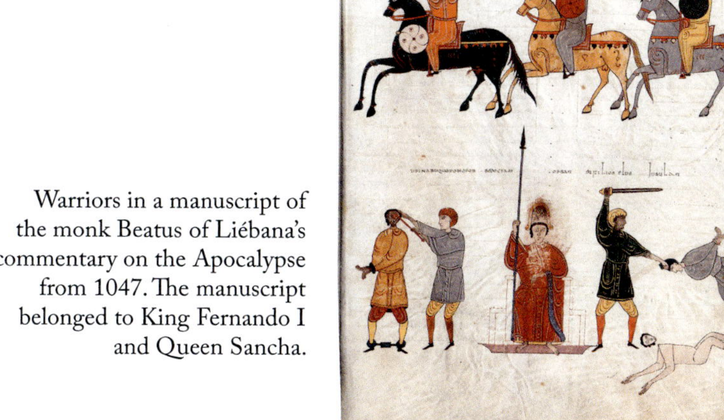

Warriors in a manuscript of the monk Beatus of Liébana's commentary on the Apocalypse from 1047. The manuscript belonged to King Fernando I and Queen Sancha.

The Golden Hall in the Aljafería Palace, in the taifa of Zaragoza, built in the second half of the eleventh century.

A casket from Palencia with ivory plaques; its Kufic inscription relates that it was made in Cuenca 441 H. (that is, 1049–50), commissioned by the ruler of Toledo Yahya al-Mamun.

The façade of the monastery of San Pedro de Cardeña, built in the eighteenth century; and a close-up of its statue of the Cid in the manner of Santiago Matamaros.

The grave of the Cid and Jimena in the funerary chapel in the monastery of San Pedro de Cardeña.

The grand Puerta de Santa María in Burgos, remodelled in the mid-sixteenth century. Visible are the statues of Carlos I, Fernán González, the Cid, Nuñom Rasura, Laín Calvo and Diego Porcelos.

An oil painting of Vivant Denon replacing the bones of the Cid and Jimena in their tomb, by Alexandre-Évariste Fragonard,1811, after a watercolour sketch by Benjamin Zix.

'La Tizona', the Cid's alleged sword, which is now displayed in the museum of Burgos.

The Cid Campeador Spearing Another Bull, an engraving from Francisco Goya's 'Tauromaquia' cycle, 1814–16.

One of the Cid's alleged chests, on display in the Burgos Cathedral.

El Cid's daughters, from Romance XLIV of the Tesoro de Romances,
Dióscoro Teófilo Puebla y Tolín, 1871.

Detail from the mural painting planned for the Valle de los Caídos, the colossal monument commissioned by Franco, representing him as the Cid.

A postal stamp representing the Cid, from the Franco period in Spain.

The poster for the film *El Cid*, starring Charlton Heston and Sophia Loren, released in 1961.

Ramón Menéndez Pidal with Charlton Heston and Sophia Loren on set during the filming of *El Cid*.

The statue of Jimena on the bridge of San Pablo, Burgos, created by Joaquín Lucarini in 1955.

A statue in Burgos of the Cid on his trusted horse, Babieca, sculpted by Juan Cristóbal González Quesada in 1955.

The much later *Estoria de España* presents a rosy picture of Rodrigo's treatment of Valencian Muslims after the conquest. He reassures them that they can keep their fields as before and cultivate them; he orders that tax collectors take no more 'than the tithe, according to the Qur'anic law'. He sets aside two days a week, Monday and Thursday, to hear their lawsuits 'because I want to personally resolve all your problems and be a companion for you, like a friend to his friend or a relative to his relative; I want to be your *alcalde* (magistrate) and your *alguacil* (governor)'.

This caring Cid is clearly the figment of a later author's imagination, although reliance on Islamic law and to some extent on Muslim functionaries to rule a Muslim population is not. Such pragmatic adaptation was frequent at the time. Even if the Valencians were initially governed according to their traditions and law, the Arabic authors saw Rodrigo's conquest and rule as a terrible misfortune, rather than a period of benevolent governance; they had a range of less than complimentary epithets for him. His name, Rodrigo, is rendered as Rudhrīq or Ludhrīq, qualified as an 'enemy dog', 'accursed', 'the oppressor' or 'tyrant'. The texts also add devout appeals to the divinity: 'may God destroy him' and 'may God curse him'. Even Ibn Bassām, who readily acknowledged Rodrigo's military valour and cleverness, saw him as a 'misfortune for his time', causing 'incurable damage', conquering by 'fraud, as was his custom' and labelled his Muslim allies iniquitous and vile. 'How many superb places the tyrant captured and profaned! . . . How many . . . were trampled under the feet of his mercenaries!' 'That oppressor, . . . because of his skilful acts, his qualities of fortitude and his extreme fearlessness, was one of the prodigies of his God, until shortly afterwards God made him die, passing away in Valencia by a natural death. He had, may God curse him, carried his banner victoriously, having won against groups of Christians, . . . killing their numerous soldiers with his small troop.'

Although he spent some of his life in the service of Muslim lords, and he conquered an area inhabited and surrounded by Muslims, and pragmatically employed Muslims in his service, Christianity played a significant role in Rodrigo's principality. According to the *Historia Roderici*, after taking Almenar and Murviedro, he had a mass celebrated and a church built in each place to honour God for his victories. In Valencia itself, several years after his conquest, Rodrigo converted the great mosque into a church, a common practice in the towns that fell to Christians, and it became Valencia's new cathedral. According to the *Historia Roderici*:

> in the Saracen building which they call a mosque he built a fine and seemly church in honour of St Mary the Virgin, Mother of our Redeemer. He gave to the same church a golden chalice worth a hundred and fifty marks. He also gave to the aforesaid church two very precious hangings woven with silk and gold, the like of which, it was said, had never been seen in Valencia. Everyone then celebrated mass in that church with most sweet and melodious songs of praise.

Rodrigo established a new bishopric, under Jerome of Périgord, probably a Cluniac monk from Moissac who had come to the peninsula from France earlier on the invitation of Archbishop Bernard of Toledo (who himself was from Gascony). French Cluniacs, members of a monastic order directly under papal protection, arrived in the Iberian peninsula as propagators of the papal reform movement in the last two decades of the eleventh and the first two decades of the twelfth century. This reform attempted to create more uniformity in ecclesiastical life, for example through the introduction of the Roman liturgy to various localities, and the transformation of monasticism. The local Visigothic liturgy, also called the Mozarabic or Hispanic rite, used in church services, had developed during the Visigothic period because originally there was no standard practice prescribing the exact form of church services. By the second half of the eleventh century, however, the papacy wanted all of Catholic Christendom to adopt the Roman practice. Rulers who were willing to support this change invited Cluniacs to their realm. In 1098 Jerome moved from Toledo to Valencia and was consecrated bishop of Valencia by Pope Urban II, after he was elected by the cathedral chapter. Rodrigo's donation charter to the new bishopric in 1098 detailed the landed possessions he handed over. These included gardens, estates and other lands around Valencia that he had conquered. He also permitted others to donate lands to the cathedral for the benefit of their soul. The *Historia Roderici* describes

Rodrigo's other gifts to the cathedral: a golden chalice and silk and gold-thread wall hangings.

Rodrigo's conquest of Valencia meant the creation of an independent polity. He was clearly ruling in his own right, rather than as a vassal subject of King Alphonso VI. Rodrigo held all the rights over his newly conquered domains just as Castilian or Aragonese kings did over their own. He used the title *princeps*, which by that time usually designated the highest aristocracy, including rulers such as the count of Barcelona. Without doubt this title signalled his independence from the king of Castile, who is not even mentioned in the donation charter issued by Rodrigo to the bishop and the cathedral. Rodrigo's status as a sovereign ruler is further reinforced by turns of phrase such as 'our excellence' and 'our sublimity' that are used to designate him in the charter. Furthermore, the 1098 donation charter suggests that the bishopric of Valencia was independent from the Iberian ecclesiastical hierarchy and directly subject to the papacy; this would further reinforce the autonomy of Rodrigo's new principality. Rodrigo certainly did not behave as a faithful vassal of Alfonso VI; there is no mention of the king as Rodrigo's overlord after the conquest of Valencia. Such a rise to independent lordship through successful warfare was not exceptional at the time: some other aristocrats achieved it across Europe in the period.

It is quite likely that this was not the endpoint of Rodrigo's ambitions, and that he would have tried to turn his principality into a kingdom had he not died so soon, or had he left a male heir to succeed him on his death. The framing and terminology of the donation charter of 1098 already point to such an aspiration. There are examples of this being done: on the Iberian peninsula itself, Portugal, a county in the kingdom of León, became an independent kingdom, while the Hauteville family that established the Norman principality of Sicily in the Cid's lifetime rose to royal rank in 1130. Those powerful enough to carve out substantial territorial rule and assume a royal title could eventually have their de facto power acknowledged by others. Rodrigo's pretensions to found a new royal dynasty were evoked by Muslim authors. As preserved in the chronicle of Alfonso X, Rodrigo boasted, 'I will subjugate all the lords of al-Andalus to my power, and because King Rodrigo reigned without being of royal blood, so will I reign and I will be the second King Rodrigo.' According to the account of his speech to the Valencians after their surrender to him in 1094, he said, 'I am a man who has never possessed a kingdom, and no one from my lineage ever had. But since I came to this city, I have always found it to my liking, I have desired it, and I prayed to God our Lord to give it to me. And behold the power of God: the day I came to besiege Juballa, I did not even have four loaves of bread, yet God's grace allowed me to take Valencia, of which I am master.'

Rodrigo may have meant to prepare the ground for eventually gaining the royal title from the papacy: embracing the papal push to replace local liturgy with the Roman one and placing the bishop of Valencia directly under the papacy, apart from buttressing Rodrigo's sovereignty would gain papal goodwill. Rodrigo may also have counted on his repeated victories over the Almoravids as grounds for papal support for a royal title; after all, this was exactly the period when the papacy called on warriors from Europe to fight to 'retake' the Holy Land, promising spiritual rewards for the killing of Muslims – the enterprise later known as the first crusade. Papal approval was important for the recognition of new aspirants to a royal title.

While already ruling Valencia, Rodrigo arranged his two daughters' marriages to Ramiro, an illegitimate member of the Navarrese royal family, and to the count of Barcelona. The marriages of Rodrigo's daughters were probably intended to strengthen the Navarrese and Catalan ties and reduce the likelihood of attacks against Valencia, but they could also have had the ulterior motive of linking Rodrigo's family to ruling dynasties. After all, he did not merely choose warriors from the aristocracy, but scions of ruling houses. Was one or the other also meant to take over the rulership of Valencia after Rodrigo's death? For one crucial component for hopes of royalty to be realized was missing: a male heir.

Despite his spectacular victories over the Almoravids, Rodrigo may have lost his only son (or at least the only one to survive to adulthood) to them. Only one source, the *Linage de Rodric Díaz*, mentions Rodrigo's son Diego. This vernacular text, composed according to some scholars around 1195, according to others a century earlier, and thus close to the events, was included in an anonymous Navarro-Aragonese chronicle, the *Liber Regum*, with much later embellished versions incorporated into other texts. It merely states that Diego was killed by the Moors at the Battle of Consuegra (August 1097), where the troops of King Alfonso VI were defeated by the Almoravids. Given the debatable nature of the text, it is hard to know how reliable it is, or what sources it is based on. If Rodrigo indeed had a son, his curious omission from other sources is puzzling. The reference also gave rise to much scholarly speculation: that Rodrigo had a first wife who was Diego's mother, or that Diego sided with Alfonso VI when the king and Rodrigo fell out. As so often, all historians can do is speculate. Why Diego participated in the battle is not explained in the text, and scholars hypothesized that he was either already in the service of Alfonso VI, attached to the court to complete his education or taken into the king's service when Rodrigo was exiled a second time, even perhaps as a kind of hostage, or that Rodrigo sent him with troops to help Alfonso when the king solicited aid before another confrontation with the Almoravid armies who were advancing against him. The Almoravids defeated Alfonso's army as they reached Consuegra, part of Alfonso's defensive belt. After that, in the end they withdrew to North Africa, only to return in 1099 to successfully take Consuegra. If the episode of Diego's death is true, what would the death of his only son have meant for Rodrigo? Grief? Anger that his ambitions of founding a new dynasty had evaporated?

It was not just the dynastic dream that came to an end. Rodrigo was unable to rule Valencia for long; his own life ended in 1099. He may have been about fifty years old. Unlike the later legend and then the film spinning a story of his romantic death, it was not due to self-sacrifice. While there is no information on how Rodrigo died, it seems to have been from natural causes. The many military campaigns, with the associated hardship of spending time in the cold or heat, without sufficient sleep and in physically trying circumstances, and several wounds in the course of battles undoubtedly contributed to shortening his life. Analyses of human remains from the period show that injuries and disease were frequent; life was hard and not many survived to an old age. The precise date was not recorded at the time; only a fifteenth-century chronicle claimed he died on 10 July, although its reliability is questionable, as it actually got the year wrong, placing the event in 1098.

While Rodrigo was alive, Valencia, sole Christian outpost in al-Andalus, held strong. Had he lived, perhaps he would have used his base in Valencia to create an independent kingdom; in the period, such political fortunes could be made in the peninsula, and new Christian kingdoms arose in the course of the wars and Christian expansion during the eleventh and twelfth centuries. In this case, however, a few years after his death, his widow Jimena had to evacuate Valencia, as it fell to the Muslims. It was not to be under Christian rule again until 1238, when James I of Aragon (1213–76) conquered it.

By the time he died, the historical Rodrigo had acquired a reputation as a warrior. His contemporary fame can be gleaned from brief, but significant mentions of his deeds by those not under his dominion. His Muslim enemies clearly did not like him, but just as obviously recognized his military skills. An Aragonese charter from November 1095 is dated by reference to his victory over the Almoravids who moved against Valencia and whose troops he defeated at Quart de Poblet in October 1094: 'This charter was made in 1133 of the [Spanish] era, on the day before the kalends of December, in the year when the Almoravides came to Valencia and Rodiric Didaç defeated them.' Knowledge of his conquest of Valencia started to spread; it was noted in the annals of the monastery of Saint-Maixent in France. His death in 1099 was recorded not only in diverse chronicles across Iberia but even outside the peninsula, in the monastery of Saint-Maixent. There a monk lamented his passing: 'In Hispania, at Valencia, Count Rodericus died, to the great grief of the Christians and the joy of their pagan enemies.'

The basis of Rodrigo's contemporary fame was undoubtedly military skill, both as a warrior and a strategist. He was clearly talented both on the battlefield and, when necessary, in negotiations. Rodrigo successfully carved out a territory for himself and fended off Almoravid attacks on Valencia in both 1094 and 1097, at a time when the Almoravids were widely seen as invincible, because of a series of victories against both Christians, including Alfonso VI several times, and the taifas. The historical figure thus becomes tangible through the mist of legend. Unscrupulous, opportunistic, fearless, an excellent warrior and military strategist, but certainly not someone whose main virtue was loyalty to his king or an individual motivated by an ardent Catholic faith as later legend would have it. And while we cannot be sure that he burned Valencia's Muslim judge alive, as claimed by a medieval Arabic text, that would have been more in character than catapulting bread into the city to feed the inhabitants while he was laying siege to them, as represented in the film *El Cid*.

In recognition of his martial skills, Rodrigo was known as Campeador, someone who excels in battle. Two explanations exist for this sobriquet. According to one, this vernacular term derived from the Latin term 'Campidoctor', which was used to designate him in the donation charter to the bishopric of Valencia. The same Latin word also figures in a charter by Rodrigo's widow Jimena and a panegyric poem composed probably in Rodrigo's lifetime: it seems to be the earliest title used by Rodrigo, although this choice has baffled historians. It was a rare classical Roman term to designate a military officer who instructed new recruits, who was therefore 'master of the battlefield'. Why the terminology of an obscure Roman office would have been applied to Rodrigo is unclear. According to another explanation, however, the Latin term was a neologism, based on the romance term 'Campeador' – therefore unrelated to the classical Roman title – from the word 'to fight', and designated a fighter, a battler, someone who excelled in battle. This explanation suggests that while in surviving texts the Latin form predates the vernacular one, in fact it was the latter that was in use earlier, at least orally. In any case, the vernacular term rapidly became an epithet, signalling Rodrigo's fame as an invincible warrior. It was even noted by the contemporary Muslim historian Ibn 'Alqāmā in the form al-Kambiyatūr. Later narratives claimed that both Moors and Christians called him 'el Cid Campeador'.

The Song of the Campeador (*Carmen Campidoctoris*) celebrated Rodrigo's military prowess in an archaizing framework, comparing him to heroes of classical antiquity. It was copied at the monastery of Ripoll around 1200, while the earliest proposed date of its composition is 1083. One suggestion links its creation to the occasion of the marriage of one of Rodrigo's daughters to the count of Barcelona, Ramón Berenguer III. The poem certainly celebrates Rodrigo's military merits and elevates him as an unparalleled warrior: he is placed above Paris, Pyrrhus and Aeneas, the great heroes of antiquity. The Latin poem survives incomplete, but the storyline broadly resembles that propagated by the *Historia Roderici*, and highlights the protagonist's military feats. The hero gains his title of Campidoctor after defeating the Navarrese champion when still a youngster. Famed for his victories on the battlefield, first in the service of Sancho, and, after the king's death, of Alfonso, Rodrigo's envious enemies turn the king against him. In his exile, he triumphs over both Muslims and those Christian troops that are sent against him by Alfonso.

'Campeador', however, was superseded by another moniker that, over time, became inseparable from his name. It is the one by which he is still known: 'el Cid'. There have been debates regarding the origin of the term and whether it was already used in Rodrigo's lifetime. Made up of the definite article in the Castilian vernacular and a distorted Arabic term, 'Çid' from *sayyid*, lord, a title used for the taifa rulers, it is thought to derive from an honorific title, 'my lord'. According to one hypothesis, it was the form of address that either the Muslims of Zaragoza or Rodrigo's Muslim subjects in Valencia used initially, which was then adopted by his retinue. Other scholars think it was a later invention, already part of the legend rather than reality, because the earliest sources do not use this term, nor do the Arabic sources refer to him in this way. Its first appearance was in the middle of the twelfth century, and it became firmly attached to Rodrigo only in the *Poema de Mio Cid*, in the thirteenth century. Later sources do not help. The most widely known story, according to which the defeated al-Mu'tamid of Sevilla gave him this title, when the young Rodrigo both demonstrated his superior prowess and was also merciful towards the defeated, is clearly legendary.

The matter is complicated by the fact that others were also called 'mio Cid' in the medieval sources; the earliest example is Muño Muñoz around 1100, who operated in the frontier regions of Zaragoza in much the same way as Rodrigo had. Recent research has shown that the form 'Citi', corresponding to the Arabic Sidi, 'my lord', was used as a personal name from the 1070s on. Hybrid epithets existed in Castilian charters from the beginning of the twelfth century, from which time both 'mio Cid' and other, similar constructions appeared concerning several different people, especially individuals of northern Castilian origin, many of them from around Burgos. Therefore, the origin of 'mio Cid' need not be directly from the Arabic, used by Muslims; it was also a loan word from Arabic used in the vernacular Romance Castilian language. It points to a local Castilian custom for addressing nobles. It may be that the title was already conferred on Rodrigo in his lifetime, but in that case it merely corresponded to local Castilian usage for the nobility. Ironically, in that case, it may not have been a unique title elicited by Rodrigo's exceptional qualities. The historical Rodrigo, however, was soon superseded by the mythical Cid, who was certainly peerless.

3

A Saviour Sent by Divine Providence

Shortly before Rodrigo's death, a document drawn up to record his endowment of the cathedral of Valencia and its bishop gave birth to his emerging myth. The donation charter includes a narrative framing of Rodrigo's deeds that made him the protagonist of a divine plan; it is the earliest transformation, turning Rodrigo into a larger-than-life hero. He is no longer an opportunistic warrior, but a Christian saviour.

The first aspect of Rodrigo's life that blurred into legend, which underpinned his transformation into a hero fighting for the faith, related to his warrior qualities; and in this, legend was not far from reality, merely turning his victories into more heroic deeds, to paint the image of an unvanquished warrior. He is *invictissimus princeps Rodericus Campidoctor*, an undefeated prince and master of the battlefield in this document. The charter, however, does much more than praise Rodrigo's warrior qualities. Its prologue (translated by Simon Barton in his article 'El Cid, Cluny and the medieval Spanish Reconquista') provides a historicizing backdrop to Rodrigo's conquest of Valencia, placing the story of Christianity in the Iberian peninsula in a providential framework. As this text would have it, the peninsula, designated with the classical term Hispania, had already been evangelized during the age of Christ's first disciples by apostolic preaching. Yet, after a while, charity grew cold, iniquity increased and divine precepts were forgotten. For these lapses, divine punishment swiftly smote the populace. Those who did not voluntarily serve the Lord were forced to become the servants of slaves: Hispania fell before the cruel swords of the sons of Agar. Agar is the biblical Hagar, a slave handmaiden to Sarah who, according to the Bible, bore Ishmael for Abraham; medieval interpretations made Ishmael the ancestor of the

Arabs, and, more broadly, of Muslims. The conquest is therefore depicted as an Islamic one, and as divine punishment for the Christian inhabitants, the Muslims being denigrated as the descendants of a slave concubine. The peninsula thus endured four centuries of calamity before God finally took pity on his people and raised up Rodrigo to be the avenger of their shame and the propagator of the Christian faith. With divine help, he achieved exceptional victories and finally captured the most opulent city of Valencia. 'Moreover, having overcome the army of innumerable Moabites and the barbarians of all of Hispania' without incurring any losses, he dedicated the mosque that had been considered among the Agarenes as a house of prayer to God as a church, and endowed it.

Rodrigo has now become a God-appointed champion for Christianity, ever victorious. The end of Visigothic Iberia through the Arab-Berber conquest is also reconceptualized. The success of the conquerors over the Visigoths is represented here as divine punishment for the wrongdoing of Christians, which implies that if God is placated, the punishment will come to an end, with the return of the peninsula to the Christians. Rodrigo, therefore, fulfils a role in a grand divine plan, rather than merely waging opportunistic warfare, however successfully. This was a major step in the recasting of the Campeador, the basis for all future legend-making.

Why was it not enough to claim that a successful Christian warrior conquered Valencia? Why would churchmen want to turn Rodrigo into a Christian champion sent by God? Such charters were meant to be legal proof of the ownership of lands that were acquired as gifts. In some, there were narratives about the recipient's deeds showing they merited the donation, or about the counter-gift, such as a monastic community's prayers for the donator. But extensive praise for the person giving the gift, elevating him to the role of divine saviour, is unusual. The narrative prologue that extolled Rodrigo preceded the legally most significant part of the charter: the details of the endowment Rodrigo made to the cathedral and its new bishop. Rodrigo's donations included various landed properties around Valencia granted to the bishopric from his own possessions. The Catholic ecclesiastical community of Valencia had a vested interest in portraying Rodrigo in a good light. Plunder from a mere warrior who had been fighting rather indiscriminately and happened to take Valencia from Muslims, but whose checkered past clearly demonstrated that this was motivated by opportunism rather than an ideological war for Christianity, would not look nearly so good as the pious donation of a God-appointed hero. No wonder the clerics who wrote the charter recording this donation in 1098 wanted to present the donator not as a mercenary conqueror but as someone sent by divine providence to restore Christian rule. The new bishop and perhaps other clerics in Valencia were members of, or at least influenced by, Cluniac monasticism. The Cluniacs were the most significant monastic movement at the time; they disseminated ideas of monastic reform and were closely involved in the spiritual care of Europe's elites in return for large donations. The clerics would have been eager to base their privileges in Valencia on rock-solid foundations.

It is in the context of ecclesiastical privileges, therefore, that the ruthless and successful warrior Rodrigo became a 'most invincible prince' raised up by God finally to avenge Christians and expand the faith, defeating the barbarians. Moreover, the charter also made a claim for the Valencian bishopric's independence from the local hierarchy, and the bishop's consecration by the pope himself. In the Catholic hierarchy, each bishopric was subordinated to an archbishopric; direct dependence on the pope instead would be a significant privilege. The bishopric of Valencia was restored after Rodrigo's conquest of the principality; in Visigothic times, Valencia had been a suffragan, that is, subordinate, of the archbishopric of Toledo. The charter may have claimed a status that did not match reality, but it is also possible that Rodrigo managed to gain papal approval for such a new status for his bishopric. For ecclesiastical independence, and direct dependence on the papacy was a privilege, and a Christian hero was more worthy of the granting of such a request. Perhaps Rodrigo wanted to bolster the independent status of his principality by creating a bishopric that would be separate from the Castilian hierarchy, and from the oversight of the archbishop of Toledo, which would also contribute to political independence. It is equally possible that Bishop Jerome had ambitions beyond a mere bishopric, and suggested it would be more favourable to be under direct papal authority. Jerome could have found the model for such a relationship in the status of the monastery of Cluny itself, which had been placed under the protection of the papacy by its founder and was directly dependent on the pope ecclesiastically. Whether the charter made a grandiose claim or reflected a new reality, after Valencia's fall, when Jerome was reassigned to another bishopric, he was firmly designated as a suffragan of Toledo. While the ambitions for ecclesiastical status were either short-lived or remained an unfulfilled aspiration, Rodrigo's promotion to a Christian hero was durable.

This was partly due to the fact that the transformation did not merely concern one individual. Rather, it dovetails with the emerging myth of the Reconquista itself. Rather than being a common feeling motivating all Christian warriors since the early eighth century, the notion that Christians were fighting for religious reasons against Muslims, to retake territory that had once been theirs, appeared in the late ninth/early tenth century at the court of Oviedo, and was further developed in the late tenth century. It started to make a stronger mark in texts in the late eleventh century. This idea about Christian war was not called the 'Reconquest' at the time; the noun itself was coined at the end of the eighteenth century, although the verb form 'to reconquer' occasionally appears in the medieval sources. The term has a bad reputation because of its nineteenth- and twentieth-century ideological usage, the claim that it shaped Spanish national character, and its exploitation by a dictatorship. Some scholars therefore argue that it is irrelevant to the medieval history of the Iberian peninsula. However, the conceptual content of the term, Christians fighting against Muslims to retake land, was clearly present in many medieval sources. Yet its presence is no straightforward sign of the real motivations of people at the time, nor does it mirror reality.

The idea of a 'restoration' or reconquest motivating the Christians of the peninsula emerged gradually, and often at odds with the evolving real events. Towards the end of Rodrigo's life and in the following century, we often find the lofty rhetoric of fighting for the Christian faith clashing with the chaotic free-for-all of fighting on the ground. Indeed, the most fascinating aspect of the alleged Reconquest is that it was a rhetoric that existed in parallel with a reality that it did not match. This can be appreciated through one example: King Pedro I of Aragón's conquest of the city of Huesca.

Huesca belonged to the taifa of Zaragoza and therefore we may think that this was a Christian conquest of a Muslim territory. Pedro even became a vassal of the pope to strengthen his position as a Christian warrior. However, Zaragoza paid *parias* to Alfonso VI, and the siege, when it started in 1096, was anything but a straightforward act of the 'reconquest'. Pedro supplemented his own army with troops recruited from across the Pyrenees in Gascony. The defenders included both al-Mustaʿīn of Zaragoza, and two of the most significant nobles of the kingdom of León-Castile, Count García Ordóñez of Nájera and Count Gonzalo Núñez of Lara with their troops, therefore Christian armies were engaged on both sides. Pedro won, according to legend, with the heavenly aid of St George. Huesca was incorporated into the kingdom of Aragón; Pedro bragged about the large number of Muslims who had been killed, and the donation charter to the cathedral of Huesca in 1097 blithely referred to 460 years of Muslim oppression of Christian territory in the Iberian peninsula. In many modern accounts, Pedro's victory over Huesca is but one in the history of the Reconquista, yet he was fighting against Christians as well as against Muslims in the battle. In this way, messy realities started to be forced into the straitjacket of religious warfare in narrative accounts, very similarly to the prologue of Rodrigo's donation charter. What on the ground was a complicated and shifting pattern of alliances and opportunistic territorial aggrandizement started to be presented in the narrative sources written by Christian ecclesiastics as divinely ordained war, motivated by Christian faith.

Such formulations of religious war were not only at odds with the realities; they also started to foster a textual rivalry. Before the charter providing Rodrigo with such a lofty status was written, the king of León was already styled the legitimate heir of the Visigoths. This idea was formulated at the royal court and was an early form of the rhetoric of religious reconquest, as Alfonso would have then been retaking lands that rightfully belonged to him. The donation charter to Valencia, however, did not refer to Alfonso's role as heir to the Visigoths; Rodrigo's ambition was not loyal vassalage to Alfonso VI, and therefore adopting such a Leonese viewpoint would not have suited his interests. But the idea of centuries of subjection and a God-sent saviour in the person of Rodrigo hails from the same kind of thinking, and indeed was conceived of and disseminated by the same kind of clerical milieu. It was part of ecclesiastical rhetoric that existed in parallel with the often more pragmatic warrior culture.

Other charters expressed similar ideas. Alfonso VI's donation to the cathedral of Toledo at the end of 1086 was prefaced by:

> This city was for 376 years in the hands of the Moors, blasphemers of the Christian name . . . I took up arms against the barbarian peoples. After many battles and innumerable enemy deaths I captured from them populous cities and very strong castles with the help of God's grace. Thus, inspired by God's grace, I moved my army against this city where once my ancestors, very powerful and rich kings, reigned, deeming that it would be pleasing in the sight of the Lord if that which a treacherous people under their faithless leader Muhammad took from the Christians, I Alfonso the Emperor, under the leadership of Christ, should restore to the worshippers of the same faith.

This text deployed the notion that Alfonso was heir to the Visigothic kings, and that this inheritance was lost to Muslims almost 400 years earlier; God himself wanted the Christians to regain their lands, because Muslims professed beliefs contrary to the true faith. Alfonso's claims were mirrored by the language of a papal letter sent to the peninsula: Pope Urban II expressed his joy on the conquest of Toledo, referring to the 370 years of captivity meted out to Christians because of their sins. Other rulers also promised to recover and expand Christian lands and fight against the 'pagans'.

Others also interpreted the wars on the Iberian peninsula through a Christian lens. The Cluniac monks in France were interested in the progress of the Iberian wars. There was a personal tie: Alfonso VI's wife Constance of Burgundy was the niece of Abbot Hugh of Cluny. The Cluniacs also had many daughter houses (that is, monasteries founded by monks from Cluny) in the Iberian peninsula, and many high-ranking ecclesiastics in the peninsula were Cluniacs. Moreover, León-Castile had been the source of significant revenues for the monastery of Cluny since the latter part of Fernando I's reign. He started to send 1,000 gold pieces a year as tribute, in exchange for Cluny's liturgical commemoration of members of the royal family; such prayer for the souls of the dead was highly prized at the time, seen as an insurance policy against suffering everlasting torments in hell. In 1077, Alfonso VI doubled that sum. The gold came from *parias* paid by taifa rulers. After the Almoravid victory at Sagrajas in 1086, the payment to Cluny had to be suspended for several years. Therefore, when Cluniac monks prayed for Alfonso's victories in battle, their prayers were not entirely disinterested. The Cluniacs also courted other Iberian rulers and offered spiritual benefits in exchange for gold. They would have been keen to promote a new patron in the person of the Campeador, Rodrigo Díaz. His military victories against the Almoravids, at a time when they were defeating all other Christian armies in the peninsula, allowed the aggrandizement of this successful mercenary as a Christian hero.

Pope Urban II also understood the fighting on the peninsula as religious war. Often seen as a prelude to the declaration of crusade, he promised various indulgences to Ramón Berenguer III of Barcelona and Ermengol IV of Urgell in 1089 to take Tarragona from the Muslims. Moreover, even after launching the first crusade to the East and Jerusalem, the pope explicitly discouraged Iberian nobles from participating, instead directing them to fight in the peninsula.

Rodrigo was, in a sense, the accidental beneficiary of this transformation; the makeover into a Christian hero was not independent of his victories, certainly, but it was also due to the emergent ecclesiastical rhetoric of his times. The view that killing 'enemies of the faith' in war was worthy of praise spread not just in Iberia, but beyond, and was soon further glorified. The papacy promised spiritual rewards, often understood by warriors as immediate entry to heaven upon death, for participation in holy war, which mobilized European warriors for crusade. The representation of Rodrigo as fighting for the Christian faith is not unique, it was even developed in a kind of competition with Alfonso VI, and certainly served particular interests. Without this context, it would seem absurd that medieval ecclesiastics started to transform Rodrigo Díaz, the successful warrior who fought indiscriminately against Muslims and Christians, into a Christian hero sent by God; against the background of his times, this metamorphosis was neither unparalleled nor illogical. It served the clerics well, and, indeed, not only the clergy of Valencia, but soon monks elsewhere were also among the earliest advocates of the Cid. Did Rodrigo come to believe the image ecclesiastics created about him in the last year of his life? Did he see himself by the end as a man appointed by God to fight against Muslim enemies? Or did he merely accept the verbal tribute offered by his clerics in the same way he had accepted the tribute of gold from vanquished Moors, because it served him well? Those are questions we shall never be able to answer.

Rodrigo's positive image underwent further developments over the following two centuries, although our own ideas of a positive hero are quite far from twelfth- and thirteenth-century ones. The texts that performed these transformations can all be linked to monastic authorship or influence and monastic repositories guarded the manuscripts made on parchment that conserved these works. The dating and authorship of all the texts are debated in scholarship, with some modern scholars preferring an earlier beginning to the panegyric transformation of the Cid. The arguments are very technical, and no knockout evidence gives absolute proof. Overall, the weight of the evidence points to the late twelfth and early thirteenth centuries as the first flourishing of a more substantial revision. Going much further than earlier celebrations of his military prowess and the God-sent saviour of the foundation charter, these later rewritings laid the ground for the appearance of a saintly Rodrigo.

Further legend-making, however, was neither linear chronologically nor inevitable. After the donation charter, other texts still celebrated Rodrigo Díaz as a superb warrior, but not as a saviour sent by God. An anonymous Latin poem composed in celebration of the conquest of Almería by Alfonso VII of León-Castile in 1147 is of particular significance in this respect. This poem was not written to praise the Cid, but refers in passing to 'Rodrigo, often called "My Cid", of whom it is sung that he was never defeated by his enemies, who subdued the Moors and also subdued our counts'. The vernacular designation Meo Cidi in the otherwise Latin text, and the clear assumption that the audience would know who he was, along with the verb 'sung', perhaps indicates the existence of oral compositions prior to 1147, songs of heroic deeds performed for entertainment. The poem certainly shows that the more widespread fame Rodrigo possessed by the time of his death did not die with him; yet this fame consisted as much of defeating Christians as of victories over Muslims. The earliest longer narrative of his deeds, called by modern scholars simply 'the history of Rodrigo', *Historia Roderici*, survives in an early thirteenth-century manuscript found at the monastery of San Isidoro in León. Some historians have argued for a dating as early as the beginning of the twelfth century, and others as late as the 1180s, with the latter more generally accepted nowadays. It is therefore possible that even in the late twelfth century, and in a work written about the deeds of Rodrigo for posterity, Rodrigo Díaz could still be represented closer to the historical reality. This history, while it disculpates Rodrigo from wrongdoing, with evil rivals at the royal court of Alfonso being responsible for poisoning the king's mind against him, does not completely whitewash Rodrigo's actions. It recounts his devastation of the Rioja region and his service of Muslim rulers. But it already emphasized that he was ever victorious: 'while he lived in this world he always won a noble triumph over his enemies: never was he defeated by any man.'

Likewise, the *Crónica Najerense*, another Latin chronicle produced at the Benedictine monastery of Santa María la Real de Nájera in the last third of the twelfth century, contains a celebration of Rodrigo's warrior qualities, this time focusing on one event, the Battle of Golpejera that pitted King Sancho of Castile against Alfonso of León. The chronicle's Rodrigo fights fourteen enemy warriors one after the other, armed only with a lance, to free his king, Sancho, after they had insulted Rodrigo by suggesting he must be mad to want to fight single-handed against fourteen men.

The language of these compositions, Latin, and classical influences attesting to some knowledge of Homer and Virgil, at least in the *Carmen Campidoctoris*, are a giveaway of ecclesiastical authorship. Despite such clerical origin, these texts celebrate Rodrigo's military success, and while they portray a superhero in a sense, an undefeated champion, they do not transform their protagonist into a spiritual model. The reason for such restraint was probably linked to the impetus for commemorating him. The period following

Rodrigo's death was a chaotic one, witnessing war between Aragón and León-Castile, the Almoravid defeat of Alfonso I of Aragón in 1134 and the growing independence of Portugal. Alfonso VII of Castile – grandson of Alfonso VI who ruled in Rodrigo's lifetime – turned fortunes around, and in 1147 conquered Almería. Rodrigo, the famed Campeador, seems to have remained a reference point as a peerless warrior throughout the turbulent years of the first half of the twelfth century and beyond.

Somewhat later, however, Rodrigo was turned into not just a Christian warrior fighting for the faith, but also a paragon of Christian virtue, motivated by loyalty to the king, who had unjustly exiled him. He also became a Castilian patriot, and, soon, almost a saint.

4

The Earliest Legends: A Paragon of Christian Virtue?

The Cid's military exploits, so clearly the basis for his fame in his lifetime, naturally feature prominently in the legends; they were exaggerated ever more and used by a variety of texts emanating from different localities. Some imaginary feats resemble those of modern-day Marvel superheroes, as in a story where the Cid single-handedly vanquishes fourteen enemy warriors. But other, and sometimes contradictory, transformations created a quasi-saint and an insubordinate rebel as well. While even the earliest stories cannot be blindly trusted – both panegyric of a hero or condemnation of an enemy can be exaggerated and may not be truthful – the legends from the thirteenth century go beyond trying merely to exculpate Rodrigo, putting all blame on envious enemies or a weak king, as twelfth-century texts had done. They imagine a hero who never existed, and never could have existed. One monastery in the region of Burgos, now relatively obscure, played a key role in creating the mythic Cid. The legends written at or promoted by the monastery included the best-known stories about the heroic Cid and became the basis for all later transformations.

The monastery of San Pedro de Cardeña is hard to reach today; without a car, one has to walk many kilometres from the nearest bus stop. Nor can published opening times be taken for granted, as the monastic community can close to the public with no notice whatsoever. I discovered this on a cold March morning, when, having checked at the tourist office in Burgos that the monastery was indeed open, I made my way there. I learned from a caretaker that there was no point waiting in the falling snow: San Pedro was not going to open that day, or, for that matter, that week. I could take a peek into the church from behind the locked grille and then return months later. Finding locked doors yet again on my next visit, I begged for entry, and an elderly monk and a young postulant finally took pity on me, so I was able to visit the elusive site. The buildings have been transformed since Rodrigo's lifetime. The monument over his now empty grave stands in a baroque chapel; the earliest extant part is a twelfth-century cloister, and the closest we get to the Campeador's era is the remains of an eleventh-century tower. Yet this monastery was one of the fundamental places that launched the myth of el Cid.

The first step towards the monks' involvement was the arrival of Rodrigo's remains in San Pedro de Cardeña. When he died, Rodrigo was lord of Valencia, and was buried there. However, the town, so deep in Muslim al-Andalus, was soon reclaimed by the Almoravids, and its Christian inhabitants went north to Castile. Rodrigo's widow Jimena decided to take her husband's body with her and she had it reburied in San Pedro de Cardeña; thus began the long history of the Cid's association with the monastery. Jimena's choice of the site for Rodrigo's reburial has never been explained; the hypothesis is that it was the closest large monastery to his place of origin. The monks, however, were not content merely to have the grave in the monastic church; stories were woven around Rodrigo, linking him in life to the monastery, so that his resting place no longer appeared accidental, but a consequence of strong pre-existing ties to the monastery. At least from the thirteenth century, the monks fostered the Cid's cult, composing and copying texts lionizing him.

This medieval monastic legend-making was not exclusive to the Cid. The Benedictine monastery of Arlanza hitched its fortunes to the posthumously glorified count Fernán González in a similar way. The monks forged documents from Fernán González to benefit the monastery, claimed he was its protector during his life (for which there is no proof), and further embroidered his myth as the first count of Castile, producing the *Poema de Fernán González*. The monasteries of Santo Domingo de Silos and San Millán de Cogolla also fostered myths related to Fernán González in the middle of the thirteenth century, in response to the crisis threatening monasteries at the time. The mythic reworkings of the story of the Cid were not unique; but his story triumphed over a longer time period, outshining the others in the end.

For the monks of San Pedro de Cardeña there may have been a particular trigger to reinforce their desire for the Cid's patronage. In 1142 Alfonso VII gave San Pedro de Cardeña to the monastery of Cluny in exchange for stopping his yearly payment of tribute. Abbot Martín I protested, but was forced into exile with his monks. They appealed to the pope, asserting their right to their possessions independently of the king, an appeal upheld by Pope Eugenius III. So, three years after being forced out, the monks were allowed to return, but the Cluniacs departed with the treasures of the monastery. Moreover, the monks were still threatened by the bishop of Burgos's support for Cluniac ownership. In 1190, Alfonso VIII confirmed some of the monastery's privileges. Around that time, a new work associated the Cid firmly to San Pedro.

The first serious large-scale revamping of Rodrigo's image came in a text that is as controversial as it is famous. The *Cantar* or *Poema de mio Cid* is a vernacular epic, renowned in Spanish literary history and translated here by Peter Such and John Hodgkinson, which created a Cid who began to bear no resemblance to the historical Rodrigo. In order to appreciate the legendary Cid who emerged, it would be helpful to know who made these changes and why. Yet any guess comes from analysing the work itself, because no external information exists about the epic poem, and, despite ongoing scholarly debate, nothing is certain about it.

The work's various titles are the creation of modern scholars; the original title is missing, since the sole surviving manuscript copy lacks the first page. Its date of composition has been hugely contentious. It survives in a single fourteenth-century manuscript that is clearly a copy. Yet at the end, a line closes with 'Per Abbat wrote it in the month of May in the [Spanish] era 1245'. The Spanish era (which, for unknown reasons, calculated the years from 38 BCE and was in use until the fifteenth century) date converts to 1207. Per Abbat was a Castilian lawyer of the early thirteenth century, and was probably an earlier copyist of the text, although one opinion has it that he was its author. The scholar Ramón Ménendez Pidal, an advocate of an extreme early dating, wanted to see in the *Poema* a faithful rendition of an oral epic poem that was composed close to the Cid's lifetime, first written down around 1140 and subsequently copied. More persuasive evidence suggests a late twelfth- to early thirteenth-century composition, based on the analysis of the language of the poem, on its references to bureaucratic procedures and law and on borrowings from twelfth-century Old French epic poetry. The poem also clearly displays evidence that its author was a Castilian, through good knowledge of eastern Castilian topography and references to places and people. The envisaged audience of the epic composed in the vernacular would have been Castilian as well; such works were recited aloud for the entertainment of the warrior nobility and reflect this in their subject matter, structure (in this case, tripartite: the 'Song of exile', 'Song of the marriage' and the 'Song of the affront at Corpes'), language and humour.

Debate continues about the text's unknown author. While there exist arguments for and against the authorship of a monk or cleric linked to San Pedro de Cardeña, the *Poema* clearly depicts very close links between the monastery and Rodrigo in his lifetime that differ substantially from the account of the *Historia Roderici*, which only mentions his posthumous reburial there. It is plausible that the monks influenced the birth of the epic. The monastery's scriptorium produced manuscripts in the same period that the *Poema* was written, which includes, for example, the Beatus of San Pedro de Cardeña from the last third of the twelfth century, a richly decorated copy of Beatus's commentary on the Apocalypse. The souring of relations with royal power due to Alfonso VII's attempt to give the monastery to Cluny may have inspired the emphasis on the monastery's independence from royal power expressed in the *Poema de Mio Cid*, where, against royal prohibition, the abbot of Cardeña is willing to let Rodrigo stay at the monastery before he leaves for exile, when nobody else is prepared to help him. Additionally, according to one theory, the *infantes* of Carrión are the villains of the *Poema* because the historical counts had close ties to Cluny. Above all, San Pedro de Cardeña is mentioned numerous times in the text and gains prominence in the hero's life. The *Poema* claimed that Rodrigo spent his first night in exile at Cardeña and left his wife and daughters at the monastery during his exile; that he sent money there to pay for their maintenance; and he sent for them to San Pedro after his conquest of Valencia. San Pedro is thus the scene of many touching episodes, not least the Cid's farewell to his family and Jimena's tearful prayer. One of his faithful followers even prayed to St Peter to guide him to Rodrigo and found the Cid at the monastery just before he went into exile.

In fact, there is no evidence that Rodrigo had particular ties to the monastery. There are no signs of any special relationship during his life, although quite good evidence exists concerning benefactors of the monastery at the time. The copies of charters from the tenth and eleventh centuries kept at the monastery, in the Becerro, a cartulary made at the end of the eleventh century, which reproduced close to 200 documents written between 899 and 1085, pertaining to monastic properties, contain no donation from Rodrigo. Indeed, donations were made to Cardeña by a number of his contemporaries, but not by Rodrigo. Moreover, as a surviving charter of donation shows, Rodrigo and Jimena in fact directed their patronage elsewhere: in 1076 they gave gifts to the monastery of San Sebastián de Silos (the later Santo Domingo de Silos). Finally, the accounts of San Pedro de Cardeña made in 1338 include lists of revenues from donated lands and rights that can be substantiated with earlier documents: none is tied to Rodrigo.

The only historically attested links between Rodrigo and San Pedro de Cardeña were the result of Rodrigo's actions in the service of King Alfonso VI. He confirmed Alfonso's charter of donation and privileges to the monastery in 1072, and, on royal command, together with another royal appointee, acted for the monastery in a lawsuit in 1073 that pitted the monks against some members of the lower nobility. The *Poema*, in contrast, creates a dense web of links.

It is not simply the role of Cardeña that changed. The Rodrigo of the *Poema* is a Christian hero who fights against the Muslim enemy; a loyal vassal to his lord King Alfonso VI, even when the latter treats him unjustly; and a proud Castilian. The period of his life when he served the Muslim rulers of Zaragoza was written out of the story. This is already much more of a mythical image of the Cid than the one conveyed by earlier texts. Rodrigo is portrayed as a pious Christian, who prays often. Early in his exile, the Archangel Gabriel appears to Rodrigo in a vision while he is sleeping, telling him to ride forth, 'For never has man ridden at so fortunate a time / while you live all will go well with you.' Rodrigo repeatedly thanks God for his victories, and wants to regain Valencia for Christendom.

Rodrigo's many victories against Muslims are highlighted. He fights predominantly against Muslims, and the one positive Muslim figure, Avengalvón, pays tribute and is submissive to the Cid. His battle cry is Santiago, St James the Apostle, who was supposed to have been buried in Santiago de Compostela, and who acquired the epithet 'Matamoros', 'Moor killer', in the peninsula. The author of the *Poema* described how, prior to battle, mass was celebrated for the warriors, and the celebrant, Bishop Jerome (Jeronimo), gave the remission of sins to those who would fight against the Almoravids, echoing crusade indulgences. Bishop Jerome, as 'a good Christian', also asked the Cid for a favour: to allow him to lead the attack and strike the first blows, since he had come to 'kill a few Moors'.

The *Poema*, as epic poetry for entertainment, serves up strong stuff when it comes to his victories over the Muslims. Graphic descriptions of killing include:

> My Cid wielded his lance and then drew his sword;
> he killed Moors beyond reckoning,
> as their blood flowed down to his elbow.

And, in one encounter, the Cid

> dealt him a mighty blow
> he cut through the gems of the helmet;
> passing through the helmet and cutting everything else away,
> the sword sliced through him down to the waist.

Such violence, to us, represents extreme cruelty, but perhaps for audiences at the time it was uproariously funny.

Yet parts of the original story survived, notably the link between killing and looting: for the clerical authors of the period, killing Muslims and taking booty from them were not incompatible with Christian virtue; on the contrary, very much a sign of it. Rich plunder clearly demonstrated divine favour in action. While this represents some continuity with Rodrigo's era, there was a marked shift in the attitude to the Muslim enemies. In the thirteenth century, the Christian anti-Muslim rhetoric that had already appeared in Rodrigo's donation charter to the bishopric of Valencia started to saturate the texts. Yet even explicit religious enmity did not override the pragmatic actions for gain; in the thirteenth century booty taking was still compatible with honour. However strange to modern audiences, the latter was both a sign of divine favour and the means for attracting and retaining the loyalty of a military retinue. A plunderer, as long as he confined his activities to Muslim lands, was a paragon of Christian virtue.

Rodrigo's loyalty to King Alfonso is exemplary, even though he is unjustly sent into exile by the king at the start of the epic poem. The Cid does not wish to fight against the king; he keeps sending him gifts of booty while in exile, and even after the conquest of Valencia he declares his loyalty and subordinates himself to the king. His achievements and continued gifts to Alfonso finally lead to a royal pardon. Rodrigo's love for Castile is also underscored, and his origins firmly tied to Vivar, near Burgos, through the recurring expression 'the man of Vivar'. In order to accentuate his social ascent and accomplishments, the *Poema* also changed Rodrigo's social status, and represented him as a member of the lower nobility, an *infanzón*, rather than as a member of the higher ranking aristocracy.

The final change concerns the Cid's relations with his family. The *Poema* depicts the Cid's reunion with his wife and daughters after his conquest of Valencia, and a large section is dedicated to an entirely invented story concerning his daughters' fate. After granting his forgiveness, the king asks that Rodrigo acquiesce to the marriage of his daughters to the *infantes* of Carrión; although he has grave doubts, he complies and a double marriage is celebrated. The last part details the assault against the Cid's daughters by their husbands and his subsequent successful endeavours both to punish the culprits and restore (and even enhance) his daughters' status through remarriage to members of the royal dynasties of Aragón and Navarra. The *Poema* took considerable liberties with historical personages and events to aggrandize Rodrigo and portray him in a much more favourable light. Many of the individuals, including Álvar Fáñez and the counts of Carrión, were real people, yet they never played the roles attributed to them. Álvar Fáñez was not Rodrigo's right-hand man, and the counts were neither *infantes* (royal heirs) nor did they marry Rodrigo's daughters, much less attack them.

Why the *Poema* was written is difficult to answer; why it would have appealed to its audience is easier. The background to the interest in a revamped Cid lay in the changing political landscape of Castile; a heroic past was crafted in response to crises. The Almoravids were replaced by the Almohads, al-Muwaḥḥidūn, a new rigorist movement that advocated a stricter adhesion to Islam, which started in the Maghreb in the early twelfth century; they also took over al-Andalus by 1172. In 1195 Alfonso VIII of Castile joined battle with the Almohads at Alarcos, and was defeated, raising fears not just in Iberia, but beyond. Many years of preparation and papal pressure led to a united Iberian military enterprise. The Christian kings of the peninsula overcame their differences and in 1212 the Almohads were defeated at Las Navas de Tolosa. The Christian conquest of al-Andalus took off; by the middle of the century, all but Granada was in Christian hands. In light of this, at the end of the twelfth and in the early thirteenth century, at the court of Alfonso VIII, the example of a Christian hero dedicated to fighting against Muslims, who was also a Castilian patriot and absolutely loyal to the king, would have been more than welcome. Against fractious aristocrats who had tried to gain power during Alfonso VIII's minority (which came to an end in 1169), here was the exemplar of a perfect vassal. In contrast to those who were still engaged in fighting against Christians, here was the ideal combination of heroism and reward. The poem linked warfare against the Moors to rich pickings, booty and conquest, offering an attractive model for aristocratic behaviour from the court's point of view.

The rewritten Cid also served Castile's conquest of the past, as David Porrinas González argued. Castile gained a preeminent position on the peninsula through territorial conquests in the thirteenth century. Castile's newfound status, however, was not matched by a suitably glorious past. Historically, it emerged as a kingdom much later than León or Navarra. It was a frontier zone of León initially, then a lesser partner in the personal union when Fernando declared himself king of León and Castile. Castile became the hegemonic power on the peninsula after a definitive union with León and success in the 'reconquest' in the thirteenth century. Castilian kings compensated for their realm's lack of importance in the past by laying claim to the Visigothic heritage and conjuring up the image of an Iberian peninsula united under their rule. They asserted Castilian leadership in the wars against Muslim al-Andalus. Finally, legend pushed the institutional origins of Castile further into the past; the mythical early judges of Castile were invented, supposedly elected by the population in the ninth century, thereby creating de facto independence from the royal court of León; and Count Fernán González (c. 910–970) was turned into the supposed first independent ruler of Castile. Converting the Cid into a patriotic Castilian was also part of this reshaping of the past, not without an element of rivalry between Castile and the other Iberian kingdoms who could lay claim to him, since the Cid was the grandfather of García Ramírez el Restaurador (1134–50) of Navarra.

The *Poema*'s Cid became the basis of future representations, and still largely determines the image most people have of him. Yet it was far from the endpoint of Rodrigo's metamorphosis. The next stage of his transformation can also be firmly tied to the initiative of the monks of Cardeña. Sometime after the middle of the thirteenth century, texts depicting Rodrigo in a strongly hagiographic light – suggesting he was a saint, but without saying so, since officially sanctity had to be conferred by papal canonization – were written at San Pedro de Cardeña; within a short time, these texts were incorporated into (and are transmitted to us in this form) the official histories produced at the court of Alfonso X and Sancho IV. A chronicle, the *Estoria de España*, was commissioned by King Alfonso X; a first version was written in the 1270s, which was reworked in subsequent decades and which also inspired various other fourteenth-century chronicles. The original *Legend of Cardeña* does not survive, but the version incorporated into the royal chronicle is still extant.

By then, the Benedictine monks of San Pedro de Cardeña treasured the body of Rodrigo Díaz as that of a saint. The dead Cid strapped to his horse still defeating Muslims is one of the most potent images we have of him; it is the brainchild of the monks of San Pedro. Over the centuries, they created a cult site not only for the Cid but for his entire family and even for his horse. All this despite the fact that, in the end, the Cid was never canonized. Local cults of people promoted for ecclesiastical recognition as saints, who failed to gain that status, or only obtained it after centuries, existed elsewhere as well. In such cases, the candidate was already treated as a saint locally, even without official canonization. Some cults were eventually suppressed, and others gained papal recognition, an official declaration of sanctity. What distinguishes the Cid is that this was just one of his faces, one of his many guises, whereas other prospective saints tended not to be so multifaceted.

The monks of San Pedro exploited an excellent opportunity: being close to the Camino de Santiago, the pilgrimage route to Santiago de Compostela that drew a large number of pious pilgrims, they would tap into that source of income with an alluring saintly hero's body. Medieval saints' cults centred on the bodily remains of the saint, often displayed in reliquaries, and drew the faithful who both prayed there for the saint's intercession for healing or aid, and went there to offer gifts of gratitude after miracles were granted. Non-pecuniary interests were at play as well. Possessing the tomb of such an important individual enhanced the monastery's prestige during difficult times. The monastery's fortunes, as those of many other ecclesiastical institutions, had declined substantially since the burial of Rodrigo. The centre of the kingdom moved from Burgos to Toledo, shifting the geographical focus of the monarchy; San Pedro de Cardeña had to compete with other monasteries, San Pedro de Arlanza and Santo Domingo de Silos, for royal favour and patronage, as well as for pilgrims. In such a context, the monks of San Pedro discovered in the Cid's relics a valuable asset. They were interested not just in the Cid, but in the potential inherent in promoting holy figures more generally, since around the same time they also started to foster the cult of the 'two hundred martyred monks' allegedly killed at the monastery in 834 by a Muslim army, as well as of the eleventh-century abbot Sisebut.

The *Leyenda de Cardeña*, or *Legend of Cardeña*, incorporated stories from and adopted the whitewashing strategies of the *Poema*, and presented the Cid as a Christian motivated by his faith and a loyal vassal of King Alfonso VI, with envious nobles at court intriguing against him. It enhanced other stories, for example, the angel's promise that Rodrigo would always be rich and honoured as long as he lived is an improved heavenly offer compared to that made by the *Poema*'s Gabriel. Above all, the *Leyenda* is a pretty heavy-handed attempt to retrospectively create an even closer connection between the living Rodrigo and the monastery than the *Poema* would have it, while turning Rodrigo into a saint. It not only propagated the fictitious close ties between Rodrigo and the monastery; it comprehensively rewrote the story of his death and its aftermath, teeming with the miraculous on a scale that would later become unpalatable. While one of the best-known episodes linked to the Cid – his posthumous victory over Muslims – was included in the film featuring Charlton Heston, much of the rest of it has been discreetly forgotten.

The *Leyenda de Cardeña* provided a fictitious account of why the monastery was Rodrigo's last resting place, one that is much more favourable to Cardeña than the truth. According to this story, Rodrigo himself chose to be buried there and left money and gifts to the monastery in his last will. There is thus no prior burial elsewhere; nor is it Jimena, but Rodrigo himself, who chooses San Pedro. According to this story, King Búcar, lord of Tunis, was preparing to attack Valencia, threatening to kill the Cid, who was preparing for the fight. Before it could take place, the apostle St Peter appeared to Rodrigo. St Peter, the heavenly gatekeeper, carried his keys with him for easy identification, and was surrounded by marvellous light. He foretold Rodrigo's death, warning him that it would occur within thirty days, but also granted him a posthumous victory against Búcar, with the aid of the apostle St James. St Peter specifically said that this vision was granted to the Cid because of the reverence he had always shown to the monastery of San Pedro de Cardeña. The Cid proceeds to say his farewells, confesses his sins and prepares for death. For seven days he takes no nourishment but for drinking a little myrrh and balsam mixed in water, that he had received from the sultan of Persia. His body and face became more beautiful each day. This curious self-embalming while alive is to be completed after death: he instructed his wife and his closest followers to anoint him with the rest of the myrrh and balsam after his passing. The legend's author explicitly compares the process to mummification, as had been practised on the 'kings', that is pharaohs, in Egypt.

This legendary version of Rodrigo further commands that his death be kept a secret, and when Búcar arrives at Valencia with his troops, that Rodrigo's own dead body be attached securely onto his horse Bauieca so it cannot fall off, his sword Tizon should be put in his hand, and Bishop Jerome and Gil Díaz (a convert from Islam) should guide his horse. In this way, they should lead the troops to attack Búcar; Rodrigo reveals to his closest circle that victory in this posthumous battle was promised him in his vision. Rodrigo then made his last will, with his first demand being that he be buried at San Pedro de Cardeña, and bequeathed many goods to the monastery. He also enjoined Jimena and Gil Díaz to remain in the monastery after his death. He then devoutly took his last communion, offered his soul to God and died. His body was anointed according to his wishes, and placed in a church where prayers were said over him for three days, after which Búcar arrived with his troops and attacked Valencia.

For nine days the defenders of Valencia fought the Moors; since the Cid did not participate, the attackers began to think that he was not going to fight. In the meantime, the Cid's body was being prepared. His eyes were open, his beard was long and he appeared to be alive. His body was set in the saddle of Bauieca and secured in place, his sword in his hand. The bishop and Gil then led the horse with the Cid's body, along with hundreds of warriors, out of the gate at night, so that by daybreak the troops were ready to attack the Moors. The chronicle invented a company of female archers in the Muslim camp, who are defeated by the troops from Valencia. When the remaining soldiers of Búcar's army start to flee, the Moors are confronted by sixty thousand knights, whiter than snow, led by one who holds a white banner in one hand and a sword that seems to be made of fire in the other; they slay many and put the rest to flight. After the intervention of this heavenly host led by St James, the Valencian troops continue to slaughter the enemy, until finally Búcar and the survivors manage to get back onto their ships and escape. The Christian troops take so much plunder from what the enemy have left behind that even the poorest become rich that day.

This retelling also deprived Muslims of a triumph in their retaking of Valencia. Instead, the fall of Valencia to the Muslims is a consequence of Rodrigo's decision about his burial place. The Christian evacuation is now due to the funeral, rather than a military necessity. After the Cid's death, Jimena and the Cid's followers carry out the rest of his wishes and take his body to San Pedro for burial. The grieving inhabitants all want to accompany Rodrigo's body on his last journey from the city to the monastery of San Pedro, about 416 km as the crow flies. As a result, the entire city of Valencia is emptied of its residents. Eventually, the original Muslim inhabitants of the town who had relocated to a nearby settlement realize that Valencia is completely empty, and move back in, occupying the city without resistance. In this way, the legend even eliminates the fall of Valencia; its return to Muslim hands is neither an enemy victory, nor a Christian defeat.

According to the tale, Doña Jimena then remained at the monastery and spent the rest of her life in prayer there until her own passing, her only wish being to be buried next to the Cid. She is turned into a recluse, instead of governing Valencia as she did in reality. This storyline also mirrors and enhances that of the *Poema*, which confined Jimena to San Pedro during her husband's exile. Gil Díaz remained there, too, taking care of the Cid's horse, even making sure Bauieca was put to stud, so as to perpetuate the lineage of such 'a noble horse'. Bauieca died two years after the Cid, and Gil Díaz buried him to the right of the monastery's entrance, planting two elm trees on the grave. Four years later, Jimena died, too.

The most outlandish part of the legend concerns the fate of the Cid's body. Jimena had refused to have Rodrigo's body put in a coffin, since it was fresh and appeared to be alive. His body stayed on his horse after the last battle while his daughters and sons-in-law, the *infantes* of Navarra and Aragón and finally King Alfonso himself paid their respects. It was then transported to the monastery on horseback. After weeks of travel, at San Pedro de Cardeña Rodrigo was finally removed from the horse, but he remained in the saddle, and in this way he was placed in front of the altar of St Peter. His body was honoured with vigils and masses, and was finally installed, in a sitting position on an ivory stool, and holding his sword Tizon in its scabbard in his left hand, next to the altar. When Jimena died, she was buried at the Cid's feet. The body sat there for ten years, attracting many people who wanted to see it, including Jews and Muslims. Each year, a great feast was held, when the poor were fed and clothed and the abbot of the monastery preached to the crowd outside.

The legend claimed that one year, the seventh after the Cid was placed on the ivory stool beside the altar, as everyone was outside on the occasion of the yearly feast a Jew entered the church, and, seeing that he was alone, said to himself: 'this is the body of that Ruy Díaz el Cid; they say nobody could pull at his beard in his whole life. I'd like to pull it now and see what he can do to me.' As he reached for the Cid, before his hand could touch his beard the Cid's right hand dropped the cords of the mantle he wore, grabbed the hilt of his sword and started to pull it out of its scabbard; the Jew, frightened, fell down screaming. Those outside heard the noise, and the abbot himself stopped his sermon to see what had happened. The Jew was found at the feet of the Cid, scared almost to death. The abbot saw that the Cid had started to pull out his sword, and the Jew's account made all present marvel and give thanks to God for the great virtue the Cid's body demonstrated. Nor was anyone able to take the Cid's hand from his sword, pull the sword out completely or return it to its scabbard. The Jew, impressed by this miracle, converted to Christianity. The Cid's body remained next to the altar for another three years. Finally, ten years after his death, the tip of his nose fell off and the monks decided that, since the body had become so unsightly, it was finally time to bury him. With great reverence and ecclesiastical celebrations, therefore, they buried him in front of the altar next to Jimena.

This tale of the body of the Cid, so bizarre to modern readers, propped up the implicit claim to sanctity – an uncorrupted body, its ability to act, the miracle concerning the Jew all echo various medieval ideas about saints. Moreover, most of it, including the missing tip of the nose, was modelled on an eleventh-century story about Charlemagne, who had been canonized as a saint by the time the monks were composing the *Legend*. The central element of the story, the attempt to pull the Cid's beard, shows a curious amalgamation of social norms and religious ideas. Having one's beard pulled was considered a great dishonour at the time, but also alluded to Jesus. In medieval societies where adult men wore beards, these denoted maturity, virility and in some places high social status; that is why pulling someone's beard was considered an outrage. This is best demonstrated by a fictional story relating to John, future king of England (1199–1216). He arrived in Ireland where the Irish lords were ready to accept him as their overlord, but upon his arrival members of his entourage pulled the beards of some of the Irish who came to greet them. This resulted in the Irish refusing to submit to John and deciding to resist the English. In the *Poema*, honour is even explicitly linked to avoiding such an atrocity: the Cid proudly declares that nobody ever plucked his beard. The association with Christ comes from the Christian interpretation of some of the passages written by the prophet Isaiah, which referred to the sufferings of the Messiah. These were understood to foretell the sufferings of Christ before the crucifixion; one of the torments inflicted on him was pulling out hairs of his beard. The figure of the Jew, the enemy of Christ and the Christian faith in medieval representations, at once recalled the crucifixion and attested to the sanctity of the Cid, a sanctity San Pedro's monks could not quite make official. Who better to witness a miracle than someone hostile to Christianity?

The *Legend of Cardeña*, incorporating many of the traits of the Cid from the *Poema*, was given a more official stamp of approval, and a means for wider dissemination, as it was included in the court chronicles composed during the reign of Alfonso X the Wise. Alfonso personally visited the monastery of Cardeña in 1272; he even asked that the Cid's body be reinterred in a more prominent part of the monastery. He was a fan of the Cid, but also undoubtedly found the model of a loyal, invincible warrior worthy of promotion. That is why the *Leyenda* was extensively incorporated into the chronicle composition of the history of the Iberian peninsula overseen by Alfonso. This assured a prominent place for the Cid that the monks alone would not have been able to achieve. The twelfth-century rift that opened up between the interests of the king and those of the monastery was healed through the legendary Cid produced by the monks.

The monastery of San Pedro de Cardeña did not have a monopoly on the Cid; for example, another ecclesiastical community, clerics of the bishopric of Palencia, also tried to gain prestige from an association to the Cid through *Las Mocedades de Rodrigo*, a vernacular epic poem that survives in one copy from the end of the fourteenth or beginning of the fifteenth century, translated here by Matthew Bailey. According to modern scholarship, a learned author transformed an earlier oral composition by adding the material on Palencia, with the aim of affirming the legitimacy and rights of the bishopric in the fourteenth century. In this way, the foundation of the bishopric of Palencia in the archdiocese of Burgos, and its restoration in the eleventh century, was inserted into the epic. In the text as we have it, Rodrigo's deeds are interwoven with the history of Castile and León and their oppression by the Moors, and the history of the bishopric of Palencia, both laced with liberal doses of invention. The text is thus a curious literary hall of mirrors, where Rodrigo's deeds glorify Castile-León as well as the bishopric of Palencia. Further, the Cid, without any historical basis, is presented as a patron of Palencia, and protector of its bishop against usurpers. Turning a well-known hero into the special protector of the bishopric served the purposes of the ecclesiastics of Palencia at the time of the writing. It was a time of trouble more generally in Castile, with fighting for political power, and a time of crisis for the bishopric itself, which suffered from attacks by nobles and had to accept subordination to the archbishopric of Toledo, after a failed bid to be recognized as an archbishopric. Other sources also tied Rodrigo to Palencia, claiming his marriage was performed there. The myth-making was quite successful: by the sixteenth century, it was widely believed that the Cid had married and lived in Palencia.

Las Mocedades de Rodrigo also shows that the Cid's image was evolving in different directions. The main thrust of the epic probably comes from an oral composition, and concerns the youthful exploits of Rodrigo. The work created a fictional youth for a well-known hero, attesting to a medieval appetite for prequels; a fourteenth-century author then added a genealogy. Genealogies were important for their legitimizing function, a proof of nobility and of the right to wield authority. The Rodrigo of the *Mocedades* is the grandson of one of the legendary judges of Castile, Laín Calvo, and great-grandson of a king of León, based on a myth already relayed in some previous sources. Because of his lineage, he therefore enjoys a high status from the outset that surpasses even the aristocratic standing of the historical Rodrigo. But he is arrogant, insubordinate and the very opposite of the saintly character dreamed up at San Pedro de Cardeña; indeed, he is more than once called 'a devil'.

Although in a different way from the *Legend of Cardeña*, Rodrigo's deeds in the *Mocedades* are just as incredible. He appears on the scene at the age of twelve, after a spat between his father, Diego Laínez, and Jimena's father, Count Gómez de Gormaz. The count stole Diego's livestock, and he retaliated by raiding Gormaz. After setting fire to some houses, Diego's men took not only the count's livestock but also some of his men with their belongings, and for good measure the washerwomen washing at the water's edge. In the medieval texts women are always a foolproof way of dishonouring an adversary. The furious count challenges Diego by referring to him as 'you son of the town judge' and the two sides agree to pit a hundred of their men against each other. As Rodrigo rides out with the hundred of his father's warriors, in his first battle, he is the first to exchange blows with Count Gómez and kills him. At Jimena's request, then, the king decides that Rodrigo should marry her.

The piece is wonderfully optimistic about royal power. When Diego receives the royal summons to go to the court accompanied by his son, with the messenger stating that he would attain eminence there, Diego immediately concludes that the king wants to have him killed in revenge for the death of the count of Gormaz. 'I am fearful of these letters that are full of lies, / for in these matters kings have very evil ways. / Any king you serve, serve him without trickery, / and be wary of him as of a mortal enemy.' Accordingly, he tells Rodrigo to take refuge at his brother's and, should the king indeed bring about Diego's death, Rodrigo, with his uncles, should avenge him. The king is also represented as a coward; despite his father's warning, Rodrigo accompanied him to court, taking three hundred armed men, and frightened the king badly, showing up with a longsword.

Rodrigo is both insubordinate and impulsive. In some ways, he is a caricature of the Cid who imposes the oath on King Alfonso VI, and of the heroic warrior. He refuses to kiss the king's hand, declaring that he is not the king's vassal. He declares both his displeasure when King Fernando oversees his engagement to Jimena and his determination 'not to lie with her' until he wins five battles. The king exclaims: 'This is not a man, he has the look of a devil!' Rodrigo makes good his word and defeats several raiding Muslim troops, as well as a warrior of the king of Aragón who had challenged King Fernando to give up Calahorra. Yet he refuses to give a large share of the booty to King Fernando, and even frees a Muslim king he captured in battle, who becomes his vassal and pays him tribute. Rodrigo also drags a count out of the church where he sought refuge (violating sanctuary), pulling him out 'by the beard from behind the altar'. A part of the text is therefore structured around rebellion against authority, exalting disobedience; according to one modern hypothesis, this was to indicate immature youth, as well as to provide a story of initiation, in line with medieval romance literature on heroes.

Yet these stories are interwoven with others that show divine approval of Rodrigo. In what seems almost a fairy-tale episode, prior to his duel with the champion of Aragón, Rodrigo goes on a pilgrimage to Santiago de Compostela, and on his return meets a leper who asks for help to cross a ford. The leper is scorned by everyone else, but Rodrigo feels sorry for him and helps him across, and then into a cave, where Rodrigo falls asleep. The leper then whispers in his ears: 'I am a messenger of Christ, I am not a leper. / I am Saint Lazarus, God sent me to you.' He then breathes on Rodrigo, telling him he will succeed in any undertaking while possessed of a fever as a result of this. The foretold success comes to pass after the king of France, the German emperor and the pope demand that the five kingdoms of Spain pay tribute to France. The Hundred Years War, raging in Europe at the time, may have influenced the invention of such an international coalition. The tribute they want, however, is clearly demeaning: it includes fifteen virgin noblewomen a year. King Fernando asks Rodrigo's advice; Rodrigo counsels war. So the five kings of Spain, numerous counts and their troops ride to France. The king wants him to carry the banner, but Rodrigo declines: 'I am a squire and not a knighted warrior.' This uncharacteristic humility is immediately contradicted by events.

The count of Savoy, who already knew Rodrigo's reputation, but not what he looked like, approached Rodrigo to try to entice him over to his side before knowing who he was, only to be mocked. Once he is defeated and discovers Rodrigo's identity, he exclaims: 'I fought with a devil.' The count promises Rodrigo his daughter's hand, making him his heir, in exchange for his freedom. Seemingly accepting the deal, Rodrigo simply passes the young woman to King Fernando to take as his concubine, once more using a female body to dishonour the father. He then leads the Spanish troops to Paris, to confront the French king and the pope. Rodrigo's stature becomes evident as the dignitaries cannot at first tell which of them is King Fernando and which Rodrigo. The pope seems unable to decide exactly what he wants: first he suggests that the French king should trick Fernando into a four-year truce, after which they would take his kingdom; then he proposes to honour Fernando and make him emperor of Spain. Rodrigo cuts in, 'Cursed be your offer, oh Roman Pope!' saying the five kingdoms of Spain already kiss Fernando's hand, so he does not need papal recognition; he has come to conquer the German empire. He then demands battle and promises to seek out the French king on the battlefield. Battle is to be joined the next day, but, in a miraculously short time that would surely be popular with women were it possible to patent it, the count of Savoy's daughter, who had become Fernando's concubine only a few weeks earlier, gives birth to his son. The pope quickly takes charge and baptizes him with the king of France and the German emperor as godfathers, thereby preventing war, and they agree on a very long truce.

The Rodrigo of the *Mocedades* is irascible, insubordinate, a law unto himself, but fearless and a peerless warrior. Diverse explanations have been proposed in modern scholarship for such a representation: competition for the attention of the audience through creating increasingly extreme stories, a celebration of qualities dear to the authors of epic poetry (passion, transgression, revenge) or even a sarcastic take on the *Poema*'s Cid. It is hard for modern audiences to appreciate the humour of a past age; but the bizarreness of this text may well derive from a less than reverent attitude towards the hero in the oral tradition. The clerical reworking incorporated that tradition, even while adding the elements that made the fictional Rodrigo significant for the bishopric of Palencia. The legends of the hero, so removed from the historical Rodrigo, therefore meandered in diverse directions.

The monks of San Pedro de Cardeña, however, continued to play an eminent role in stimulating the cult of the Cid. Around 1400 they composed an epitaph for him: 'I was victorious . . . over Búcar and 36 pagan kings. Of these, 22 died on the field of battle. I defeated them in Valencia after my death, sitting on my horse. Together with this, I won 72 battles in the field.' In the seventeenth century, doubts grew, even in other Benedictine monasteries, about some of the more spectacular deeds of the Cid. So in the eighteenth century, the monks redoubled their efforts in the face of criticism. Between 1719 and 1721 Francisco de Berganza, a monk of San Pedro de Cardeña, wrote a history of the monastery; supposedly a rigorous work depicting the historical Cid, it incorporated all the legendary elements, including the story of the Cid going on pilgrimage to Santiago, meeting a poor leper on the way and insisting on taking him along, sharing his bed and his plate with him. The leper then turns into St Lazarus and promises the Cid military victories over all his enemies as reward for his charity. Maintaining ties to their legendary patron remained important for the monks, in the face of periodic litigations over properties and income, and disagreements with the royal court.

The monks also translated some of the stories of the *Legend* into visible monuments as a means of reinforcing their ties to the Cid. The text described the heavenly host who helped the dead Cid's troops, and their leader, the apostle St James, known in the Iberian peninsula at the time as Santiago Matamoros, St James the Moor-slayer. He was thought to have helped Christian troops against Muslims many times during the medieval period. He also became a model for representing Moor-killing heroes. The eighteenth-century façade of the monastery, completed in 1739, features a monumental statue of the Cid depicted in the same way as Santiago: a warrior on horseback, killing Muslims. It also echoes the seventeenth-century façade with the sculpture of Fernán González replicating the imagery of Santiago Matamoros at Arlanza. The *Legend of Cardeña* had also created the figure of a Muslim *alfaquí* (an expert in Islamic law) of Valencia, converted to Christianity by the Cid, who took the name Gil Díaz, and eventually buried the Cid's horse Bauieca in front of the monastery, in a 'grave' that took on a physical reality much later.

Moreover, the cult of the Cid developed into the honouring of his extended family. Curiously, this unites features of saints' cults, where the relics of saints and their burials are the focus of veneration, and the creation of aristocratic family pantheons, uniting the tombs of multiple generations in one location. The *Crónica particular del Cid*, printed in 1512 and financed by the monastery of San

Pedro, included a section on the tomb of the Cid and those buried at the monastery. The author was on a mission to confer as much prestige on the monastery as possible. He affirmed the ancient foundation of the monastery by the wife of the Visigothic king Theoderic of Italy in 537; the martyrdom of 200 monks by the Moors in 834, who are buried in the cloister; the refoundation of the monastery by King Alfonso III of León in 899. The long list of kings and queens buried in the monastery starts with Sancha, the alleged founder, Theoderic's wife, and continues with many kings of León, and the various family members of the Cid: Jimena, his son Diego, his daughters, his son-in-law Sancho of Aragón, numerous counts and countesses of Castile and other nobles, an alleged bastard brother of the Cid with his large family, including the Cid's many nephews; Jimena's parents; and two saint abbots of the monastery, Sisebut and Sancho, the latter being merely a legendary figure. The text records the inscription on the Cid's tomb – 'invincible warrior, famous for his battles and triumphs, this tomb encloses the great Rodericus Díaz' – and goes on to compare the Cid to the glory of ancient Rome and Charlemagne. In 1736, a new funerary chapel was constructed in the monastic church, a pantheon reuniting the remains of those who had been buried in the church, although many of these alleged burials were fictitious. The Cid, along with Jimena, was in the most prominent place.

The monks of Cardeña presented a quasi-saint already in the *Legend* written about the Cid. By 1327 at the latest, there is evidence of a yearly commemoration of Rodrigo at Cardeña, with a mention that the tomb was in front of the altar. Not content with the strong hints of Rodrigo's sanctity, the monastery soon wanted to promote him for official canonization. Thanks to monastic reform and the consequent remodelling of the church, in 1541, the remains of Rodrigo and Jimena were moved. As the tomb was opened, a fragrant smell reportedly arose from the coffin, typical evidence of sanctity. Also, after a period of drought, rain finally fell, and this was attributed to the merits of Rodrigo. The abbot was already speaking of Rodrigo as a saint and the monks chanted the liturgy accordingly. People were scandalized, however, that the remains were moved to a less prominent location; the local authorities of Burgos protested, and finally King Carlos I himself intervened, demanding that the remains be moved back to the centre of the main chapel. Ideas about the sanctity of the Cid therefore must have been more widespread. Indeed, at the end of the fifteenth century, the *Historia de los hechos del Marqués de Cádiz*, which celebrated the deeds of Rodrigo Ponce de León – one of the leaders of the royal armies against Granada, the war that completed the Christian 'reconquest' of Spain – wrote of the 'most saintly knight Çid Ruy Díaz'. At the request of the monks of Cardeña, in 1554 Philip II initiated the canonization at the papal court, but amid political upheavals in Italy, his ambassador had to leave, and the case was ultimately abandoned.

Despite the lack of papal recognition and some texts to the contrary, the Cid had been progressively moulded into a Christian hero. This makeover served not just the interests of religious institutions, but probably had its origins closer to home.

5

Cherchez la Femme

The works composed about the Cid in the two centuries following his death established many elements of the myth as we know it. It is rather surprising that someone who neither attained the rank of a king nor lived the life of a cleric should become the subject of such extensive textual commemoration after his death in this period. Chronicles and lives of saints were normally written about those who were royalty and members of the clergy at the time, or about entirely fictitious figures, and it was rare to have an aristocrat, however successful on the battlefield, memorialized to such an extent. How to explain this anomaly? It seems to arise from the memory of a warrior who alone had considerable success against Muslim advances on the peninsula in the late eleventh century and the agency of his descendants. El Cid became a paragon in the period when the papacy advocated a united Christian front against Muslims in the Iberian peninsula, in the decades leading up to the Battle of Las Navas de Tolosa in 1212. That was a turning point in the wars on the peninsula, leading to the rapid collapse of most of al-Andalus, with the exception of Granada, by the middle of the century. In the decades of Christian uncertainty and preparations for war that would unite, however fleetingly, all the Iberian Christian rulers in one camp, the story of an earlier successful Christian champion was useful. His memory was therefore progressively cleared of the elements incongruous with such a role: his employment in Muslim service, his insubordination to his king and his lack of devout Christian piety.

Yet, despite his primarily military fame, it is more than probable that women, Rodrigo's wife and two daughters, contributed to the early reformulation of his image in a major way. We have mostly circumstantial evidence that they must have been instrumental in the early myth-building; ironically, they barely appear in the historical sources. But the role of women in medieval society in maintaining family memory is well known. Rodrigo never became a king. Through the female line, however, he did become the ancestor of kings, who probably profited from an association with the legendary Christian hero. One element alone stands out from the sources themselves: that Jimena took her husband's body with her when evacuating Valencia and reburied it in San Pedro de Cardeña.

The women of Rodrigo's family are obscured in the medieval narrative sources, and appear as generic stereotypes rather than individuals with agency; this conforms to a general trend, as shown by historian Jeffrey Bowman, with twelfth- and thirteenth-century histories 'erasing women from the political landscape', expunging exactly those tenth- and eleventh-century aristocratic women who had played significant roles. The earliest narrative, the twelfth-century *Historia Roderici*, hardly refers to them at all. Jimena appears as a relative of King Alfonso, daughter of the count of Oviedo, given by Alfonso in marriage to Rodrigo. Her role in this marriage is of interest simply in terms of what she brings to Rodrigo: children and honour. Accordingly, space is allotted only to cameo appearances: 'She bore him sons and daughters.' Her imprisonment on the orders of the king at the time of Rodrigo's unjust second exile is worthy of inclusion only because of the dishonour this brings Rodrigo. The most detailed episode concerns her actions as a grieving widow. Yet here, too, she serves to highlight Rodrigo's greatness. With North African troops marching against Valencia, 'deprived of so great a husband, finding herself in her affliction so hard-pressed and unable to find the remedy of consolation in her unhappiness, [Jimena] sent the bishop [of Valencia] to King Alfonso to ask him for pity's sake to help her'. When the king arrives, 'Rodrigo's unhappy wife received him with the greatest joy, and kissed his feet. She implored him to help her and all the Christians who were with her.' This proves to be impossible and he takes her and all the Christians, with their goods, to safety in Castile, along with Rodrigo's body. The text accords even less importance to Rodrigo's daughters; they are merely mentioned as being imprisoned along with their mother early on.

Paradoxically, the text that dwells in the greatest detail on these women is the one that erases their personalities the most. In the *Poema de Mio Cid*, the Cid's wife Jimena is characterized as a 'wise and noble lady', and the Cid says of her: 'my wife is a worthy lady.' Yet her role is a passive one, to pray and wait for her husband. His daughters feature prominently in the same source, but only as the subjects of horrendous humiliation that triggers the Cid's retaliation. The author could not even get their names right: the historical María and Cristina become Elvira and Sol. The female members of Rodrigo's family are most conspicuous by their near-inexistence in their own right in the texts composed about him.

The role of these constructed literary figures is to enhance the hero's reputation. The *Poema*'s Doña Jimena is the symbol of obedience, loyalty and patience. She is the perfect noble wife. We first meet her at the monastery of San Pedro de Cardeña, praying for her husband at matins. The Cid has been exiled and is preparing to leave Castile. On his way he stops at the monastery to say goodbye and provide for his wife and daughters, instructing the abbot to look after them and giving him a sum of money for their upkeep. Jimena comes to meet the Cid entirely distraught, sinks to her knees crying, and asks her husband to counsel her. In despair, she acknowledges 'we must be separated during our lifetime', a sentiment echoed by her husband; they both pray to be reunited.

Yet *his* role is active, even in these circumstances, guiding her, providing for her. In contrast, her longest speech in the *Poema* is a prayer in San Pedro on the morning when the Cid leaves to go into exile: enumerating a long list of biblical miracles, she begs Christ and St Peter to watch over her husband and bring him back. She is nobly submissive, kissing her husband's hands as he leaves, tears pouring down her face. Her figure thus enables the Cid to act as the protector of his wife and children, doing his duty.

Once the Cid conquers Valencia, he sends to the monastery for them, asking the king to allow them to join him, a request he grants. Álvar Fáñez, who was sent with warriors to take the ladies to Valencia, buys the 'richest garments' for them to wear, and they are escorted to the Cid. Great emphasis is given to the expense and honour involved in escorting them as well as to their reception. Jimena and the Cid's daughters (who are not even named at this point) are instrumentalized: they are merely a means to display the Cid's riches and status. Upon arrival, Jimena once more throws herself at the Cid's feet and thanks him for saving her 'from very great dishonour'. The Cid refers to Valencia as the inheritance he won for them. He then takes them to the highest point in the citadel, whence they can see the city, the rich plantations, and the sea, and praise God for these gains. In this way, the readers of the *Poema* and those who listened to it as it was recited experienced the Cid's new fortunes through the eyes of his wife and daughters.

When, shortly after that, Emir Yusuf of Morocco besieges Valencia, the Cid declares that his wife and daughters should watch him fight: 'They shall see what life is like in these alien lands. / With their own eyes they shall see full well how we earn our bread.' Once again, he takes them up to the citadel, only this time to see the land covered by the enemy's tents. Doña Jimena, alarmed, exclaims: 'What is this, Cid? May the Creator save you!' The Cid, however, makes light of the situation, joking: 'you have hardly arrived and they want to make you gifts! / Your daughters are of age to be married and they are bringing you a dowry!' The Cid sees the attack as an opportunity to gain great and wonderful riches, as well as to display his prowess to his wife. He encourages her to watch him fight. Jimena is 'so terrified it seemed her heart would burst', but the Cid convinces her of impending victory so she loses her fear and becomes joyful. It is as if even her emotions followed her husband's dictates.

After the Cid is indeed victorious, he addresses a remarkable speech to Jimena and his daughters, part joke, part bragging, all the while holding his bloody sword in his hand. He declares that he has won renown and riches for them; while they held Valencia, he triumphed in battle. 'Pray to the Creator to grant me a long life, / for through me you will acquire honour and men will do homage to you.' Kneeling before him, the women acknowledge 'we depend upon you'. We are told repeatedly that the Campeador loved his wife and daughters 'with his heart and soul' and took care of them. Their main role is to gratefully accept and acknowledge that fact.

There is one fourteenth-century literary work that paints a different picture of Jimena – at least at first glance. In the *Mocedades de Rodrigo*, after the young Rodrigo kills Jimena's father and also captures her two brothers, taking them home to Vivar, Jimena, who is the youngest of three sisters, dresses in mourning and goes to Vivar to beg for her brothers' release. This is granted, and the brothers immediately start to plot a night-time attack against Vivar. Jimena, however, dissuades them by promising to seek justice at the royal court. She rides, with a suitable retinue, to the court at Zamora and pleads with the king to grant her justice. King Fernando is concerned that Castile will rise up against him, but Jimena offers him the perfect solution: give her Rodrigo as a husband. The king readily acquiesces and oversees their engagement. While in this text Jimena has all the agency, rather than being a passive pawn, the difference is more illusory than real. Firstly, after this episode Jimena completely drops out of the story. Secondly, giving her the decisive voice in obtaining marriage to Rodrigo is part of the satirical tone of the work and looks suspiciously like a stock misogynistic trope, that of women ruling over men. One of the most famous iterations of the idea was the story of Phyllis humiliating Aristotle, who had tried to warn Alexander the Great against her wiles, by riding on his back. This kind of female agency humiliates and ridicules the male protagonist; Rodrigo, by refusing to obey her wishes, demonstrates that he cannot be subdued by a woman. Jimena, despite her seeming agency, merely serves to enhance Rodrigo's character.

If Jimena is repeatedly treated as a mere backdrop so as to highlight the Cid's valour, this is even more true of the Cid's daughters. They remain nameless for most of the *Poema*. They are entirely passive participants as the Cid expresses his love for them and his duty to care for them. When they arrive in Valencia, they are presented by their mother as 'fine girls, well instructed to serve you and God'. It is indeed instructive for the reader that in this phrase obedience to their father takes precedence even over obedience to God. They appear with their mother in all the scenes where she plays a role, saying nothing, kissing their father's hand, crying or being joyful as befits the situation. After his victory over Emir Yusuf, the Campeador first marries off her wife's ladies-in-waiting to his vassals, providing them with rich dowries, before telling Jimena: 'I shall deal with the future of your daughters later.' We are not told what husbands he would have had in mind for them, however, because his daughters' marriages end up being decided by shameless schemers.

After the Cid's conquest of Valencia, when his fortunes are vertiginously rising, two high-ranking noblemen at the royal court, the *infantes* of Carrión – Fernando and Diego González – secretly discuss the idea of marrying his daughters 'for our own gain'. They tell nobody, conscious of the great difference in their social standing by birth. The *infantes* are figments of the poet's imagination. Although there were historical figures who were the sons of the count of Carrión, members of the nobility of the kingdom of León, they were not called González. They would not have been called '*infantes*' either, titles only appropriate for the sons of kings. Yet their exaggerated title serves a role in the poem: by elevating their social position, in sharp contrast to their contemptible character, they showcase the Cid's perfection, who, though allegedly born in the lower nobility, is much nobler than they are in comportment.

Fernando and Diego finally decide to act after the Cid gains the riches of the besieging Moroccan troops through his victory; this sustained increase in his fortunes counteracts their scruples, for, if they marry his daughters, 'we shall grow in honour by it and so we shall prosper'. Because of this they ask for King Alfonso's intercession; he sends assurances to the Cid that he would gain more honour and wealth through such an alliance. As this request comes at the same time as King Alfonso's admission that he had wronged the Cid, for which he offered his full pardon, the Cid is in something of a quandary. On the one hand, he is grateful to be restored to a position of honour by the king, and he acknowledges that, since his social superior proposes the marriages, he must consider them. On the other hand, although he sees the *infantes* as 'proud and powerful members of the court', left to his own devices he would not agree to such marriages. The Cid then goes to meet King Alfonso in person, which is the occasion of his public restoration to royal favour and great celebrations. The king repeats the offer to marry the Cid's daughters to the *infantes*, but while he starts by asking, he ends up commanding, as he considers 'the marriage to be honourable and to bring great prestige'. Significantly, it is also at this point that the Cid's daughters are named, as if the impending marriages finally conferred on them their individuality.

The Cid responds by claiming that his daughters are still young, but 'Both they and I will do as you desire; / I now place Doña Elvira and Doña Sol in your hands; / give them to whomsoever you will, for with that I am pleased.' The Cid expresses a vassal's obedience to his lord, and the daughters' obedience to their father. The latter is simply taken for granted, since the Cid left his family in Valencia and consults neither the daughters affected, nor his wife before agreeing to Alfonso's request. The Cid with a large company and the *infantes* then return to Valencia to celebrate the marriage forthwith, where Álvar Fáñez acts as the king's representative, giving the girls away. The Cid greets his wife and daughters with 'My honoured wife, I am come! Thanks be to the Creator! / I bring you sons-in-law through whom we shall gain honour. / Be grateful to me, my daughters, for I have married you well!' The women kiss his hand and express their gratitude, especially because Elvira and Sol will 'not know want'. The Cid emphasizes that it was not he, but the king who arranged these marriages; while this may on the surface look like an emphasis on the honour bestowed on them, it is also a mechanism for distancing the Cid from the responsibility for what is to come. The splendour of the fifteen-day wedding celebrations is stressed, the *Poema* enumerating the fine clothes worn by all and the rich gifts given to the guests. This emphasis on fine clothing and the display of wealth was important to indicate the Cid's status and power, and it is hard to escape the conclusion that the women fulfilled the same function.

The *infantes* stay in Valencia for almost two years after their marriage until an unfortunate episode reveals their cowardice. Once, while the Campeador slept, a lion broke out of its cage. As the Cid's men surrounded the couch on which he was sleeping to protect him, Fernando González hid under the couch in terror, and Diego González first ran out the door screaming, then hid behind a wine press. When he finally emerged, his cloak and tunic were covered in dirt, mirroring the stain on his honour. In the humorous scene that follows, the Cid finally wakes up and is surprised to find himself surrounded by his men; when they tell him what has happened, he approaches the lion who hangs his head in shame.

The Cid takes him by the neck and leads him back to his cage. The Cid then calls for his sons-in-law, but they are nowhere to be found; finally, they emerge, pale and shaken. Members of the court mock them, and although the Cid forbids such mockery, the *infantes* are aggrieved and feel insulted.

At the same time, another Moroccan army arrives to besiege Valencia, under Búcar. The Cid and his men are delighted, looking forward to more booty, but the *infantes* are terrified, afraid of dying in battle. One of the Cid's vassals overhears them and reports to the Campeador, who tells his sons-in-law to stay in Valencia, adding, 'I am brave enough' to defeat the Moors. They cannot face such dishonour and participate in the battle, only to demonstrate their cowardice once again. Fernando rides towards the enemy, though not exactly bursting with enthusiasm; but when a Moor actually rides at him, he flees. However, when one of the Cid's men kills the Moor and offers to pretend the deed was done by Fernando, he happily acquiesces and then boasts about his victory. The *infantes* then quietly let the Cid and his men get on with it and defeat the Moroccans, and only show up to the division of the booty.

The Cid thinks they gained honour and prestige in the battle, saying, 'They are now fine men – in future they will be even more highly esteemed.' Although he intended it as praise, Fernando and Diego, only too aware of their duplicity, take this badly. However, they accept their share of the booty, which makes them very wealthy. The Cid's men who fought bravely know the truth, and their mockery day and night 'taught the *infantes* a cruel lesson'. They, however, hatched a wicked plan to retaliate. They pretended they wanted to return to Carrión to show their wives the estates they had there. The unwary Cid lets his daughters go and even bestows rich presents on his sons-in-law: a huge dowry, horses and garments of silk. Finally, he even gives them his two swords, Colada and Tizón. In reality, however, the *infantes*, who initially sought honour through marriage to the Cid's daughters, now want to dishonour the Cid through them. They constantly repeat their keen awareness of their own higher social standing when justifying their plans for vengeance.

Elvira and Sol take leave of their parents, still obedient instruments of their father's will: 'Now you are sending us to the lands of

Carrión / and it is our duty to fulfil your command.' Their own agency is expressed in one single desire: they beg their father to send envoys to them once they are in Carrión. The Cid suspects that not all is well, and he sends his nephew Félez Muñoz to accompany his daughters; the parting is difficult, with both father and daughters weeping. The Cid's last words to them as they leave, 'may all you do be such as to give us pleasure', reiterate the belief that their role is to be subordinate and obedient. Their subordination, however, takes a different turn as they are used by their husbands as mere instruments to dishonour the Cid.

The vileness of the *infantes* is further demonstrated as they plot to kill Abengalbón, the Cid's Moorish friend who put them up during their journey and treated them well out of friendship for the Campeador. They are overheard, however, and their conversation is reported to Abengalbón, who in disgust orders them to leave. Fernando and Diego stop with their escort in the oakwood of Corpes, and disguise their evil intent by spending the night making love to their wives. They then send everyone ahead and remain behind with their wives, purportedly to continue their lovemaking. Finally alone, they can put their plan into practice. In a particularly sadistic way, they first inform their wives that they would now take revenge for having been humiliated over the incident with the lion, before tearing the rich garments from the women until they are in their underwear. Sol begs them simply to decapitate them with the swords they had received from the Cid instead of battering them, which would bring dishonour upon the husbands themselves, and for which they 'will be accountable at an assembly or at the royal court'.

The *infantes*, however, go ahead with their vengeance by beating Elvira and Sol with straps and using their spurs to cut into their flesh. 'They beat them until they are numb, with their silken undergarments all covered in blood.' Remarkably, throughout this ordeal it is the 'pain in their hearts' for the dishonour of their husbands and of their father that the women feel. When the *infantes* have exhausted themselves beating Elvira and Sol, and the latter can no longer speak, Fernando and Diego leave their wives for dead, at the mercy of wild beasts. They are very proud of themselves; seemingly having forgotten that they were the ones who had wanted to marry the Cid's daughters, they now talk of their marriages as something that had been imposed on them, and that was not in accordance with their higher social status. It is only thanks to the astute Félez Muñoz that the Cid's daughters are rescued. He had misgivings and had hidden in the forest, and when he saw the *infantes* ride away, he searched for Elvira and Sol. Having found his cousins, he revived them and carried them on his horse to safety.

The women are still mainly passive, like the early Disney princesses, simply benefiting from being saved. They merely ask for water and express the hope that their father would reward Félez. They are sheltered in a nearby community and nursed back to health. The episode of the 'Afrenta de Corpes' is an intriguing literary composition: one could assume that women who are degraded in this way would not be marriageable again and the dishonour to the whole family would be enormous; why invent such a story about the daughters of a hero who is represented in the best possible light? Scholars have speculated that the author may have been inspired by either saints' lives, where female saints are tortured; or literary models, where a fictional, innocent young lady, a princess or queen, is unjustly persecuted and suffers horrendous torments before her ultimate triumph. There are notable parallels in this respect between the *Poema* and the French *Chanson de Florence de Rome*, for example. In such tales, undeserved suffering evoked ideas of beauty and innocence, making it more understandable that the author would invent such a story about the Cid's fictional daughters.

The Campeador's first reaction when he hears the news is to vow that the *infantes* would not succeed in dishonouring him; he would yet marry his daughters well. He then sends a strong military escort to bring Elvira and Sol back to Valencia. When the leaders of the host meet the grieving sisters, one of them consoles the Cid's daughters in what today would be considered a particularly tone-deaf pronouncement: 'You have lost a good marriage, but you will be able to gain a better one.' When they arrive back in Valencia, the Cid embraces and kisses them, once more hinting that he had been uneasy about his sons-in-law from the outset: 'I accepted the marriage, and dared say no more.' He then reiterates his hopes of a better marriage for both, as well as declaring his intention to take revenge for the deeds of the *infantes*. Thankful to their father, and reunited with their mother, the women once more become passive pawns awaiting new husbands.

Arguing that what dishonours the vassal dishonours his lord, and stating, 'He married my daughters to the Infantes, not I', the Campeador asks King Alfonso's help in receiving justice. The king recognizes the legitimacy of the request and calls a court to Toledo, specifically commanding the *infantes* to appear there. Fernando and Diego fail to wriggle out from attending. Describing at length the great finery the Cid wore and the large number of his men who accompanied him, the *Poema* relates how the court gathered and the king appointed some nobles to be judges in the suit. When asked to state his case, the Cid merely demands his two swords back, since the *infantes* are no longer his sons-in-law. Imagining that they can come to an agreement with King Alfonso over the rest, the *infantes* quickly acquiesce. The Cid then demands they repay him the dowry he had given them; Fernando and Diego try to refuse, as they had already spent the money. The judges, however, deem the request just, so the *infantes* offer to give Rodrigo some of their estates in exchange, and finally repay him in horses and arms.

It is only after this that the Cid finally raises the issue of satisfaction for the mistreatment of his daughters. García Ordóñez, the Cid's old enemy, addresses the king to dismiss the Campeador's request: 'Those of Carrión are of such descent / that they ought not to want his daughters even as concubines', echoing the *infantes*' self-justification after they left their wives in the Corpes woods. Fernando himself speaks out, adding insult to injury: 'We should have married daughters of kings or emperors', the daughters of mere *infanzónes*, lesser nobles, do not suffice. They therefore gained, rather than lost, honour by abandoning their wives, he argues. Pedro Bermúdez, the Campeador's nephew and loyal warrior, then intervenes, and recounts the treachery of the *infantes* that hitherto was not known to the court: how Fernando only pretended to kill a Moor in battle and then boasted of his valour, taking credit for someone else's deeds; and how he hid, a coward, from the lion. Pedro then challenges Fernando to a duel. Diego doubles down on their interpretation of events, adding that they did not repent of abandoning the Cid's daughters. He, in turn, is chastised for his past cowardice and challenged to a duel by Martín Antolínez, the Cid's faithful vassal. Verbal taunts fly, before King Alfonso announces that the duels will be fought. These are judicial duels, to determine guilt with the aid of God. In this way, it is men who must fight over honour, which can be lost through the treatment of women, but cannot be restored by them. In the realm of fiction, women can only contribute to the hero's honour through obedience and a good marriage.

As if on cue, two messengers then arrive at court, one from the prince of Navarra, the other from the prince of Aragón – real *infantes* – and ask for the hands of the Cid's daughters in marriage to their lords, 'to be queens of Navarra and Aragón'. The Cid defers to King Alfonso, and the king – the reader hopes with better judgement this time – immediately grants the hands of Elvira and Sol to the princes, since, as he tells the Cid, 'by it you gain in honour, possessions and lands'. Álvar Fáñez then asks permission to speak, and, once he receives it, expresses his own grievance. Since he had represented King Alfonso, handing over the Cid's daughters to their first husbands, he challenges them as evil men and traitors. With not a little *Schadenfreude*, he reminds Fernando and Diego that 'Before, you had them as your wives to hold in your arms, / but now you will kiss their hands in homage and call them your ladies; / you will have to serve them, even though it causes you distress.' Finally, the king appoints the time and place of the duels. The *infantes* insist that the duels take place in Carrión, and would have tried trickery to win, but Alfonso is there with his troops to protect the Cid's champions. Three of the Cid's men duel the *infantes* and their kinsman Asur González and defeat them all.

It is a version of all's well that ends well: the dishonour that the attack on his daughters had brought upon the Cid is removed through vengeance. However, this vengeance is not private, but overseen by the king, so the Campeador gained the king's justice and reinforced the rule of law and royal authority at the same time. Moreover, he sees his daughters married to worthier and higher ranking husbands: 'My Cid marries his daughters more prestigiously than before.' The just recovered Elvira and Sol once again have no say in the matter; they must be thankful to their father.

Not only do our modern sensibilities quail before the image of the subservient, obedient wife and daughters, but eleventh-century sources contradict such ideas about real women at the time. The shadow of the historical figures, in particular Jimena, still just about emerges from the fog of later legend that turned her into an essentially passive figure, waiting for Rodrigo to return from exile, and then from battle. Yet we can know very little with any certainty. Jimena is mentioned a few times in contemporary documents. She descended from an aristocratic family, but the precise reconstruction of her lineage is an open question. One of the narratives, the *Historia Roderici*, claimed she was related to Alfonso VI of León, and while the exact degree of the relationship has been debated, her family was clearly a high-ranking one. The various modern reconstructions make Jimena the daughter of Diego Fernández, the count of Asturias or Oviedo, and of Jimena, the daughter of Alfonso V of León; or of Diego Rodríguez, count of Oviedo, and Cristina, Alfonso V's granddaughter. In either case, she would have been called Jimena Díaz, according to the patronymic naming system, from her father's name, Diego. Whether she was a cousin or niece of King Alfonso VI, Jimena's family was certainly connected to royalty. Her date of birth is unknown; many aristocratic women married at the age of fifteen or sixteen, and perhaps she did, too.

We don't know the exact date of her marriage to Rodrigo, only that it took place probably in 1074 and definitely by 1076. Even the precise date of her death is lost, and medieval sources provide varied, erroneous dates, although it must have occurred between 1113 and 1116. A charter containing the marriage contract between Rodrigo and Jimena, whose authenticity has been contested, but is upheld by recent research, provides some information. According to local practice, a husband gave his wife a gift, the *arras*, upon their marriage, as a kind of pledge of the property she would now share with him. The charter, written in the first-person singular, states that Ruderigo Didaz accepts Scemena, the daughter of Didago, prince of the Asturian lands, as his wife, emphasizing her virginity, and gives her various properties that are listed. She is made an owner, together with her husband, of his lands and goods. Further, should she survive her husband and not remarry, not only will she retain the properties, but 'you will have all furnishings, the silver and gold, the horses and mules, the armour and arms, and all the ornaments that are in our house, and without your will you do not have to give any of this to anyone unless to our children; and after your death, this will all go to the children who are born to me and you'.

Far from being the passive recipient of her husband's care for her, Jimena's voice resonates in the charter. 'And if it should happen that I Scemena accept another husband [after Rodrigo's death], I shall give up all these . . . to the children who will be born to you and me.' Husband and wife mutually declare the other to be their only heir. Jimena will inherit all if she does not remarry. 'I Scemena Didaz similarly make you, my husband, owner of all my properties and inheritance . . . all furnishings, the silver and gold, the horses and mules, the armour and arms, and all the ornaments that are in our house, and should my, Szemena Didaz's death occur before yours, my husband Ruderigo Didaz, all my inheritance belongs to you, and you will have the right to do with it as you wish. And after your death, all the children who will be born to you and me will inherit.'

Thus the very language describing Jimena's wishes mirrors that of Rodrigo's. Despite its apparent directness, Jimena's voice is refracted through a language that was not hers, Latin, and the clerical scribes who produced the document, using formulas. Even so, the image conveyed is rather different from the literary constructs. Although it does not amount to complete equality, nonetheless a much greater balance between the spouses puts paid to the passivity and dependent status of the *Poema*'s fictional Jimena. Agency rather than dependence is also visible in what we know of Jimena's life after her marriage. She did not patiently wait in a monastery during Rodrigo's exile; she seems to have returned to her family's estates. Once she was established in Valencia, she had a share in ruling it: Rodrigo's donation charter to the bishopric of Valencia specifies he is acting 'together with my wife Jimena'. And after his death, it was Jimena, rather than one of Rodrigo's sons-in-law, who ruled Valencia for three years.

Two years after Rodrigo's death, on 21 May 1101, Jimena reconfirmed Rodrigo's previous donations and gave a tenth of her present and future goods to the cathedral of Valencia for the benefit of the soul of her deceased husband, herself and her family. The charter declaims her motivations:

> I, Eximina Didez, not coerced or persuaded by anyone, but out of my own free will, with the consent of my children and trusted men . . . as remedy for the soul of my lord and husband Ruderico the Campeador, and for the souls of myself, my sons, daughters, and grandchildren [donate to the cathedral various properties]. I, the aforesaid Eximina, willingly give all this and swear, and command my children to swear and to confirm that as long as I live and hold honour, I shall fulfil all these things, as I promised to God and to our mother the Church.

Moreover, it is not just in her own and her family's name that she confers these goods to the Church, but also in the name 'of our princes'; that is, vassal nobles dependent on her, who must similarly give a tenth of the estates they hold from her.

At the end of the charter, conforming with the requirements of the age, various witnesses are listed. Between the text and the names of the witnesses, sprawls in crooked lines and a very different script in poor-quality ink that faded over time: 'God is true. I, the abovesaid Eximina, who ordered this document to be made, signed it by my own hand.' It is the hand of someone who is not used to putting pen to parchment. Jimena may even have copied the letters, putting spaces in the wrong place, misspelling some words. Yet she assumed full responsibility for ruling Valencia, and did not flinch from the unaccustomed task of writing in order to do so. She was used to commanding; in the charter, she repeatedly referred not only to her daughters but to her sons, although by then none she had given birth to were still alive. She had, however, two sons-in-law, and they are the ones she commands to honour her donations to the Church, as well as ordering the nobles who were her vassals, just as they had been her husband's, to align with her wishes.

Jimena's 1101 donation charter optimistically envisaged future conquests 'which, with God's help, we shall make by land or sea'. She seems to have intended to continue enlarging the territory under her rule. This, however, was not to be. In the summer of the same year, a large Almoravid army arrived to besiege Valencia. Jimena asked for the help of Alfonso VI, who arrived with his troops in March of the following year. The Almoravids lifted the siege, but Alfonso decided that he could not maintain the defence of Valencia, so far from his own domains, and instead opted to evacuate the city. In the following month, treasures and charters, valued possessions and movable goods were packed up, and under the protection of Alfonso's army the inhabitants of Valencia set off for Castile. Alfonso ordered the city to be burned: if he could not prevent the Saracens from taking it, at least he was not going to leave them anything.

What did Jimena feel as she left a burning Valencia behind? More grief, losing the city that witnessed her husband's greatest triumphs? Despair at not being able to hold onto it? Resignation to God's will? One thing is clear: it was not just her household goods and the accumulated riches that she saved from Valencia; she took the Cid's body with her. 'Accompanied by her husband's knights, she bore his body to the monastery of San Pedro de Cardeña. There she gave it honourable burial, granting for the sake of his soul no small gifts to the monastery.' Was this simply the action of a bereaved widow, who wished to save the remains of her loved one from possible annihilation or the vengeance of the conquerors? Or was it also a calculated move to foster his cult, perhaps at the inspiration of Bishop Jerome?

Of the many remaining years of Jimena's life, almost no trace remains. She lived to see a granddaughter, the issue of María and the count of Barcelona, married to the count of Besalú in 1107. She outlived her daughter María. She last appears in 1113, when she sold one of the properties, Valdecañas, that had been listed in the charter of Rodrigo's property gifts to her upon her marriage, to the cathedral canons of Burgos. It was witnessed by the abbot of the monastery of San Pedro de Cardeña. In this last charter, she refers to herself as 'I, Scemena, the wife of Rudericus Didaz'. A final expression of loyalty? Or a sign that she was active in cultivating Rodrigo's memory, or even his legend? Her continued ties to San Pedro, as signalled by the abbot's signature as a witness to the charter, raise intriguing possibilities of Jimena's role in transmitting ideas about the hero. She then disappears from the records and probably died not long afterwards. According to later tradition, she was buried alongside her husband at San Pedro de Cardeña.

Yet a grave in the Benedictine monastery of San Juan de la Peña of a Jimena Gómez bore an inscription according to which 'Here rests Eximinia Gomez, the wife of Rodericus Cid, commonly known as Ruy Díaz'. This gave rise to the idea that Rodrigo married twice, first to Jimena Gómez, and, after her death, to a second wife, Jimena Díaz. A much more convincing explanation is that the inscription in San Juan de la Peña is apocryphal, the product of thirteenth-century imagination, an attempt by yet another monastery to hitch its fortunes to the hero, by laying claim to at least Jimena's remains, even if the Cid himself was beyond reach.

The historical Jimena was no submissive, doe-eyed wife. Indeed, the Jimena of the *Mocedades* who rides to the royal court to demand Rodrigo as her husband, however distorted a mirror, is closer to the historical figure in her militant agency compared to other literary renditions. The real-life Jimena came from the aristocracy, and aristocratic women at the time inherited, owned and transmitted property – the parity of inheritance among sons and daughters was usual – and played active roles, even in politics. Lordship gave women political authority alongside their husband, or even in their own right. Aristocratic women also gave donations to religious institutions, instigated litigation, sold properties and administered justice. They had economic, social and political power. Jimena's contemporary, Urraca (1030s–c. 1103), sister of Alfonso VI, transmogrified into a seductive vixen in the film *El Cid*, regularly witnessed and signed charters issued by her parents. She sided with Alfonso in the sibling infighting that followed their parents' death. She was among those her brother consulted once he gained power, and she features in his early charters. She attended royal councils, gave donations to bishoprics and monasteries and confirmed donations of Alfonso VI. A magnificent chalice, housed in the museum of the Basilica of San Isidoro of León (and believed by some to be the Holy Grail), bears an inscription naming her as the donator. She was buried in the pantheon of the kings of León in the same basilica, and the inscription on her tombstone celebrates her donations and dedication to St Isidore.

Her namesake and another contemporary of Jimena, Queen Urraca (1081–1126), daughter of Alfonso VI, acquired the nickname 'the Reckless'. Married to Raymond of Burgundy, she ruled Galicia together with him. After his death, she began to rule alone at the age of twenty-six; within a year, when her brother Sancho died, she became heir to the throne of the kingdom of León. Her father came up with the plan to have her marry the king of Aragón, Alfonso el Batallador (the Battler or the Warrior), but did not live to see the realization of the marriage. Styled 'the queen of the whole of Spain', Urraca became queen of León and Castile, and married Alfonso. The mutual antipathy of the spouses was all but instantaneous. Various important groups of the nobility and the pope himself were also opposed to the marriage, and it disintegrated spectacularly, leading to repeated clashes and wars between the troops of Urraca and those of Alfonso. The marriage was ultimately annulled because of their consanguinity; according to the rules of the Catholic Church at the time, people related to each other within seven degrees of kinship were not allowed to marry, and if they did because they had no knowledge of the relationship, but later discovered it, their marriage was deemed to be invalid, a useful escape route for many members of the elite. Urraca did not just want to escape her marriage to Alfonso; she had had enough of marriage, full stop. She took a lover from the aristocracy, and after his death, another, Pedro González de Lara.

The world of Jimena was therefore in a sense closer to our own than to the subsequent literary representations, a world where aristocratic women were not toys for men to honour or push around, but one where women made decisions and acted on their own volition. Jimena's active agency at the start of Rodrigo's transformation seems to have been crucial. What of their daughters? The *Poema de Mio Cid* confirmed: 'Now, the kings of Spain are of his line.' His daughters' marriages were negotiated by Rodrigo, and seem to have united them to men who had similar aspirations to the Campeador. Rodrigo's daughters indeed married well; their descendants sat on the royal thrones of Navarra and Castile. Medieval women were active in the oral transmission of family histories, and it is inconceivable that Cristina and María did not pass on the memory of the incomparable warrior, el Cid Campeador. Cristina, the older daughter, married Ramiro, who was the son of an illegitimate member of the Navarrese royal family; yet, although his father was a bastard, his grandfather had been King García III of Pamplona. He was also lord of Monzón, vassal of the king of Aragón, and may well have nurtured dreams of becoming king himself, just as Rodrigo may have done. He did not rise to such a position, but his son with Cristina, García Ramírez, did end up as king of Pamplona in 1134, the kingdom that a few decades later became Navarra, and the Cid's great-great-grandson was Alfonso VIII, king of Castile. The so-called *Liber regum*, a history of the Iberian peninsula written in Navarro-Aragonese dialect between 1194 and 1209, included the 'Lineage of Rodrigo Díaz', a short biography and genealogy, in order to add renown to the reigning dynasty in Navarra. Going back in time, it listed Rodrigo's ancestors, but, embracing the present, it was already joined to genealogies of kings of the peninsula, demonstrating the Cid's rise in death, even more spectacular than his career had been in life.

María's marriage itself seems to have become the stuff of legend. The late thirteenth-century *Estoria de España* reported that she first married a son of King Pedro I of Aragón. Had that been the case, both sides could have hoped to gain from the marriage. While Rodrigo would have gained a royal son-in-law, Pedro may well have hoped for the expansion of Aragón, counting on his son's inheritance to rule both Valencia and Aragón one day. The historicity of this marriage, however, has been discounted. If the marriage is solely a fantasy, that raises the interesting prospect that someone was trying to elevate the Cid's status by connecting him to the Aragonese monarch through this marriage, yet one more strategy in creating the blossoming legend. María certainly married Count Ramón Berenguer III of Barcelona, however, and they had two daughters. María must have died by 1107, since the count married for a second time that year.

The women in Rodrigo's life were not obediently subordinate to his wishes, but more autonomous agents. Jimena and her daughters were far from passive objects whose lives were dictated by Rodrigo. While there is no definitive proof, it is likely that their early input contributed to the propagation of a mythicized version of Rodrigo. After all, a buffed-up image, in particular his disculpation from wrongdoing, served family interests. Yet they are mostly known to the public through the distorting lens of later legends; and the Cid's fictional daughters even became the object of prurient sixteenth-century sexual voyeurism, although the bashful modesty of later centuries rescued them from that indignity. Sixteenth-century printed versions of the Cid stories with woodcut illustrations liked to portray the episode in the woods of Corpes, representing Elvira and Sol completely naked. This pornographic titillation of the readers then went out of fashion for centuries. Later illustrators either refrained from representing the scene or portrayed it from a distance and in a way so that the women's bodies were covered. Painting, however, also took up the theme, focusing on the half-naked bodies of the bound, suffering young women.

The twentieth century, which witnessed the successes of feminism, such as suffrage, mass employment and sexual liberation, perversely did nothing to liberate Jimena and her daughters from the myth of obedient subservience. On the contrary, modern literature mostly contributed to reinforcing that message, even if modernizing it. Eduardo Marquina's play 'The Cid's daughters' (*Las hijas del Cid. Leyenda trágica en cinco actos*) from 1908 further embroidered the story. The Cid is only interested in marrying off his daughters to the *infantes* so that they can become queens, despite the fact that they profoundly despise their future husbands. After their disgrace, Elvira disguises herself as an unknown black knight in order to fight a duel against her former husband Fernando, and she is mortally wounded. While she takes responsibility for her own life at this point, all she finds is death. Sol is in love with her cousin, but is pressured to renounce him to accept the Navarrese monarch's offer of marriage. The anticipation of this marriage leads to the Cid's raptures of joy. Sol, however, is exhausted by the conflicting claims of filial obedience and love and dies in her mother's arms. Jimena is the passive wife and good mother without any say in the fate of her daughters. The Cid only realizes his folly after his daughters' death.

Luis Escobar's play 'Love is a runaway pony' (*El amor es un potro desbocado*) of 1959 focuses on Jimena. She worries about the opinion of other people who disapprove of her choice, and her father's opposition, but finally follows love, the runaway pony that gallops. Rodrigo and Jimena choose to live their 'cursed' love with a clear conscience, keeping faith that they are holding onto something pure. Finally, Antonio Gala, in his 1973 'Rings for a lady' (*Anillos para una dama*), sets the scene two years after Rodrigo's death, and just before Valencia is retaken by the Muslims. Jimena had only married the Cid for political reasons and waited for him for twenty years at the monastery of Cardeña. She is in love with Minaya Álvar Núñez and wants to marry him. But although Minaya loves her, in the end King Alfonso's view prevails: the Cid's myth must be cultivated carefully, and therefore nobody can officially replace him in Jimena's bed as her second husband. She must resign herself 'to be forever the spoil of a hero so that the hero can continue to be'. Though briefly emerging from the mists of time and legend, Jimena, Cristina and María continue to live on in the shadow of the hero.

6

The Legend Embodied

As the myth grew, it also took on material form. Sites mentioned in literary creations were 'identified' with real places, and objects that could plausibly be linked to the Cid were confidently claimed to have belonged to him. Places, swords and other possessions allegedly connected to the hero proliferated and made the legend more real. Tourists can visit the sites of deeds that never occurred, they can admire artefacts that seem to confirm the veracity of literary stories. The legends have taken on a physical reality.

How such fictitious stories are projected onto real places is well exemplified by the church of St Gadea in Burgos, which displays an iron bolt with the image of the 'oath of Santa Gadea': the celebrated (but apocryphal) story according to which the Cid forced Alfonso VI to swear in front of the nobles that he had no part in the death of his brother Sancho II. A sign also alerts tourists that 'in this church King Alfonso VI took his famous oath in front of the Cid Campeador'. The most dramatic description of the oath of Santa Gadea comes from the *Estoria de España*, written over the course of the late thirteenth century. After his brother Sancho's death, Alfonso calls on his vassals to acknowledge him as their king; the Castilians and Navarrese agree to do so only if he will swear he had no part in Sancho's murder. Yet at first nobody wants to administer the oath, until the Cid, who refuses to kiss Alfonso's hand, takes on the role. Alfonso is to swear the oath, along with twelve of his men. The role of the twelve as oath helpers was standard in medieval trial by oath, a way for someone to prove his innocence, with the oath helpers swearing that they believed the accused person's oath. The Cid first asked the king: 'Have you come to swear to me that you did not advise the death of the king, my lord Don Sancho?' Alfonso duly swears. Rodrigo then replies: 'Well, if you swear on a lie, may it please God that a traitor kill you, who is your vassal, as was Bellido Dolfos [the assassin of Sancho] of the king Don Sancho my lord.' 'Amen,' says Alfonso, but he turns pale. The Cid then asks once more: 'Have you come to swear to me concerning the death of King Don Sancho, that you neither advised nor ordered it?' Alfonso swears again, and the Cid is now ready to kiss his hand, acknowledging him as his lord and king. But the king does not allow him to, and from then on is hostile towards him.

The oath became a key episode of Cidian lore. A famous vernacular ballad, 'In Santa Gadea of Burgos', is even dedicated entirely to this incident, highlighting the name of the church in its title. The Cid administers the oath to the Castilian king on an iron lock and a wooden crossbow. The wording of the oath is so strong that it frightens the king. 'May peasants kill you, king, peasants and not nobles'; men who wear sandals rather than shoes, have poor quality clothes, rather than fine garments, ride donkeys rather than horses, their reins made of rope and not leather. 'May they kill you in the fields, not on a road or in a village, with a cheap knife rather than a golden dagger, tearing out your beating heart from your right side if you don't tell the truth regarding what I ask you, if you participated in or consented to the death of your brother!' The king takes fright, not so much because of the threat of assassination, but more because of the dishonour and shame this killing would entail. King Alfonso at first therefore refuses to take such an oath, but one of his knights encourages him to consent to it: 'have no care, for never was a king a traitor, nor a pope excommunicated.' The king finally swears that he had no part in his brother's murder. Yet he then lashes out at the Cid, accusing him of pressing him too hard, and administering the oath badly. He also demands, now that he has sworn the oath, that the Cid must kiss his hand. 'That will be, good king, according to the reward. For in other lands they give remuneration to the nobles.' This is the final straw for Alfonso: enraged, he tells the Cid to leave his lands and not return for a year. The Cid, however, replies that it is pleasing that this should be Alfonso's first command as king, and that he would leave for four years. He leaves without kissing the king's hand and three hundred nobles leave with him. The ballad in this way turns the oath into a pivotal episode in the Cid's life and associates it prominently with the church of Santa Gadea.

Nobody quite understands why this small, insignificant church, named after a late Roman virgin martyr, St Agatha, which in the eleventh century would have stood at the margins of Burgos, was the site of such an important oath. This is because it wasn't. The surviving church itself is from the fifteenth century, but, even more importantly, the textual tradition about such an oath started in the thirteenth century, so around 150 years after the supposed events. Some scholars believe the origin of the myth is a now lost piece of anti-Leonese writing, but the earliest existing sources that refer to an oath come from chronicles. The first extant mention is from Lucas de Tuy, a canon of San Isidoro of León, and later bishop of Tuy, who in around 1236 wrote in his *World Chronicle* that the Castilians were only prepared to accept Alfonso as king if he swore he had nothing to do with his brother Sancho's death. Nobody, however, was willing to administer the oath, until Rodrigo Díaz volunteered; from then on, Alfonso hated him. A few years later, another chronicler, Rodrigo Jiménez de Rada, repeated this story. The role of the oath in these narratives was to explain Alfonso's dislike of Rodrigo; the story was in search of a location, since initially it was not associated with Santa Gadea or even Burgos. From this kernel, the myth of the oath of Santa Gadea grew, incorporated in different versions into a number of texts. In some, the oath is only taken once, in others, three times. The object Alfonso swears on also varies: the Gospels, a lock, a lock and crossbow.

The account in the *Estoria de España* is not the product of folk traditions and oral songs based on real events, as some people once assumed. In fact, it is a fascinating inversion of the original story, in which it was Rodrigo who offered to swear his innocence to Alfonso VI in four different ways, after he was exiled a second time, deprived of all his possessions and honour, even of his wife and children. The repetitions in the oath of Santa Gadea by Alfonso VI mirror Rodrigo's written oaths, oaths that he was willing to take to clear his name; they are coupled with the various myths that grew up separately, asserting Alfonso VI's culpability in Sancho's murder.

How Alfonso's imaginary oath came to be 'located' at the church of Santa Gadea is unknown. According to one opinion, it may be related to St Agatha's story: she held steadfast to her vow of virginity and to her Christian belief in the face of threats and torture. So perhaps the church dedicated to her was seen as an appropriate place where a vow would have been administered. Whatever the reason that led to the belief that the church witnessed this episode, the invented story had very real repercussions. In the late medieval period, it actually became a place to take oaths, as fifteenth-century documents show; this was due to the myth of Alfonso VI's oath, so once again a legend took physical form. Medieval oaths were taken in juridical procedures as proof; God was supposed to punish perjury. Such oaths were normally taken on the Bible or on the relics of saints; in Santa Gadea, the iron bolt of the church door began to be used for this purpose. This was a direct translation into reality of the romance version of Alfonso's oath. A drawing in a fifteenth-century manuscript of the *Crónica del Cid* indicates that this version was widely known; while according to the text Alfonso swore on the Gospels, someone who clearly knew the version in the ballad drew the image of an iron lock and a hand in the gesture of oath-taking in the margin. The bishop of Burgos objected to the 'superstitious' practices that evolved around the iron lock of the main door of the church, which was identified as the one that featured in Alfonso's oath. Unfortunately, no details of what these practices may have been are now known, but in 1500 the bishop had the lock removed.

In more modern times, the legendary oath of Santa Gadea was invested with significance as a forerunner of parliamentary democracy, the emblem of resistance to tyranny and the symbol of legal controls over monarchical power. A vassal being able to hold a monarch to account came to symbolize the rights of subjects, and so the story was taken up in the visual arts; it became the subject of historical paintings. Marcos Hiráldez Acosta's *La Jura de Santa Gadea*, in the Palacio del Senado of Madrid, represents both the Cid and Alfonso VI as mature men, and equals, as both stand facing each other. It won second prize at the National Exhibition of Fine Arts in 1864, and a copy hangs at the Provincial Council of Burgos. Through such imagery, the legend became engrained in popular consciousness in modern times. Few would read the ballad or medieval chronicles in the nineteenth century, but familiarity with the images spread the idea of the Cid as the upholder of democratic accountability. How widespread knowledge of the oath was in society is also demonstrated by a story recounted by a certain Francisco de Paula Mellado about his travels across Spain in the middle of the nineteenth century: a beggar woman at the door of the church told him that every night at midnight frightening noises could be heard in the church, and more than once the ghosts of the Cid and King Alfonso were seen, standing exactly where they had stood when the oath was taken.

The church of Santa Gadea is not the only real location attached to a fictitious story. Tourists can also visit the gravesite of the fictional Babieca, the Cid's horse. We know nothing about the historical Rodrigo's real horses, but horses were certainly both important in war and as a status symbol, and could cost a small fortune. In the early twelfth century Queen Urraca reportedly received a horse as a gift from one of her counts that was worth 5,000 solidi, an amount that could have bought 5,000 sheep. Babieca, in the form Bavieca, first appears in the *Poema de Mio Cid* as the name of the Cid's horse; an excellent charger, the Cid is proud of him. Before this, the *Carmen Campidoctoris* mentioned an expensive North African horse 'faster than the wind' that Rodrigo bought for a thousand pieces of gold. In that text, the horse does not have a name. The *Poema*'s Bavieca is already more prominent. According to that story, the Cid won Bavieca as booty 'from the Moorish king of Sevilla', and rides him for the first time when he greets his wife and daughters upon their arrival in Valencia. 'The speed of the horse was so wonderful / that when the ride was finished all were filled with amazement.' It is Bavieca's speed that allows the Cid to overtake and kill Búcar, despite the latter's boasts about his own horse. Towards the end of the *Poema*, after his full reconciliation with King Alfonso, the king asks the Cid to demonstrate Bavieca's speed; Rodrigo then tries to gift the horse to the king. He, however, declines: 'I do not wish for this. / If he were taken from you, the horse would not have so good a lord. / Such a horse as this is for a man like you – / to defeat Moors on the field of battle and go in their pursuit. / Let the Creator not protect any man who would take him from you, for through you and through the horse we are honoured.' Sharp readers would pick up on the humour, an allusion to the start of the *Poema*, when the population of Burgos bemoan the fact that the Cid, such a good vassal, has to suffer exile; 'if only he had a good lord!'

The *Legend of Cardeña*, however, turned Babieca (using the form Bauieca) into an even more crucial character in the story of the Cid. According to the *Legend*, after his master's death Babieca not only bore his dead body in the final battle but all the way to the monastery of San Pedro de Cardeña, which necessitated weeks of travel. The *Legend* also mythologized the figure of Alhuacaxi, a Muslim *alfaquí* of Valencia; in this version, he is converted to Christianity by the Cid, and at his baptism he takes the name Gil Díaz. Having accompanied Rodrigo's corpse to Cardeña, Gil stayed at the monastery and continued to care for the Cid's horse, which nobody could ride again, until it died at the very impressive age of forty. He then buried Babieca in front of the monastery. Based on this text, a headstone was erected in the mid-twentieth century outside the main entrance of the monastery of San Pedro de Cardeña.

Spotted by lichen, the inscription, now fading, relates that, according to Alfonso the Wise's *Estoria de España*, Babieca, the famous horse of the Cid, was buried to the right-hand side of the old gate of the monastery between two large trees. Because two tree stumps were found on the spot in 1949, when excavations were undertaken, funded by the duke of Alba, the headstone was placed there. On the back of the headstone are inscribed the words from the *Poema* expressing the Cid's desire to give his horse to King Alfonso, and the king's response.

Babieca's name has been explained in many ways: from an Aragonese dialect where it would mean 'owl'; from a baseless etymological derivative of 'babear', to drool or slobber; or from a fond nickname. But the most convincing explanation is that the name is the Castilian equivalent of Bauçan, meaning fool(ish), which was the name of William of Orange's horse in the French epic poetry cycle. In other words, it is likely to be a literary borrowing. That this horse is a fictitious creation is reinforced by the excavations at the site carried out in 1949 that found – apart from tree stumps – nothing.

The monastery of San Pedro de Cardeña was not simply the cradle of an entirely mythical Cid: it continued to hitch its identity to el Cid in an ever more monumental manner. In the mid-fifteenth century, when a separate doorway was constructed for the church, the coat of arms of the Cid was carved above it, along with those of the kingdom of Castile and of the monastery of Cardeña. In 1570, when the façade of the church was completed, a full-figure Cid was also inserted into the wall, along with busts of other historical figures. Finally, a monumental statue was added above the main entrance to the monastery at the beginning of the eighteenth century, depicting the Cid in the manner of 'Santiago Matamoros'. This was a standard representation of St James the apostle, as a warrior on horseback, slaughtering Muslims, whose decapitated heads are liberally strewn under his horse's hoofs, as he allegedly appeared to help Christian warriors in battles. The Cid himself is a beneficiary of such heavenly help in the *Legend*. Here, he himself is transformed into the paragon of Christian knighthood, a warrior for the faith. Supposedly, during his visit to the monastery in 1679 King Carlos II said that the Cid was not a king, but he made kings. Therefore, this statue of the Cid holds a banner with the inscription 'Per me reges regnant': through me kings reign. The depiction provides a religious legitimation of royal power by tying it to a saintly figure and employing a biblical quotation (Proverbs 8:15), but also conjures royal protection for the monastery.

The city of Burgos, just like the monastery of San Pedro, had minimal connections to Rodrigo in his lifetime, yet eventually turned itself into the city of the Cid. The *Poema* dedicated many lines to events that allegedly took place in Burgos: Rodrigo leaves for his first exile from Burgos; the king had forbidden the citizens to sell him food or help him, and it is these citizens who lament his fate, with a nine-year-old child sent out from a house to plead with him not to harm the inhabitants, who, fearful of King Alfonso, dare not open their gate to him. It is in Burgos that the Cid tricks Jewish money lenders; and one of his loyal men, Martín Antolínez, is a 'worthy citizen of Burgos'. Rodrigo gives a gift of silver and gold to the cathedral of Burgos to have a thousand masses celebrated at the altar of the Virgin Mary. The story of the oath of Santa Gadea then created another link between Rodrigo and Burgos. Yet for centuries this did not translate into a more specific desire of the townspeople to emphasize the association between the Cid and the town. This changed after the early sixteenth-century war of the cities of Castile (1520–22), the so-called Guerra de las Comunidades.

In the early years of the reign of King Carlos I (who was also Holy Roman Emperor), a series of urban revolts broke out against the king, culminating in a battle on 23 April 1521. The urban communes were defeated, with only Toledo holding out, where resistance was finally crushed in early 1522. In the aftermath of the revolt, many town authorities were keen to both express loyalty to King Carlos I and imbue his reign with historical continuity.

In 1531, city authorities decided to erect a series of statues on Burgos's Puerta de Santa María, one of the medieval city gates, in commemoration of Burgos's reception of Carlos I in 1520. The works were finally finished in 1553. The exterior thus took on the likeness of a triumphal arch, displaying key figures associated with Burgos in two rows. It was a truly monumental effort to suck up to the king, who features prominently in the middle of the top row. The inscription emphasizes that he is 'emperor of the Romans' as well as 'invincible'. Above him is a guardian angel, and flanking him are Fernán González, alleged first independent count of Castile, and the Cid. The bottom row consists of the legendary judges of Castile, Nuño Rasura and Laín Calvo, and Diego Porcelos, founder of Burgos. The Cid is clad in armour, holding a sword and wearing a bejewelled hat that closely resembles a circlet crown. The inscription underneath reads: CIDO RVIDIEZ FORTISS CIVI MAVRO / RVM PAVORI TERORIQ(UE), that is, To Cid, Rui Diez, the strongest citizen, fright and terror of the Moors. The Cid stands on the king's left (the viewers' right), looking towards him. The inscription conveys a military, defensive message; at the same time, because of the accumulated legends, the figure of the Cid also represents the honour of Castile – since he was by then seen as a Castilian patriot – and the continued legitimate exercise of royal power, since he was thought to have exacted the oath of Santa Gadea from Alfonso VI. The Cid was invoked here as an emblem of patriotism, of honesty in the exercise of power, a legitimator who guaranteed peace and the established social order; 'a talisman against revolutionary change'. The reason for elevating the Cid, as well as Fernán González, alongside the emperor was their fabled status as early champions of

Castile. The specific model for the representation on the gate was an arch that had been erected in Burgos for the emperor's visit in 1520; on this, the two figures of Fernán González and the Cid appeared accompanied by an inscription that stated that their fame made them comparable to the emperor. The design of the gate of Santa María converted that simile into a visual form in stone.

The city then began to emphasize its link to the Cid ever more. In 1593, the council of Burgos decided to create a memorial at the entrance of some houses that had supposedly belonged to the Cid, who allegedly left them to the monastery of San Pedro de Cardeña in his testament. This idea cropped up in the mid-fifteenth century at the monastery itself; while houses belonging to the monastery that were rented out had been mentioned in earlier monastic accounts, they were not linked to the Cid in any way. This invention was part of the growing monastic instrumentalization of the Cid, to make its properties in a part of town that was in decline more appealing; the association, however, now also started to attract the interest of the urban authorities.

Around 1600, the houses themselves fell into ruin, but the memorial, with the coat of arms of the town, the monastery of San Pedro and the Cid, survived. While it is not impossible that Rodrigo had property in Burgos (he had properties in the vicinity), no such evidence survives, and thus the location is probably pure myth. Even if he held such properties, they would not have been his regular place of residence, much less his place of birth, as it was soon to be claimed. In 1784, the city government decided to clean up the ruins and erect a new memorial, which, although not in the best state of conservation, still survives. The memorial claims that it stands over the very place where the Cid was born: 'In this place stood the house where in the year 1026 Rodrigo Díaz de Vivar, called the Cid Campeador, was born. He died in Valencia in 1099 and his body was transferred to the monastery of San Pedro de Cardeña, near this city, which, to perpetuate the memory of such an illustrious site belonging to one of her sons and a hero from Burgos, erected this monument on the ancient ruins in the year 1784, during the reign of Carlos III.' While Burgos was not the only place to try to expropriate the Cid (in 1680 Palencia linked him to a house as well), it became the most successful. The city's ultimate triumph was to take possession of the physical remains of the Cid and thus become his final resting place.

Not only places but also objects 'belonging' to the Cid proliferated over time. The Cid's supposed sword la Tizón is conserved in Burgos, yet the sword's alleged connection to the Cid does not predate the fifteenth century. There is no authentic early information about what swords Rodrigo may have used. The name is first mentioned in the *Poema de Mio Cid*, according to which he gained Tizón from the Moroccan emir Búcar, who unsuccessfully besieged Valencia. The name of the sword perhaps comes from the Latin for 'firebrand'; from the fourteenth century, the form of the name changed to Tizona. Some believe that Tisó, the sword of James I of Aragón (1213–76), who conquered Valencia from the Muslims in 1238, is the same sword, but there is no evidence for that, nor did James I claim such an origin for the sword in his autobiography.

Naturally, in the warrior society of Rodrigo's age swords themselves were valued as vital instruments of war as well as status symbols. Yet named swords of famous warriors came from the domain of medieval literature about the deeds of fictional knights; therefore by the thirteenth century it would have been considered a basic part of the story for the Cid to have a named and trusted sword. The sword now exhibited in Burgos had belonged to the Marques de Falces; reportedly it had been entrusted by King Fernando II of Aragón (1479–1516) to the grandfather of the first marquis for services rendered in negotiating Fernando's marriage to Isabella. In the seventeenth century, it was kept in the castle of Marcilla in Navarra. Its owner wanted to sell it to the Ministry of Culture, but the ministry lost interest after learning that the sword had no historical authenticity; the government of Castilla y León finally bought it.

An inscription running the length of one side of the blade reads: 'I am Tisona. It was made in the era 1040'; the date is according to the Spanish system and corresponds to 1002. On the other side of the blade are the first words of the angel's greeting to the Virgin Mary in Latin, with an unexpected twist at the end: 'Ave Maria gratia plena Dominus mecum', that is, 'Hail Mary, full of grace, the Lord is with me'. The entire typology of the sword corresponds to those known from the fifteenth century. Scientific study at the beginning of the twenty-first century concluded that the blade was made of eleventh-century Damascene steel, but of three pieces that were welded together. On the whole, therefore, scholarship has concluded that this sword is a late medieval forgery, even if using fragments of an earlier medieval blade.

Throwing even more doubt on any identification, more than one sword was believed to have been the Cid's Tizón, just as John the Baptist had several heads scattered around in numerous medieval European relic collections. This shows clearly that such 'identifications' emerged late and cannot be trusted to have any historical root. This other Tizón was in the possession of Álvaro Luna (1390–1453) and was inventoried in 1503 in the Alcázar of Segovia. From its description in the inventory, it is clear that it was a ceremonial sword, decorated with Castilian heraldry; it subsequently disappeared, although some identify the blade of a sword in the royal armoury of Madrid with this other Tizón. Possessing the Cid's famed sword would have conferred prestige on an aristocrat or even a king; the desire to have such an object would have been similar to today's rich wanting to own a late celebrity's personal items. The *Cantar de Mio Cid* invested the Cid with another, earlier sword, the Colada. Supposedly, he acquired this from the count of Barcelona. So far, the Colada has failed to materialize.

Ownership of various other objects has also been attributed to Rodrigo. The *Poema* relates the antisemitic episode typical of thirteenth-century sensibilities, doubtless very humorous for contemporary audiences, in which the Cid, preparing to go into exile, devises a way to dupe two Jewish money lenders into giving him silver and gold coins; in exchange, they receive two chests supposedly full of the Cid's treasure. When, later on, the money lenders open the chests, they discover what they truly contain: sand. One of those chests is exhibited in Burgos. There is also a chess set, which, according to the *Legend of Cardeña*, Rodrigo received from the sultan of Persia. In this way, objects invented in literary stories were 'identified' with concrete items.

Other objects were connected to him without even any basis whatsoever in medieval stories, such as two crucifixes associated to him in the cathedral of Salamanca. The first evidence we have regarding the Romanesque 'Christ of the Battles' comes from the early seventeenth-century history of Salamanca by Gil González Dávila, archivist of the cathedral, published in 1606; Dávila claimed it belonged to Bishop Jerome of Valencia. In 1615, he published an entire work on the origin and miracles of the crucifix. Because of the scarcity of sources, and contradictions in the texts we do have, it isn't possible to trace the beginnings of the cult. We cannot say with any certainty if Dávila's account represents a common opinion, nor if others had already thought of the crucifix as the Cid's earlier. According to one modern opinion, the crucifix was already associated with the Cid in the fourteenth century, because King Alfonso XI (1311–50) claimed in a letter that the Cid carried a crucifix into battle; there is, however, no conclusive evidence that he was referring to the same crucifix. An inventory of the cathedral of Salamanca written in 1275 does not mention a cross belonging to Bishop Jerome or the Cid. If Dávila is correct, the association with the Cid only started in the seventeenth century; how it arose then says a lot about the making of legends.

The crucifix seems first to have gained prominence in the cathedral community's ultimately abortive attempt to foster the cult of Bishop Jerome (d. 1120). Jerome, bishop of Valencia during Rodrigo's rule, and after its fall bishop of Salamanca, was buried in Salamanca, and his remains were transferred to the cathedral once it was completed. The crucifix was above his tomb, and Dávila claimed that Jerome, while bishop of Valencia, had always taken it with him into the battles he fought alongside the Cid against the Moors, before bringing it with him to Salamanca. Dávila embellished Jerome's role in the Cid's life, turning him into the Cid's confessor and councillor, who ministered at his daughters' marriages and at his funeral; Dávila also included extensive legendary material about the Cid's death. The crucifix is therefore Jerome's, not the Cid's, but it already benefits from Jerome's connection to the legendary warrior. Dávila claims that a sweet odour rose from Jerome's grave when it was opened, referring to him as 'saint bishop'. Although he was never formally canonized, miracles multiplied at Jerome's tomb in the early seventeenth century, drawing significant donations of precious items to the cathedral. Because of its proximity to the tomb, the crucifix itself was soon invested with miraculous powers, its first miracle being recorded in 1607. Jerome's remains were then moved to a new chapel in 1608, along with the cross. In 1610 papal indulgence, and in 1614 episcopal indulgence – reducing the punishment due for one's sins – was granted to those who visited the chapel on certain days and prayed there. By 1615, eighteen miracles were attributed to the crucifix.

As the crucifix gained importance, Bishop Jerome was sidelined and no longer linked to the miracles. The publication of Dávila's booklet in 1615 on the miracles bestowed on those who invoked the crucifix, and a series of paintings in the cathedral representing these miracles, served to further boost the cult of the object itself. As a new cathedral was built, first the crucifix (1733) and then Bishop Jerome's remains (1744) were moved to a new chapel there; but the inscription over the tomb now stated that Jerome – who is called the Cid's confessor and adviser – had brought with him the crucifix, famous for its miracles, 'under the auspices of which Rodrigo Díaz de Vivar, commonly called the Cid, gained innumerable victories over the Moors, which therefore received the epithet Christ of the battles'. There were other famous miracle-working crucifixes, notably one allegedly belonging to the Catholic Monarchs Fernando and Isabella, who unified Spain in the late fifteenth century, that may have served as a model to turn this crucifix into a miraculous object that brought the Cid victory in battles.

Apart from the standard devotional context, where Christians were seeking out miracle-working relics and objects in order to be healed or saved from danger, there was a more specific political one, and this may well have strengthened the association of the crucifix with the Cid. Although the warrior Cid, a Christian hero fighting Muslims, remained relevant throughout the late medieval and early modern period – in the context first of the takeover of the last Muslim kingdom on the peninsula, Granada (1492), and then the establishment of Spain's overseas empire in the sixteenth century – he gained a new significance as a result of changing policy towards the Muslims of Spain. In the early sixteenth century, the peninsula's Muslim population was forcibly converted to Christianity, as the last step in creating a 'unified' Spain. These converts, the moriscos, revolted and many continued to plot to return at least some of the peninsula to Islam. In the early years of the seventeenth century, moriscos, under the leadership of some families from Valencia, turned to King Henry IV of France who gave religious liberties to Protestants, as well as the Ottomans for help. The plot was discovered, and in 1607 the morisco elder who was to rule in case of success was condemned at an *auto de fe*, the public ceremony during which sentences by the Inquisition were carried out, accused of having used a house in the village as a mosque. By 1608, most of the others accused of being involved in the plot had been arrested.

Dávila had already mentioned the significance of 1607, the year of the first miracle: 'the year of the miraculous manifestation of this most holy image [that is, the crucifix] will be memorable in the histories of Spain, [. . .] for the pact of the moriscos of Valencia [. . .] to conspire, taking arms against the Catholic faith and the king'. God, however, defeated their purpose, to protect the Catholic religion. And so, although the miracle itself was one of healing, 'this most holy image manifested itself with miracles, as if to warn the moriscos of Valencia [. . .] that it will return to fight against them with miracles, as it did in the past, when it removed the lordship of the city and its kingdom from the Moors, whence they descended.' There is therefore a link drawn between the Cid's conquest of Valencia and the crucifix's continued opposition to the converted descendants of Muslims who conspire against Christianity. Since the 'Christ of the Battles' itself became the purveyor of miracles around the same time as the plot of the Valencian moriscos to return to Islam was discovered, a direct association to the first Christian conqueror of Valencia, the Cid, replaced the link to Bishop Jerome, however much Dávila had insisted on the bishop's role in warfare against Muslims.

Due to its legendary link to the Cid, the crucifix was once thought to date to the eleventh century. Scientific evaluation only began once the figure of the crucified Christ was restored between 2010 and 2012. There is no consensus, but it was most likely made in the first half of the twelfth century and perhaps later (the earliest layer of pigment that had been recovered was fixed to the wood by flax oil, which was only used after the Romanesque period); certainly after Rodrigo's death. Moreover, the object does not match its supposed original function. The Christ figure alone is 76 cm; together with a cross it is about 1 m, and therefore it would have been unsuitable for being carried into battle.

Another crucifix is known as the 'pectoral cross of the Cid'. Such crosses were worn on a chain around the neck and hung down to the chest. According to a document in the Salamanca cathedral archives, it was donated to the cathedral by Martín López de Hontiveros, a professor at the University of Salamanca, in 1647; he had already maintained that it had belonged to the Cid. How Hontiveros acquired it is not known. The crucifix, however, is too large to be a pectoral cross and too late to have been the Cid's: it was made in the enamel workshop of Limoges, France, in the late twelfth or early thirteenth century.

In the Middle Ages it was already commonplace to attribute ownership of various items to celebrated heroes of the past; some of these at least roughly match the age of their alleged owner's lifetime, others are from much later. For example, numerous objects allegedly belonging to Charlemagne were actually made centuries after his death. A 'Virgin of the Battles', a statue made c. 1225–35, had been linked to Count Fernán González (d. 970) in much the same way as the 'Christ of the Battles' ended up as the Cid's. Objects were invested with added significance through a belief in such ownership; and at the same time the existence of such objects lent further credence to the stories about past heroes. While the value placed on such items in the medieval period was mostly due to the prestige they conveyed, in the modern day their possession can also confer real financial gain: 'Tizona' fetched 1.6 million euros in 2007.

Objects associated with the Cid were not just known locally, or to readers of the medieval tales; they were popularized through later literature, becoming household names. Babieca is mentioned in, among other works, popular plays such as Juan de la Cueva's *El infamador* (1581), Guillén de Castro's *Don Quijote de la Mancha* (by 1606) and Lope de Vega's *Las paces de los reyes* (1617). The Cid's swords also appeared in numerous pieces, such as Calderón's *Guárdate del agua mansa* (1657).

Ironically, while the legend was ever more embodied in physical spaces and objects, Rodrigo's actual body did not rest in peace. Indeed, his bodily remains travelled about in a manner that put to shame the *Legend of Cardeña*'s made-up stories about his corpse. While the transfer of his body to the monastery of San Pedro took place in dramatic circumstances, the Cid then remained there for centuries, although his bones were moved to different locations within the monastery. All this changed when the French troops, occupying Spain, desecrated the grave in 1808, and tossed the bones out of the sarcophagus. Intriguingly, though, two Frenchmen have separately been credited with saving the Cid's remains. Clearly, at least one (perhaps both) of these claims is wrong. Both men were drawn by the Cid's literary fame; one had antiquarian interests, the other wanted to win over the local population. Dominique Vivant, baron Denon (1747–1825), was an engraver, writer, diplomat and administrator; he became the general director of the museum later known as the Louvre. General Paul-Charles-François-Adrien-Henri Dieudonné Thiébault was a career soldier in Napoleon Bonaparte's army. He was stationed in Spain in 1808 and in his memoirs described the sacking of the tombs of the Cid and Jimena, and claimed to have saved their bones.

Vivant Denon travelled in Spain in the winter of 1808–9 in the company of Benjamin Zix, a painter from Strasbourg. Zix made a sketch, and subsequently a watercolour, depicting Vivant Denon returning the Cid's remains to his stone sarcophagus in San Pedro de Cardeña. This also inspired other painters. Alexandre-Évariste Fragonard depicted Vivant Denon Hamlet-like, in the slanting light streaming in from a window, holding the skull in front of the open sarcophagus. As the title says, he is replacing the bones of the Cid. An 1809 painting by Adolphe Roehn shows Vivant Denon in the monastic chapel, holding a skull, leaning over the open sarcophagus, which bears an inscription naming Jimena, with bones strewn around on the ground. If Thiébault's memoirs are correct, however, Vivant Denon would not have been able to find and return the scattered remains of the Cid and Jimena in the monastery of San Pedro.

Thiébault, appointed governor of Old Castile, arrived in Burgos to take over command there of the French army from General Jean-Barthélemy-Claude-Toussaint Darmagnac, and took great pains in his memoirs to emphasize Darmagnac's incompetence; every hour under his leadership produced new calamities that had to be fixed. Thiébault's interest in the Cid's remains was directly linked to his determination to show the locals that the French occupation would benefit them, rather than destroy their lives, contrasting his own administration to that of Darmagnac. He describes the desolation and ruinous state of Burgos when he arrived there: famine, plague and despair haunted the city, with death the only way out. Thousands of sick and wounded, without medicine or anyone to care for them, lay on rotting hay. The army was unable to buy provisions and pillaged the countryside, so that the whole area around the city became depopulated. There were no stores or markets; there was no administration. Brutality and violence ruled the day. Thiébault blamed Darmagnac, who also speculated in grain and other goods. He immediately informed the civil authorities that he was going to put things in order. He describes his unceasing efforts and says that, according to one of the locals, his task was more arduous than the cleansing of the Augean stables, in Greek mythology the fifth labour of Hercules. He instituted a judiciary, ensured soldiers were punished if they maltreated the locals and set out to gain the latter's confidence.

It is in this context that he described the fate of the Cid's tomb, and his actions were part of his efforts – although not devoid of self-aggrandisement – to put things right with the local inhabitants by honouring a Spanish hero. He relates how, prior to his arrival, a French regiment sacked the tomb that Philip V had erected for the Cid and Jimena at San Pedro de Cardeña, in the hope of finding gold or jewels inside it. 'I resolved to have this act of vandalism committed by the French repaired by French hands.' He ordered that a tomb be made in Burgos, which he saw as the cradle of the Cid, and which also allowed for much greater publicity than the out-of-the-way monastery. He envisaged a public space with poplars and benches between the two bridges of the city, at the Espolon, the public promenade.

> Yet the bones had been scattered, exposed to profanation; I had to think of putting them temporarily in a safe place, even if for no other reason than to be certain that they would not have disappeared by the time my monument was ready to receive them; therefore I went to San Pedro de Cardeña, accompanied by the provincial civic authorities, and drawing up a report of formal removal, I had the bones gathered into a shroud that I had brought; with great pomp, I transported

> them to Burgos, and while their new tomb . . . was under construction, I put them for safekeeping under my bed.

The author of the *Poema de Mio Cid* would either have had a fit or laughed his head off; for it was hiding under a couch that had marked the cowardice and villainy of one of the Cid's sons-in-law in the poem.

Many wanted to see the bones, but Thiébault insisted that he alone would show them to the inquisitive, presumably so as to prevent theft; and many indeed wanted to take pieces, but he gave them to no one, with the exception of Vivant Denon who travelled to Burgos at the time. He proudly asserts that he did not even take any piece for himself. When the new tomb was ready, on 19 April 1809, the bones were placed in a coffin, and Thiébault with the civil authorities, followed by a crowd of citizens, conveyed the coffin to the newly constructed tomb with full military pomp. Members of the civic authorities as well as the general gave speeches, a priest pronounced a blessing, and to the tolling of bells and the firing of cannons the ceremony ended. The memorial bore several inscriptions: one celebrating Joseph Bonaparte, installed as king of Spain by his brother Napoleon; another, General Thiébault, who had the remains transferred; and another, great men who belonged to all times and to all men. Thiébault gained exactly what he wanted: 'The ceremony, and that which gave rise to it, resulted in verses in Latin, French and Spanish written in my honour; such an homage, rendered to someone of great popular memory by a stranger considered to be an enemy, identified me to the whole population. There followed a sort of co-citizenship for me, and the monument, respected by all the parties and all the governments, is one of the three great memorials I left in Spain.' He also recounted how, after the end of the French occupation in 1818, Spaniards still remembered and honoured his enlightened governance and lauded the creation of the tomb.

It turned out, however, that the general was a tad over-optimistic. Once the French troops had left and popular opinion no longer had to respect their weapons, the Cid's remains were soon moved and the memorial was abandoned; it no longer exists. The celebrations, however, had another, unexpected, consequence. A few days after the tomb's inauguration, a learned Spaniard, whose name Thiébault does not provide, sought him out to explain to him that the Cid never existed. At first scandalized, then surprised and shaken, the general felt embarrassed. He was torn between the force of the erudite Spaniard's reasoning and his own beliefs, and cognizant of the discrepancy between the enthusiasm of the celebrations he had fully shared, and the ridicule of having paid homage 'to a chimerical celebrity'. Wasting no time, the general threw himself into the task of discovering the truth. He read all the documents he could find in Burgos, but the erudite Spaniard refuted them; he acquired prose and verse texts on the Cid, which merely made the Spaniard laugh; he cited various histories of Spain, only to be told that there were no impostures they did not contain. In despair, the general consulted many people, and was finally directed to Juan Antonio Llorente (1756–1823), renowned for his book on the Inquisition. The general asked him to give the final word.

Llorente informed him that he did not think 'that a Ruis Diaz, to whom one can attribute the actions from which the history of the Cid was composed, ever existed. Cid, that in the Moorish language means chief, victorious warrior, became the designation of an imaginary being, decked out with the feats of arms of twenty heroes, and what really made the fortune and fame of this alleged Cid was that the monks adopted him as their Don Quixote.' While Thiébault undertook his project to create a suitable memorial for the Cid's remains as part of his vision for Spain under French rule, he also seems to have been invested more personally – whether because of the Cid's military fame or because he knew Corneille's play which allowed him to feel a national pride about the hero, one cannot tell. A little chastised by the pronouncement of authority, the general nonetheless closes his account of the episode by reaffirming the Cid's place in popular memory, and implying that the existence of so many things associated with Rodrigo in themselves offer some kind of proof of his existence.

> Nonetheless, whether the Cid is historical or a fable, there is a place in the memory of people that will not be aggrandized by proof of his existence, nor diminished by proofs to the contrary. Besides, what should be done about the memories that are attached to him, the traditions that recall him, the

> monuments consecrated to his memory, the families who profess to descend from him [. . .]? What should be done about this town of Rodrigo (Ciudad Rodrigo) that is honoured to bear his first name, of a hundred stories or poems, of a thousand ballads, of the tragedy of Corneille, who, even in France, nationalized a part of the glory of this hero? What should be done about the chest still suspended above the main entrance of the cathedral of Burgos, the chest on the deposit of which the Cid was lent a large sum by his native town and which happened to contain only stones? Finally, what should one do about my tomb and the bones enclosed in it, bones, which, at least until the Last Judgement, will pass all the more for being those of the Cid and Chimène, because, until then, it is quite certain that their real owners will not come to claim them? Thus it is by pronouncing an anathema against anyone who dares doubt their authenticity that I close this digression.

General Thiébault's curse worked well. If in private some continued to doubt the authenticity of the bones, this certainly did nothing to diminish continued public adulation. Indeed, rather like the bones of saints, even though he was not canonized, those of the Cid travelled far and wide. Vivant Denon took some bones to Paris; the Hohenzollern received some bones and kept them in their cabinet of curiosities in the castle of Sigmaringen (Baden-Württemberg, Germany), until they were returned in 1882. The Cid's remains turned up elsewhere in France and in the Czech Republic, and apparently three or four men could have been reconstructed from the bones that are said to belong to him, a distinction normally reserved for some saints. Yet the odyssey of Rodrigo's remains was not over. After the French left Spain, the monks of San Pedro demanded that the bones be returned from Burgos, and, while the town tried to resist, in the end in 1826 the bones were reburied in the tomb at San Pedro. After the expropriation and dissolution of all monasteries in Spain in 1835, however, there were no monks left to oppose another transfer of the remains from the abandoned monastery. The bones, therefore, were once again taken to Burgos in 1842. At this point, Rodrigo's remains were moved into the chapel of the Casa Consistorial of Burgos.

Then, for the 700th anniversary of the foundation of the cathedral of Burgos in 1921, the remains of both Rodrigo and Jimena were transferred to the cathedral in a religious ceremony, in the presence of King Alfonso XIII, Queen Victoria Eugenia and a papal nuncio. When the remains were moved from the urn of the Casa Consistorial to the metal chest for the reburial, it was revealed that the skulls were missing, with only small fragments of them remaining, and other bones of the hands and feet were lost as well. The archbishop of Burgos, Juan Benlloch i Vivó, reverently kissed one of the bones as they were transferred to their new home. The tomb has since remained in a prominent place in the centre of the cathedral, at the intersection of the nave and transepts. The inscription on the tombstone was written by Ramón Menéndez Pidal, stating in Latin: 'Rodericus Didaci Campidoctor, died in Valencia in 1099', followed in Spanish by 'and all gain in honour through the man born in a favoured hour', one of the last lines of the *Poema*. Underneath, also in Latin: 'Jimena, his wife, daughter of Diego, count of Oviedo, born of royal stock.' As Thiébault surmised, only the Last Judgement can reveal who is buried in that tomb.

While legends of the Cid were increasingly embodied in objects, and he became a stock figure of chronicles and literary works in the sixteenth and seventeenth centuries, which consolidated his mythical image, doubts also surfaced about the exaggerated deeds attributed to him. By the nineteenth century erudite scholars even dismissed the idea that he had existed at all. For others, the objects themselves became proof of the veracity of legendary stories.

7

The Cid's Rise to Literary Fame

The first to claim international fame for the Cid was a chronicle printed in 1512, associated, yet again, with the monastery of San Pedro de Cardeña, which professed to trace his bloodline to rulers across Europe over almost twenty generations. While this was another attempt by the monastery to elevate their most important asset, the Cid's fame was indeed soon spread all over Europe by the written word. As his story continued to be disseminated by numerous literary works in Spain, it finally caught the imagination of authors elsewhere. Through the intermediary of Spanish literature, the Cid arrived on the European scene. Soon, every major European language enjoyed its own version of the Cid: French, English and German audiences were all introduced to the incomparable hero. The Cid was certainly on everyone's mind when discussing heroic, chivalric deeds; but he became ever more firmly mythologized, as already attested by Cervantes. The Cid was one of the models for the knight of la Mancha, a paragon of military valour; yet Don Quijote 'said that the Cid Ruy Díaz had been a very good knight, but nothing in comparison with the Knight of the Burning Sword, who with just one backhand had split two fierce and enormous giants in half'. The Cid thus falls down compared to an entirely fictitious hero. Moreover, Cervantes remarked that while there was no doubt about the Cid's existence, there were grave ones about the feats attributed to him. This progressive entry into complete myth made it easier to wholly decontextualize the Cid and use him in any way the author saw fit.

The first step towards international fame was the ascendancy of the Cid in the Iberian peninsula as the embodiment of the perfect knight. In the twelfth and thirteenth centuries, many chronicles had already mentioned him. He continued to be a significant warrior hero as Granada, the last Muslim realm in the peninsula, was conquered by Spain (1492); as plans were repeatedly made for a crusade against the Ottomans; as the Spanish empire was built. He was easily turned into a symbol of Christian Spanish nobility and eventually a national hero. Chronicles continued to be written and rewritten in Spain, and in the fifteenth century, el Cid took his place firmly among those invariably cited as a model knight. Chivalric literature also reinforced the binary opposition between a hero and his enemies, fixing his image as the Christian warrior, enemy of the Muslims. Rodrigo Ponce de León (1443–92), one of the principal captains of Fernando and Isabella, the Catholic Monarchs, in the conquest of Granada was called a 'second Cid'.

With the arrival of printing in the peninsula in 1474, many texts were more widely disseminated, and the Cid very quickly became the subject of printed works. The earliest in 1498 was the so-called *Crónica popular del Cid*, or, to give it its original full title, *Suma de las cosas maravillosas que fizo en su vida el buen cavallero Cid Ruy Díaz*, the 'Sum of the wonderful things that the good knight Cid Ruy Díaz did in his life'. This was a selection of stories from various earlier legends of the Cid. Another, the *Crónica del famoso cavallero Cid Ruy Díez Campeador* (or *Crónica particular del Cid*), was printed in 1512 in Burgos, funded by the abbot of the monastery of San Pedro de Cardeña; other printed editions followed in the sixteenth century. The text interweaves stories about the Cid with various other events of Iberian history in the eleventh and early twelfth centuries, specially emphasizing ecclesiastical matters and the elevation of the bodies of various early saints.

The episodes concerning Rodrigo are drawn from all the significant earlier literary sources, such as the *Poema de Mio Cid*, the *Mocedades* and the *Estoria de España*, including the *Legend of Cardeña*. Because of that, it is a virtual treasure chest of the diverse literary traditions. The chronicle includes Rodrigo's victories against 'the five Moorish kings'; Jimena's demand for him to be her husband; his pilgrimage to Santiago and encounter with St Lazarus; his duel for Calahorra; the demand from the French king, German emperor and pope for tribute; and the various victories of both Rodrigo and King Fernando. It then encompasses the infighting of Fernando's children after his death, Sancho's assassination, the oath of Santa Gadea and Alfonso's deeds.

Rodrigo's interaction with 'the Moors' is a centrepiece of the *Crónica particular del Cid*, but it very much focuses on the Moors' subjection. The hero is tireless both in fighting them and collecting tribute from them. His name 'my Cid' – which by then was his best-known designation – is elevated to be more than a mere Moorish act of submission, presumably because by then having a recognizably Arabic term as a laudatory sobriquet was not sufficiently prestigious. Therefore the naming is explained in an episode that relates how Rodrigo collects *parias* from the Moorish kings. The kings, who are his vassals, send their messengers with the payment, and, calling him the Cid, want to kiss his hand. However, he directs them to King Fernando, demanding that they kiss his hand first. Fernando then declares that because the Moors call him 'my Cid' he should henceforth be thus known. In this way, a well-regarded Christian king ultimately endorses the hero's epithet.

Other changes were also made compared to the texts the *Crónica* drew on, all of them contributing to enhancing Rodrigo's standing as a warrior. The *Poema*'s stories about Rodrigo's exile are incorporated, but embellished: the Cid fights against the Moors during his exile, destroying their lands, taking forts and finally conquering Valencia, governing and defending the city. With a delightful twist, the Cid's service to the taifa of Zaragoza is revised so that he makes the Moorish king of Zaragoza his vassal, and after that king's death, his son entrusts Zaragoza to the Cid. All this reinforced the image of the Cid as a Christian hero fighting Muslims. The narrative of Rodrigo's fight with the count of Barcelona is quite extensive, describing how the Cid wins the sword Colada. The story of the *infantes* of Carrión, their deceit and punishment and the more noble second marriage of the Cid's daughters follows the *Poema*. From the *Legend of Cardeña*, the chronicle reprises the story of the Cid's final days and victory after death, although in this version Jimena herself also sallies forth with the army accompanying her husband's corpse for the battle with the Moors. The account concludes with the section on the events that follow the evacuation of Valencia. This includes the transport of the Cid's corpse to Cardeña, Jimena occupying her last years with good works at the monastery, her death and burial, and Babieca being cared for by Gil Díaz. The miracle of the Jew and the Cid's beard features as well. The chronicle thus inscribed the Cid's story in the hagiography of the peninsula, preparing the request for his canonization, while at the same time ending with a reference to Don Sancho of Navarra, great-grandson of the Cid, therefore tying the hero tightly to the present as well.

A lengthy and mythical genealogy of the Cid is appended to the work, which claims that both on his father's and mother's side his lineage goes back to the mythical judges of Castile; it also enumerates his direct descendants, including his son Diego who left no children, before going on to more distant progeny. However, the genealogy uses the names Elvira and Sol for his daughters and mixes literary fiction with historical truth. According to this description, Sol was married to *infante* Don Sancho of Aragón; they became rulers of Aragón but left no progeny. Elvira wed *infante* Don Ramiro of Navarra, and they became rulers of Navarra. Their son García, the Cid's grandson, is the ancestor of astonishing numbers of royalty in the Iberian peninsula and beyond. In the first generation, these are King Sancho of Navarra, the *infante* Alfonso, Blanca, who marries the king of France, and Margarita, who marries the king of Sicily. The Cid's descendants become rulers of Aragón, León-Castile and Portugal, including such eminent royals as Alfonso X 'the Wise' of Castile and Fernando II, better known to the English-speaking public as Ferdinand the Catholic who unified Spain with his spouse Isabella. Their diffusion is also truly international, with royalty and aristocracy descending 'from the blood of the Cid' in Champagne, France, and England, and as far away as Constantinople. By the thirteenth and fourteenth centuries, the Cid's offspring rule from St Louis IX, king of France, and his heirs in France and Sicily, to Charles Martel, nominally king of Hungary at the end of the thirteenth century, as well as Louis, who truly ruled Hungary in the fourteenth century. With a vengeance, the Cid is a progenitor of kings.

The chronicle also popularized an image of the Cid resembling Santiago Matamoros, the invincible and even holy warrior: a woodcut illustration represented him as a knight on horseback, with the dismembered bodies of his enemies below the horse's hoofs.

Other printed chronicles appeared, with ever grander titles, such as Diego Ximénez Ayllón's *Los famosos y heroycos Hechos del Invencible y esforçado caualleroo, honra y flor de las Españas, el Cid Ruy Diaz de Biuar*, in other words, 'the famous and heroic deeds of the invincible and hardy knight, the honour and flower of the Spains, the Cid, Ruy Díaz of Vivar' (1568, reprinted in 1579). An appetite for chivalric tales clearly left its mark on the presentation of the Cid; this was a period when Baldassare Castiglione's very popular *Il Cortegiano*, inspired by the Spanish court, tried to establish the image of the ideal courtier, and romance literature featuring knights enjoyed great success. The Cid, who by this time had become a sort of national warrior hero, was the logical candidate to be enshrined in the growing literary output as the perfect knight.

Other important sources of literary inspiration were collections of ballads, which soon inspired playwrights. Many legendary Cid stories were propagated by vernacular ballads, another sign of the Cid's popular fame in the peninsula, especially from the fourteenth century onwards. These introduced, for example, the theme of Urraca's unrequited love for Rodrigo in *Afuera, afuera, Rodrigo*, as well as Rodrigo's insolence towards Alfonso, whom he arrogantly insults as he demands his oath concerning his innocence in Sancho's murder, in *En Santa Águeda de Burgos*. An ever-increasing number of ballads were collected and published: the *Cancionero de Romances* (1547/8), Lorenzo de Sepúlveda's *Romances nuevamente sacados de historias antiguas de la cronica de España* (1551) and the *Romancero General* (1600). An entire collection was dedicated just to the Cid in 1605: Juan de Escobar's *Romancero e historia del muy valeroso caballero el Cid Ruy Diaz de Vibar, en lenguage antiguo*, which includes 102 texts. A few of the ballads collected were composed between 1450 and 1550, but most of them date from after 1550. Escobar's collection made various textual changes, and was reprinted twenty-six times. While he was not alone in wanting to collect ballads about the Cid, not everyone did so this successfully. For example, Francisco Metge's *Tesoro escondido de todos los más famosos romances ansí antiguos como modernos del Cid* from 1626, prior to its modern printing, was only known from one copy.

The theatre picked up on the ballads and legends, including the youthful deeds of Rodrigo, the death of King Sancho and the oath of Alfonso. Twenty-two theatre pieces on the Cid have been preserved from the 'Siglo de Oro', Spain's Golden Age of drama, starting in the late sixteenth century and going on to the late seventeenth. The number written in that period was even higher, since some of them have been lost; this blossoming is testimony to the great interest in the Cid. Their range was extraordinary, too. There were dramatic pieces, such as the *Comedia de la muerte del rey don Sancho y reto de Çamora* by Juan de la Cueva in 1579, where the Cid is distinguished not only by his physical force but also by his sober rationality. Another example is the anonymous piece focusing on the Cid's great triumphs, including the conquest of Valencia, and his death, *La Comedia de las hazañas del Cid, y su muerte, con la tomada de Valencia*; written in 1603, it was based on the *Poema* and the *Legend of Cardeña*. The Cid 'exemplified a catalogue of chivalric virtues'.

But seventeenth-century theatre also opened up the story of the Cid to farce. Theatrical performances consisted of a prologue, an act, a short farce, then the second and third acts, and finally the so-called *mojiganga*, a ridiculous short piece. There were also sacramental spectacles, which consisted of only one act together with a final comical part. Therefore the same theatrical event included pieces with very different purposes, for example representing the main character in one part as a saint, and in another as a kind of clown, such as the *Auto sacramental del Cid* and the *Mojiganga del Cid para fiesta del Señor*. The *Auto sacramental* was a popular form of religious theatre of an allegorical nature, usually focusing on the eucharist. In the *Auto sacramental del Cid*, the figure of Rodrigo becomes, on the allegorical plane, Christ; his father Diego Laínez, God the Father; his adversary Count Lozano, the devil; and the patiently waiting Jimena, the community of Christians, demonstrating their faith. The *Mojiganga*, on the other hand, started with the Cid's father bemoaning not a loss of family honour, but flea bites; it included a mock bullfight that parodied the Cid's fight against the Moors; and Count Lozano, Jimena's father, hides under a bed and dies after the Cid hits him over the head, but is later resurrected to celebrate the wedding. In this way the Cid could simultaneously serve as an allegorical eucharistical figure, and a burlesque character of comedy. On the allegorical plane, Christian faith receives its reward, and theological virtues are exalted. The burlesque has been interpreted as a carnivalesque 'safety valve' for society to let tensions escape; it parodied strict social norms and gave audiences something to laugh at after they had watched a serious drama.

The Cid also cut a ridiculous figure in Jerónimo de Cáncer y Velasco's drama *Las Mocedades del Cid*, written before 1655, which makes fun of the traditional values of honour, fighting and the status of women. The Cid is not sure where Valencia is, and the Moors hand over the keys to the city without a fight.

These theatre pieces developed various and sometimes contradictory images of the protagonist: that of the warrior Cid, the courtier Cid, a saintly and a burlesque figure. Because theatre was performed not just at court, it brought the Cid to all types of audiences: to members of confraternities, which had permanent locations for theatrical performances, including the patios of their hospitals; to spectators at religious feasts, such as Corpus Christi, dedicated to the consecrated host and immensely popular. Posters and proclamations created the publicity to draw in spectators. The audience consisted of people of all social ranks, who came to be entertained, and thus the stories spread to the population at large. The legendary Cid came to be known by all.

One seventeenth-century work combined the ludicrous and the philosophical questioning of truth through the figure of the Cid. Francisco Santos wrote many volumes of short stories, often with an allegorical meaning. His *El Verdad en el Potro y el Cid Resuscitado*, 'Truth on the Rack, or the Cid come to Life again', written in 1679, is a satirical vision in which Truth, embodied as a beautiful woman, is tortured on the rack to give an account of things as they truly are. One of the people risen from the dead who surround her is the Cid; he is roughly spoken and unhappy about new developments in the world. He particularly objects to the accounts of him in ballads. When he hears that he insulted the pope in the ballad based on the *Mocedades*, he exclaims: 'Do they pretend I was ever guilty of such effrontery? I, whom God made a Castilian, – *I* treat the great Shepherd of the Church so? – *I* be guilty of such folly? By Saint Peter, Saint Paul, and Saint Lazarus, with whom I held converse on earth, you lie, base ballad-singer!' When it is time to return to the grave, he leaves gladly, declaring that he would not want to live in this world.

The Cid now embodied both the sublime and the ridiculous. On the one hand, 'to be a Cid', 'second Cid' or 'a new Cid' were expressions commonly used to describe valour, a courageous warrior and virtuous nobility. On the other hand, many comical expressions were linked to him as well; for example, someone who falsely claimed to have an illustrious lineage was said to 'descend from the leg of the Cid's horse'. As an offshoot of the *Mojiganga*, the Cid also came to be associated with bullfighting; from the middle of the seventeenth century, he was invoked in the corrida (bullfight), and the bullfight became an allegory not just of battling the devil, but also of the Christian retaking of Spain. From allegory, it was a short step to depicting the Cid as an actual torero (bullfighter). In the second half of the eighteenth century Nicolás Fernández de Moratín wrote a poem, the *Fiesta de toros en Madrid*, that depicts a corrida at the Moorish court where no Moorish torero is able to defeat the bull, but then the exiled Rodrigo is victorious; the events represent the Reconquest. The celebrated Spanish painter Goya's Tauromaquia cycle from 1814–16, which depicts scenes of bullfights, includes an engraving of El Cid Campeador spearing a bull. Dramatic pieces and historical novels of the nineteenth century also employed the theme: in Fernández y González's *Cid Rodrigo de Bivar*, published in 1875, Rodrigo has to fight four bulls simultaneously. The Chilean writer Vicente Huidobro's novel *Mío Cid Campeador* (1929) even turned Rodrigo into the inventor of the bullfight, because 'in this man were all the things of his race. All the good and all the bad. The past, present and future of Spain is in synthesis in him.' The Cid started to stand in for national identity.

Many theatre pieces by the most famous playwrights of seventeenth-century Spain – Guillén de Castro, Lope de Vega, Tirso de Molina – dramatized episodes of the Cid's story. Of these, it was Guillén de Castro's play *Las Mocedades del Cid*, published in 1618, that became the key vehicle for the Cid's conquest of Europe. This was the piece that inspired Corneille, whose *Le Cid* was crucial in establishing the Cid as a hero outside Spain. Guillén de Castro adapted some of the ballads, relying especially on the stories from the *Mocedades*, and incorporating elements from knightly romance, yet revising the Cid's character more in line with the *Poema de mio Cid* to turn him into a loyal and measured man of the king instead of an insolent rebel, in spite of the title. While he retained the story of the Cid killing the father of his future spouse in revenge for the dishonour he had shown Rodrigo's father, he portrayed the Cid as discreet and restrained, a statesman and the perfect Christian knight, more courtier than warrior.

According to the norms of the period, honour included the need for vengeance; for Castro there was no conflict of values. He also insisted on the Cid's religiosity, and incorporated his charity to the leper. In short, the Cid combined all the chivalric virtues of the age. Castro also introduced a love triangle, with Urraca also being in love with Rodrigo; but when she learns of his love for Ximena, her love turns into hatred. Yet Castro fashioned a conflicted love interest between the main protagonists: Rodrigo offers himself to Ximena, telling her she can kill him in revenge for her father's death, but she is incapable of doing so. However, Ximena repeatedly demands a judicial duel from the king after her father's death. The king finally transforms what would have originally been a duel between representatives of Aragón and Castile, where Rodrigo was to fight the champion of Aragón, Martín Gonçáles, into a judicial duel for Ximena. Rodrigo's victory means that he can claim Ximena in marriage, and her conflict between love and honour is also resolved in this manner. The great innovation of Castro was to turn the Cid into a noble courtier instead of a heroic warrior, in line with the society of his time, as well as to represent the protagonists as being in love, so that the requirements of love and honour clashed, although this aspect of the play was subordinated to the Cid's exaltation. However, it was this that inspired Corneille, whose *Le Cid* was first performed in 1637 in Paris. While there was an earlier French work, François Loubayssin de la Marque's *Les Advantures heroyques et amoureuses du conte Raymond de Thoulouze et de don Roderic de Viuar*, the heroic and amorous adventures of Count Raymond of Toulouse and Rodrigo, from 1619, it was Corneille's Cid that propelled Rodrigo onto the world stage.

The story allowed Corneille to develop his interests in topics already present in his earlier plays. Corneille stripped from the play many of the original elements, such as the encounter with St Lazarus, and many Spanish references, to focus on the central conflict. He concentrated the events into one day, and elevated the conflict between love and honour as the central theme. He also created perfect parallels to the main pair of lovers, with Urraque being in love with Rodrigue and Sanche with Chimène. This allows for an even deeper exploration of the various facets of conflict between love and honour, as it is not just the two main protagonists who embody this inner struggle. Urraque is a much nobler character than in Castro's play, who voluntarily renounces her love for Rodrigue because of the mutual love of Rodrigue and Chimène; she is also conscious of her social standing and royal duties, which dictate that she must be victorious over herself. She declares herself ready to die rather than do something unworthy of her rank, such as loving a mere knight; her courage outweighs her love.

The tragedy is triggered by Gomès, count of Gormas, Chimène's father. When the king elevates Rodrigue's father to a position that Gomès believed was due to him, the count insults Don Diègue and slaps him. Drawing his sword, Diègue demands satisfaction, but Don Gomès easily knocks his sword out of his hand and does not even deign to duel with him, an old man. Diègue then demands that Rodrigue avenge him, and thus begins the cycle of inner conflicts for the two main protagonists between duty and love. Rodrigue immediately identifies the bind he is in: honour and love pulling in opposite directions, he must live in infamy or betray his love. Gomès likes and respects Rodrigue; chose him as his son-in-law to be, rather than Sanche, because he wanted his daughter to marry 'a perfect knight'. When Rodrigue challenges him to a duel, he tries to deter him: Rodrigue is inexperienced, while the count has never been defeated.

After Rodrigue triumphs in the duel, killing the count, both Chimène and Diègue appeal to the king, she to revenge her father's death, he to pardon his son. Although she seeks Rodrigue's death to gain justice, Chimène still loves him; 'in my enemy, I find my love'; 'I demand his head and fear I shall have it / my death will follow his, yet I want him punished'. Her confidante tries to dissuade her from following such tyrannical logic, and encourages her to give up her demand for revenge, but she persists, so Rodrigue offers his sword still smeared with her father's blood, and tells her she can kill him in revenge. He does not repent of the duel with Chimène's father and tells her he would do the same again; he was obliged to punish the man who dishonoured his father. Indeed, had he not acted in this way, he would have forfeited his own honour and thus Chimène's hand. A true Catch-22 therefore: not killing Don Gomès would have rendered Rodrigue undeserving of Chimène, but killing Don Gomès made it inevitable that she, in turn, would demand revenge.

Chimène herself does not blame Rodrigue and freely admits that the outrage her father committed had to be revenged. Yet, by the same logic Chimène must show herself worthy of Rodrigue by engineering his death. Despite being repeatedly urged by Rodrigue to kill him with her own hands, Chimène is unable to strike the man she loves. Albeit initially, Chimène subordinates herself completely to her father's will, accepting the suitor he chooses for her, Chimène is no mere trophy to be taken by the victor; the duel is not the decisive factor in gaining her. The psychological torment resulting from the lovers' dilemma is developed in great detail, and especially Chimène gains significance. Her predicament between love and honour is highlighted; this love is problematic and painful. She becomes a central character along with Rodrigue, not merely a means to his glorification. Strong heroines were in vogue, corresponding to the growing influence of women in politics and on the literary scene in Corneille's time; he himself benefited from female patronage. The king represents more of an absolute monarch than a medieval ruler, and noble warriors are turned into courtly aristocrats. Don Gomès does not respect the king, Don Fernand, and wants to take the law into his own hands, which contrasts with the Cid's absolute loyalty to the king, even to the point of being willing to give his life for him. On the other hand, Don Diègue declares love to be nothing but gratification, while honour imposes a duty. The two main protagonists, however, give equal weight to both love and duty. Further, the Cid is not merely concerned with his own honour; he is also a loyal subject who above all wants to act for the good of the state.

A Moorish attack gives Rodrigue the chance to redeem himself by a glorious victory. Since he now becomes Castile's main support and hope, he should not be punished; otherwise, the motherland would be delivered to the enemy. Even so, Chimène pursues her duty of revenge, again demanding justice from the king. She now proposes that the royal knights fight Rodrigue and that she will marry the winner. The king is unwilling to risk losing Rodrigue, and states that 'the Moors in their flight carried away his crime'. Only when Diègue weighs in as well, afraid that such a decision would impugn their honour, does the king reluctantly agree, but on one condition: Chimène must choose one champion only; if he wins, she will have to marry him, but 'choose well, for after the duel, demand nothing more'. Chimène chooses Don Sanche as her champion. Rodrigue visits Chimène to take his leave, revealing that he will not defend himself in the duel, to allow Chimène to have her revenge. Chimène at first argues that he will lose his honour if he is defeated, but then changes tack and asks him to fight for her, so that she does not have to marry Don Sanche, whom she dislikes. When Sanche comes to her after the duel, Chimène believes Rodrigue dead, and can now freely confess her love for him in front of everyone; she has done her duty, and only wants to enter a convent to lament her dead father and dead love. Sanche, however, had in fact been defeated, but Rodrigue refused to take his life and sent him to Chimène; since she jumped to the wrong conclusion and didn't even let him finish one sentence, he could not explain what happened. Because she publicly proclaimed her love for Rodrigue, the king has no regrets about demanding that they marry. Chimène protests the haste: 'the same day put my father in a coffin and Rodrigue in my bed'. The king therefore gives Chimène a year to mourn her father, in the meantime sending Rodrigue off to fight the Moors.

Corneille's Cid whipped up furious debates, the 'querelle du Cid'. The piece was immensely popular, but critics attacked it for multiple reasons. Corneille was accused of being a mere plagiarist and to have broken the rules governing plays at the time, of verisimilitude, which required that drama resemble life, and decorum – to show only what was 'suitable' and for characters to act according to social expectations based on their social position and gender. Ironically, the critics assumed that the events in the play were factual, taking the accumulated literary fictions Corneille relied on as historical reality, but maintained that Corneille should have changed various aspects of the plot to fit the dramatic rules. The storyline of a noblewoman marrying her father's killer evoked special ire: the figure of Chimène was branded as 'unnatural', wanton, a monster, a parricide, and a prostitute. The play's denouement was unacceptable. Various ideas were advanced as to how Corneille should have changed the plot to conform to dramatic rules.

Indeed, several authors proceeded to rewrite the play, to remedy the failings of Corneille. Urbain Chevreau's *La Suite et le mariage du Cid* (1638) eliminated the love-honour conflict and turned Urraque into a vengeful and vicious woman, willing to kill Chimène. In the same year, Nicolas Desfontaines' *La vraie Suite du Cid* turned the play into a comedy that multiplied the rivals for Chimène's love, where Don Fernand tries to enlist Rodrigue to help him conquer Chimène. In the end, not only are Rodrigue and Chimène united, but Urraque and Sanche also find partners and the piece ends with the marriage of three couples. Perhaps the most thorough rewriting to conform to dramatic rules and morals is Thimothée de Chillac's *L'Ombre du Comte de Gormas et la Mort du Cid* (1639), according to which the ghost of Chimène's father curses her and prophesizes revenge by her brother. The count's son indeed kills the Cid in a duel, and Chimène repents and enters a monastery. The play may have satisfied the critics who demanded conformity to dramatic conventions, but it quickly sunk into oblivion (as did the other 'corrections' of the plot), unlike Corneille's tragi-comedy. Parodies of *Le Cid* were also written in the seventeenth century as vehicles of political or personal satire.

Once the Cid made it across the Pyrenees, there was no stopping him. A translation of many of the ballads into French was published in 1783. This was presented as giving direct access for readers to the original genre and the pure material that had been the basis of literary adaptations, although in reality the collection consisted more of rewritten, rather than merely translated, texts. An obstinate, questioning Cid who is willing to argue his opinions was offered as having an educational value for the sceptical youth of the times. The collection also attracted a readership of bourgeois women. The French adaptation of 1783 in turn gave rise to a German adaptation, the *Romantische Geschichte des Cid*, published in 1792. This, together with the *Romancero* of Sepúlveda from 1551, inspired Johann Gottfried Herder to write a revised history of the Cid. In keeping with the Romanticism of the period, he increased the emotional language and adopted an elevated style, while omitting all negative descriptions of the Cid. He also secularized the Cid, a trend that had already been evident in the French adaptation of 1783. Romanticism held ballads to be the original expression of the spirit and voice of the people. Accordingly, Herder believed that the ballads reflected the Spanish national temperament, focused on Christian chivalry and the passion of love. This was in line with ideas on national character at the time, attributing essential characteristics to each nation; even today's reader can identify some of the stereotypes established at the time, which had a long afterlife. Herder's Cid was a great success, and it was reprinted many times. Through it, many other German authors, including Goethe, learned about the Cid and started to make references to his story in their own work.

The Cid was also exported to England in the age of Romanticism; the poet laureate Robert Southey's *Chronicle of the Cid* of 1808 was a translation of medieval stories, including the *Legend of Cardeña*, largely as transmitted through the *Chronica del famoso cavallero Cid Ruy Díaz Campeador*. It started to make the Cid popular with the English-speaking public. This was followed by others. In 1823, John Gibson Lockhart's translation of *Ancient Spanish Ballads* included eight texts on the Cid. The writer Joaquín Telesforo de Trueba y Cosío, who immigrated to England in 1824 because of his liberal political views, published in the 1830s a three-volume collection on Spain, entitled *The Romance of History*, which included a variety of Spanish tales in English; he was influenced by Walter Scott's writing. One of these, 'The Knight of Bivar', focused on the same story as Corneille: Rodrigo's killing of Ximena's father, and his subsequent marriage to Ximena. However, he added elements that would appeal to nineteenth-century audiences of 'historical' novels. The maiden in distress motif was a clear favourite, and, accordingly, in the tale Ximena is not merely responsible for getting justice from the king for her father's death, but is also the unwilling subject of her cousin Don Suero's pursuit. It is hard to tell if Suero is more attracted by the fair maiden or her substantial estates, and when she spurns his courtship, he threatens her.

Suero 'with the most arrogant demeanour' tells Ximena that 'the welfare of our house requires that we should be joined in wedlock. For the last time I come to prefer that as a request, which, if refused, I shall henceforward enforce as a command. Reflect seriously on your ultimate decision; for a rejection of my suit will entail upon you trials and hardships, of which, at present, you can form no idea.' Ximena seems to adopt a 'bring it on' attitude: 'Begone, proud Sir.

Dare you threaten the heiress of Gormaz in her very mansion? Thy vaunts I despise! – do thy worst! – and trust not too deeply to my apparently helpless situation; for though a woman, and an orphan, I have good friends and retainers, who will not suffer the Lady Ximena to be injured with impunity!' Don Suero's response, 'you know not into what an abyss those imprudent words may precipitate you! Learn that my titles to the signories of Gormaz are as good as yours, and that I have greater strength to support them!' elicits the astonished 'Usurper! And wouldst thou, in very sooth, attempt to despoil me of my inheritance?' Don Suero then plays his trump card: 'That inheritance you may still preserve. Disperse those unseemly frowns, which so ill become your beauteous brow, and accept the devoted love of the impassioned Don Suero!'

It is hardly surprising that Ximena is less than willing to fall for such a declaration of love and sends Suero packing. From then on, he is intent on plotting dark schemes of revenge and intrigues to gain Ximena's estates. At an opportune moment, he occupies Gormaz and Ximena's estates with his armed followers, and, as the closest male descendant, declares himself the legitimate heir of Ximena's father. Her vassals take the field but are outnumbered and defeated; Ximena herself is captured and is offered the unpalatable alternative of marrying Suero or being kept a prisoner until she pays a ransom and renounces her inheritance. Ximena's kinsman, Garci-Gomez, who had already been defeated and wounded by Suero, volunteers to be Ximena's champion in a duel to the death with Suero. All fear the outcome, as Garci-Gomez is sickly and, although imbued by a heroic spirit, is much inferior to Suero in his warrior standing. When the duel takes place, in Burgos, in the presence of the king, Suero is unhorsed and hurled to the ground, but then the victorious knight is revealed to be not Garci-Gomez, but the Cid. The substitution is of course decried, especially by Suero's party, as illegitimate, but Rodrigo accounts for it as a divine miracle: when he arrived in secret in Burgos that day, he came across a crowd surrounding Garci-Gomez, who had fallen off his horse, just as the first trumpet call announcing the duel was sounded. Garci-Gomez lived only long enough to transfer to Rodrigo the scarf given to him by Ximena as her pledge, and to ask that he undertake the duel in his stead; he then breathed his last. Both the crowd and the king now approve of Rodrigo's actions; it is decided that Suero can have another duel with Rodrigo, but he wisely declines.

Ximena, who had been honour-bound to pursue Rodrigo in revenge for her father's death, now owes him her liberty and the restoration of her estates. Indeed, she had continued to love him and admire his courage and noble character even while demanding justice against him. The king now urges them to be wed; as justification, he advances not just the fact of their mutual attraction and earlier betrothal, but also the rationale that the Cid would be able to protect her landed possessions. The author tried to make this palatable to readers of the period by stating, 'In those ages refinement was totally unknown, and a deed which would shock the feelings of any modern female, soon began to wear no very formidable aspect in the eyes of Ximena.' He also added that Ximena waited another two years (which made it three since her father's death) before she consented, and the wedding took place another three years later, thereby creating a suitable distance between Rodrigo killing her father and marrying her. 'During that time he achieved many of those feats of arms which have rendered his name one of the most illustrious in Spanish history. That name was a sound of terror to the Moor, the sure harbinger of victory to the Christian.' Trueba y Cosío declares that the Cid lived to a ripe old age, omits the stories that would follow the marriage, and directs the readers' attention to a possible trip-cum-pilgrimage: 'The mortal remains of Rodrigo Diaz de Bivar were carried from Valencia, with great pomp, to the convent of San Pedro de Cardeña, near Burgos, where the sepulchre of the famous knight is still visited by all who respect valour and worth.'

In the nineteenth and early twentieth centuries, other work in England, Italy, France, Germany, the USA and beyond continued to make use of the stories around the Cid in literature, drama and historical novels, while of course Spanish works continued to be written as well. Some of these involved tendentious selections to portray the Cid in a specific way to fit the authors' agendas: they picked themes that corresponded to their own situation and concerns. Others rewrote the story to make it palatable to nineteenth- and twentieth-century readers. For example, Victor Hugo's *Le Romancero du Cid* (1859) includes poems that focus mainly on the contrast between the loyal and honest Cid and the cowardly, ungrateful king. Hugo, writing in exile after the 1851 coup of Louis-Napoléon Bonaparte, gave an actualized significance to the Cid's reprimand to the king. French parodies of the Cid also appeared in the twentieth century, including Jean Camp's *Le Cid est revenu* (The Cid Has Returned), a short story published in 1931. In this work, the famous philologist Aurelio Presagios of the University of Matapozuelos writes the true history of the Cid, but loses his manuscript of the *Poema*, which then causes the inhabitants of a whole village to hallucinate that they live in the time of the Reconquista; Rodrigo has to choose between marriage to Chimène and prison, perhaps a dark reflection of modern existentialist angst. Vicente Huidobro's story *Mío Cid Campeador* (1929) made various changes to the storyline, to make it more acceptable to contemporary audiences: it is Jimena's godfather, not her father, who is killed. The injury to the Cid's daughters at Corpes takes place in a dream of Jimena, forewarning the pair that the *infantes* of Carrión are villains, so they can be exiled before they do any damage. Yet, despite some use of irony in the text, Rodrigo is still a loyal vassal, and his exile makes it possible for Spain to become Spain; he is predestined to be a hero from birth; all Spain is his cradle.

Other artistic genres further contributed to the Cid's international fame. He was celebrated in operas, notably Jules Massenet's *Le Cid* (1885), and Mariano Capdepon's *El Cid* (beginning of the twentieth century). According to one opinion, the famous Wild West outlaw Billy the Kid (William H. Bonney, 1857–81) took his sobriquet from 'Cid'. While this is far from certain, the Cid had other more definite American admirers. An American sculptor, Anna Hyatt Huntington's, interest in the Cid led to the creation in 1927 of a bronze statue of him on horseback, holding a shield and a lance with a flag, and with an enormous crucifix hanging around his neck, which further popularized the Cid in the United States, but also ended up in several cities in Spain. The prototype was erected in South Carolina. Anna Huntington herself made several copies; one was set up at the Hispanic Society of America – a society founded by her husband, Archer Huntington – in New York. Another of the bronze statues was given as a present by the Hispanic Society of America for the Iberoamericana exhibition, and was set up in Sevilla in 1929. Several casts were made, with statues being erected in the USA, in San Francisco and San Diego, and even beyond, in Buenos Aires, Argentina. Then, in 1964, the Hispanic Society of America entrusted a Spaniard, Juan de Ávalos, to make a copy of the statue that stood in Sevilla, and that replica was then erected in Valencia. Anna Huntington, who was most famous for her animal sculptures, many of which still grace American public spaces, was perhaps more interested in the horse than in the Campeador. In any case, King Alfonso XIII reputedly told her that he had often wondered what the Cid's famous horse, Babieca, might have looked like, but now he knew, because the only horse worthy of the hero was the one she had sculpted.

Scholarship also discovered the Cid early on, and quickly became international. The 1779 publication of the first edition of the *Poema de mio Cid* by Tomás Antonio Sánchez made the text available to modern audiences; although the stories of the *Poema* had been incorporated into so many later texts, by then the original had almost been forgotten. The published text prompted interest from literary scholars, such as the American Hispanist George Ticknor, who made use of it for his *History of Spanish Literature*, published in 1849, the first scholarly overview of the field. His description of the *Poema* designates its subject as 'the great popular hero of the chivalrous age of Spain':

> From a very early period he has been called El Cid Campeador, or The Lord Champion. And in many respects he well deserved the honorable title; for he passed almost the whole of his life in the field against the oppressors of his country, suffering, so far as we know, scarcely a single defeat from the common enemy, though, on more than one occasion, he was exiled and sacrificed by the Christian princes to whose interests he had attached himself, and, on more than one occasion, was in alliance with the Mohammedan powers, in order, according to a system then received among the Christian princes of Spain, and thought justifiable, to avenge the wrongs that had been inflicted on him by his own countrymen. But, whatever may have been the real adventures of his life, over which the peculiar darkness of the period when they were achieved has cast a deep shadow, he

> comes to us in modern times as the great defender of his nation against its Moorish invaders, and seems to have so filled the imagination and satisfied the affections of his countrymen, that, centuries after his death, and even down to our own days, poetry and tradition have delighted to attach to his name a long series of fabulous achievements, which connect him with the mythological fictions of the Middle Ages . . .

Some of the other early scholars admired the Cid equally as much. For example, his early biographer Victor Aimé Huber, who wrote the first German scholarly biography of the Cid in 1829, *Geschichte des Cid Ruy Diaz Campeador von Bivar*, described how Spaniards pay tribute to the Cid as the most noble, devout, loyal and brave of all; and they are not wrong. 'History honours the hero by attesting that reality did not detract from the legend.'

While literature and other media carried the Cid's fame far and wide, works also continued to be written in Spain itself. Dramas from the nineteenth century onwards also featured some of the other characters, such as the Cid's daughters, Jimena and even Urraca, a trend that continued in the twentieth century. There were also particularly topical aspects of the Cid's story that could be utilized for their resonance in contemporary society and politics. For example, in *La Jura en Santa Gadea* by Juan Eugenio de Hartzenbusch Martínez (1845), Rodrigo displays all the qualities of a mature statesman, at the helm to resolve grave political problems. He bemoans the fact that King Fernando was a better father than king and left his realm divided between his children, creating endless political problems. He is also unimaginably steadfast and loyal, having loved a girl whose name he does not know, and whom he had not seen for seven years, at the start of the play, which prevents him from accepting the proposal to marry the widowed queen and thus gain a royal title. He finally comes across his love by chance, but as soon as he discovers her identity his duty separates them. The tension between Rodrigo's obligation to exact Alfonso's oath before he allows Castilians to offer their homage and accept Alfonso as their king, and his love for Jimena, Alfonso's cousin, is exploited by Alfonso. He knows of their secret love but tries to marry Jimena off to one of his faithful vassals. Rodrigo is willing to give up everything, to be exiled, in order to honour his public duty. Putting all political matters right without wanting to rule was surely a most appealing proposition for many in mid-nineteenth century Spain.

Other work, such as the historical novel by Manuel Fernández y González, *Cid Rodrigo de Bivar (El Cid Campeador)*, from 1875, both changed the plot to match ideas of justice and turned Rodrigo into a representative of Spain itself. Don Gómez writes a testament in which he orders Gimena to marry Rodrigo; but after Rodrigo kills her father, Gimena is offered a choice – to marry him or kill him with her own hands. Rodrigo goes from one battle to another to try to expunge the dishonour Don Gómez had brought upon his family; he is miraculously saved from his enemies by the Virgin when he prays to her. The marriage of Rodrigo and Gimena is even seen as predestined by the will of God. Yet, in the end, Gimena's curse that she had uttered against her father's killer comes true and Rodrigo is killed by the Moors. The end of the piece puts Rodrigo firmly among the figures of the Reconquest. His service to the Moors is admitted, but presented as part of his strategy to ruin them, justified by the end result. He is a loyal vassal of the king and his exile displeases God; yet it does not impede his historic mission against the Moors. Rodrigo was predestined for that role; he made good use of the power he received from Providence, he represented reason and justice, and people owed their liberty, independence, strength, respectability and glory to him. This may seem like overkill, but there is even more. Following some of the later medieval texts, the Cid is depicted as originating from the lower nobility, but whereas in earlier representations that was merely meant to make his rise even more spectacular in a rags-to-riches manner, here it is to make him more 'of the people'. He represents the entire character of the people: 'Decir Cid es decir Castilla', 'To say the Cid is to say Castile'. In the twentieth century, the Spanish philosopher, writer and classicist Miguel de Unamuno's Cid, who is a mystic, was added to the repertoire. Spanish-language literature in Central and South America also started to feature the Cid, such as the Nicaraguan Rubén Darío and the Chilean Vicente Huidobro.

The Cid therefore arrived in the twentieth century already internationally famous. As his legend burgeoned to ever greater extremes, and was put to good use by a variety of groups and institutions, so doubts about his very existence emerged. Scholars began to scrape away at the legendary accretions, but reconstructions diverged. With the objective of disentangling the historical Cid from the legendary hero, a war of words had begun.

8

The Historian

In contemporary times, the Cid found his most ardent champion in the most unlikely place. A philologist, literary scholar and historian in the early twentieth century made it his life's work to elevate Rodrigo to a position he imagined the man merited. His book on the Cid became the most influential work on the topic for generations. Ramón Menéndez Pidal (1869–1968) was the son of a lawyer, and held the chair of Romance studies at the University of Madrid. He gained international recognition and prizes as a scholar. His story may seem like one of success, but beneath, measured by the standards of common humanity, it is a rather tragic one. He idealistically set out to redeem his nation; and ended up becoming a useful tool for a dictatorship.

Ramón Menéndez Pidal was writing in the period that witnessed the crumbling of the last vestiges of the Spanish colonial empire. Once one of the largest in the world, the Spanish empire fell into steep decline in the nineteenth century. Napoleon's invasion and subsequent fighting in the peninsula triggered wars of independence in the American colonies, which successfully detached themselves from Spain; in 1836, Spain finally renounced all claims to continental America. Santo Domingo was next to gain independence by 1865, and then Cubans fought repeated wars with the same intention. In 1895, another war of independence broke out and the prime minister, Antonio Cánovas del Castillo, vowed to defend Cuba 'to the last man, to the last peseta'. Accordingly, Spain sent an army a quarter of a million-strong to Cuba to defeat the uprising. Fighting continued for years. At the beginning of 1898, an American battleship was sent to Havana in response to the US consul-general's communication, who feared for the lives of Americans there. An explosion blew up the battleship a few weeks later in Havana harbour – whether due to an attack or some problem on the ship itself has never been definitively established – and this triggered American intervention.

American expansionism had already created an appetite for war; now Congress declared its support for Cuban independence, including military support, if needed, and demanded Spanish withdrawal. The Spanish government refused, facing dishonour and fearful that a revolution would topple the government at home if it ceded Cuba without a war it could only lose. As a consequence, war broke out between those unequal sides, the USA, a rising power with naval superiority, and Spain. Within less than four months, Spain was defeated in a 'splendid little war' – from an American perspective. With its fleets destroyed, and more than 60,000 Spaniards dead, Spain had to sue for peace, relinquishing any control over Cuba. Cánovas was no longer there to protest; he had been assassinated by an anarchist the previous year. In the Treaty of Paris of 1898, Spain also ceded ownership of Puerto Rico, the Philippines, and Guam to the US. As the last fragments of the Spanish empire crumbled and the country experienced the defeat as a national humiliation, a crisis of identity gripped Spain. It was a stupendous fall: in 1810, the Spanish empire extended to more than 20 million sq. km, over 13 per cent of the entire world. After the defeat of 1898, the remaining Pacific colonies – the Carolines, Marianas and Pelews – were sold to Germany, and only Spain's African colonies remained.

The events of 1898 were not the only cause of Spain's malaise; indeed, 1898 was more a consequence than a source of the country's difficulties. Economic, social and political crises dogged Spain throughout most of the nineteenth century. The most serious problem was the inability of the liberal state to entrench itself, leading to repeated political crises. The direct reactions to the lost war were shock and outrage; the military and politicians were blamed. The deluded belief that Spain was still a significant power could not be maintained, especially as it was losing its once vast early colonial empire in a period when other great European powers were busy building theirs. Everything was called into question: 'national character', the political system and nationhood itself. A popular magazine claimed that a life-or-death question now faced Spaniards:

'whether we continue to exist as a nation or not.' Seen as a national humiliation, 1898 triggered a flurry of responses demanding modernization and cultural renewal, while 'Regenerationism' set out to identify the causes of Spain's decline and to find remedies. Spanish ideas about possible solutions, however, diverged.

Diverse groups imagined very different futures. Some wanted 'Europeanization', social, economic and political modernization, and an end to corrupt clientelism, while others turned to nostalgic reconstructions, wanting to revive a mythical past, claiming that the real problem was the loss of ancient virtues, or flaws in the Spanish character. The unity of Spain itself was increasingly questioned. The Catalan values of modernity, industry and thrift were put forward as the basis for the regeneration of Spain, in opposition to Castilian hegemony, and led to demands for autonomy. Basque separatism also appeared. A divide opened up and became entrenched between the Catholic, Castilian, rural, aristocratic and anti-commercial views of a traditional elite on the one hand and liberal and progressive ideas on the other. Over the next decades, polarization continued, with an ever-growing range of groups and movements opposing the conservatives. Republicans wanted to change the political system; regional nationalists saw their own province as of paramount importance; organized labour movements, especially socialists, wanted to change the structure of society; diverse anarchist groups participated in organizing strikes and carried out political assassinations.

Uneven modernization contributed to deepening the political and cultural divide, as some parts of Spain underwent rapid economic and social transformation, while other areas were untouched by change. Popular protests were rife. The First World War increased the division, with a greater concentration of workers in industry, and the attendant unionized labour movement. All this, as historian Sebastian Balfour argued, 'exacerbated an already existing crisis of modernization in Spain, widening the gap between city and countryside, industry and agriculture, workers and employers, and between the industrial bourgeoisie and the landowning oligarchy who controlled the political system'. Politically, proponents of a modernized, democratic system, with devolution as an integral part of governance, were in a minority, based in cities; on the other side were the advocates of tradition, order and centralization. There was no meeting of the minds between labour movements, Catalan regionalists, Republicans and military juntas. After a number of crises, and the fall of several governments, with King Alfonso XIII's acquiescence Miguel Primo de Rivera gained power in a military coup in 1923 and continued in office until he was forced to resign in 1930. He presented himself as a Catholic patriot who would solve the country's problems, caused by liberal politicians, through a dictatorship.

In his manifesto to the people upon seizing power, he referred to the disaster of 1898 as the start of the crisis he allegedly was going to solve.

> To the country and army of Spain: The moment more feared than expected has arrived (because we would have wanted to always live according to legality and for it to govern Spanish life without interruption) to recognize the anxieties, to attend to the clamorous request of those who love the Homeland; they see no other solution for her than to liberate her from the professionals of politics, from those who for one reason or another offer us the picture of misfortunes and immoralities that began in the year '98 and threaten Spain with an impending tragic and dishonourable end.

The fear of labour movements bringing revolution and the fall of the monarchy pushed conservatives to find an authoritarian solution, which was also accepted by many others, hoping to avoid a revolution.

We can only understand Menéndez Pidal's work against this background. He was not merely looking to study the past; he fervently wanted to help his compatriots, providing a moral compass based on history. As he put it, 'Although busy in the study of the past of our people, nothing preoccupies me as much as its present and its future.' Menéndez Pidal was already a highly respected academic. In 1893, he won first prize for the best philological study, which he had written on the *Poema de Mio Cid*. He worked for two decades on the edition and study of the *Poema*, which was published in 1908–11. It became the basis of his advocacy for the Cid. He expounded his vision of the past first in the short *El Cid en la historia* in 1921, and, especially, in *La España del Cid*, first published in 1929, and running to seven editions.

In the panegyrical *The Cid in History*, he extolled the literary significance of the Cid, and his centrality for the nation, since his 'memory is something inseparable from our very existence as Spaniards'. Menéndez Pidal even praised his hero for stimulating a greater literary output for his homeland than any other nation's hero, and celebrated the Cid's influence on international literary production. Most importantly, however, Menéndez Pidal argued that while one knew nothing about other literary heroes such as Achilles, Siegfried and Roland, there was reliable information about the historical Cid. While he acknowledged that reality and legend were confused almost from the outset, he bemoaned the fact that histories written by the Muslim enemies of the Cid, distorted through a hostile lens, contain more material than the earliest Christian texts. He made similar accusations against all those who did not see the historical Rodrigo as a hero: Aragonese Benedictine authors and the Catalan Jesuit historian Juan Francisco de Masdéu y Montero (1744–1817) – because of their geographical origins from other parts of Spain, they could be accused of negative bias towards a Castilian hero – and scholars working on Arabic texts, especially the Dutch Orientalist Reinhart Dozy (1820–83), whom he labelled 'a rabid Cidophobe'. He set out to refute the various conclusions Dozy drew from the Arabic sources by vindicating the Cid's deeds and accusing his enemies of crimes that had necessitated Rodrigo's actions.

Menéndez Pidal embraced the perfect knight as if he were historical reality, even turning Rodrigo into a connoisseur of the law. 'We can see that the life of the Campeador evolved entirely as a development and normative solution of the legal problems that public and private life imposed on him.' He also claimed that while Rodrigo was willing to live together with the Andalusian Muslims who were just as Spanish as the Christians, after these Muslims committed 'one of the gravest historical errors' in Spanish history by inviting the Almoravids, things changed dramatically. The Campeador behaved very differently towards the invaders and their local allies by necessity, and their relations were characterized by 'irreducible struggle, irreconcilable rigour'. He maintained that early poetry and historical facts coincided exactly and so the poetry was 'a historical source of singular value'. His final conclusion was that the Cid's 'example will live on in national history' and 'the spirit of the hero will continue to animate our national consciousness'.

By the time Menéndez Pidal was writing, there was a wide range of opinions about the Cid. From the seventeenth century on, increasing doubts were expressed about the veracity of his deeds, with some even doubting his existence. There was also the negative view about him that Menéndez Pidal criticized. Yet others still saw him in a positive light. Emilio Castelar, professor of history at the University of Madrid, republican politician and president of the First Republic for a few months in 1873, said in a speech in the Cortes that el Cid was the symbol of Spanish virtues and the 'personification of our nationality, because the people invest him with all their thoughts, . . . the archetype of our race and the sun of our glory'. Yet even positive judgements did not necessarily amount to adulation. Perhaps the most famous assessment came from Joaquín Costa Martínez (1846–1911), jurist, historian and politician, who championed the 'regeneration' of Spain as a remedy to its decline. He was a proponent of a 'republican Cid' as an icon for moral public life; yet he also wanted to expunge other elements of national discourse linked to the Cid. He sought solutions to the problems of his times, the political crisis of Spain, in education, secularism and progress, instead of fixating on a heroic golden age in the past. He wanted the help of the hero in transforming Spain: 'The hero of Vivar more than once abandoned his grave to mount his warhorse, always when national independence was imperilled by foreign invasion . . . Today, we need to resuscitate the other Cid . . . he of Santa Gadea.' This Cid, he suggested, lived in the breast of all Spaniards: it was sufficient to open their hearts to him. On the other hand, he expressed the need to abandon the violent and imperial traditions of Spain and accept its new realities at the beginning of the twentieth century: 'In 1898, Spain had failed as a warring state, and I put a double lock on the tomb of the Cid so that he would not ride again.' This is the aphorism that is often picked up by those who want to open those locks, although it is frequently distorted to include seven locks instead of two.

Menéndez Pidal therefore not only battled against negative views but intended to elevate the Cid to a height of which even his admirers were critical. He picked up and elaborated on the themes of *El Cid en la historia* in his monumental *La España del Cid*, a detailed biography of Rodrigo as well as a history of the period. Yet for its author, 'the Cid's Spain' was a programme rather than simply a past epoch. As he saw it, and declared in his book, Spaniards had forgotten the remarkable deeds of the Cid, and he had to bring the hero back to the centre of national consciousness. He wanted to rehabilitate the Cid, and restore him to his rightful position. 'I intend, above all, to purify and revive the memory of the Cid, who, being one of the most consubstantial with and formative of the Spanish people, is in great need of renewal.' He also acknowledged a concern that was more than historical: 'when I was writing my book, I felt that to the initial historical interest, something of a pious interest was added.'

As in the previous volume, but in greater detail, Menéndez Pidal criticized earlier historians who dismantled the legends, and accused them of malevolently attacking the Cid. His two primary targets were the Catalan Jesuit Masdéu, who had even doubted the Cid's existence, and Reinhart Dozy, who, working from Arabic sources, had presented the Cid as a cruel and greedy mercenary. Masdéu's work, a critical history of Spain published between 1783 and 1805, claimed that 'of the famous Cid, we have not even one report that is secure or evidence based, or that merits a place in the memory of our nation'. 'Of Rodrigo Díaz el Campeador, we know absolutely nothing with any probability, not even his existence.' Dozy summed up his findings based on the portrayal by Ibn Bassām: the Cid was an 'adventurer, who fought as a real mercenary, sometimes for Christ, sometimes for Mahomet, only concerned by the pay he would get and the pillaging he could undertake; he violated and destroyed many churches, he, this man without faith or law, broke agreements and the most solemn oaths; he burned alive his prisoners or had them torn apart by his mastiffs'. Menéndez Pidal dismissed these results as not scholarly at all and claimed to go back to the roots to establish who the 'real' Cid was.

In fact, he lionized and idealized the Cid, falling in love with his subject matter. The Cid's 'spirit with his internal fire illuminates like no other the collective national consciousness'. In his desire to rehabilitate the Cid, he wanted to see the main source of the positive narrative, the thirteenth-century epic poem, as much earlier than it was and ultimately based on authentic oral information. He argued that it was written down about forty years after its hero's death, and contained truthful information lost to later epochs. He had developed his views on the reliability of poetry early on in his life. In 1893, finding a medieval text that was similar to a sixteenth-century ballad, he concluded that chronicles, epics and ballads (*romancero*) were linked and could all be used as historical sources. During his honeymoon in 1900, he came across the living tradition of *romancero* in Castile, hearing a washerwoman sing about events that occurred four centuries earlier, which he recognized contained historical information. He thus saw his convictions confirmed, that medieval poetry was a vehicle for authentic folk memory and that the oral transmission of reliable historical information culminated in later written poetry. Turning the *Poema* into 'authentic testimony' with supposed roots close to the Cid's lifetime allowed him to present the Cid of legend as reality; this became an enormously influential portrayal.

Although he did not rely on the *Poema* alone, and used other medieval sources as well, he was tendentious in their interpretation, because for him the Cid could do no wrong, but was the incarnation of heroism and important virtues. These virtues included courage, pride, piety, patriotism, chivalry, generosity, and being a loyal vassal, a loving husband and father. Various problems in this analysis have since been pointed out by scholars. For example, Menéndez Pidal argued that Rodrigo conquered Valencia on behalf of Alfonso VI and held it as his vassal, which is a key plank of his argument that Rodrigo remained faithful to Alfonso; his proof for this relied on later sources that are directly contrary to the sources closest in time to the historical Rodrigo. The campaign that according to Menéndez Pidal the Cid waged in alliance with Pedro of Aragón against the Almoravids to the south of Valencia during the winter of 1097, which would be proof of his unwavering service to the Christian cause, never took place. Menéndez Pidal even thought that genuine information was transmitted about the oath of Santa Gadea, and claimed the ballad about the story as a source of the thirteenth-century Bishop Lucas of Tuy's narrative, whereas the ballad's date of composition was much later, at the end of the thirteenth century at the earliest.

For Menéndez Pidal, the Cid embodied the soul, the character of the nation; a man whose example 'illuminates the national spirit'. This Cid was to play an active role in Menéndez Pidal's present. In what he branded an age of scepticism and lack of solidarity, suffering from a 'weakness of the collective spirit', the Cid's deeds and virtues were to help social cohesion, inspire, and be a model for patriotism and national unity. Menéndez Pidal's Cid was a leader in the fight against the Muslims, a Reconquest spearheaded by Castile, which was also facilitating the national reunification of Spain, and throughout these wars he remained faithful to King Alfonso VI. He acted for the good of the nation, and even of Europe as a whole.

Menéndez Pidal held up this Cid not merely as an exemplar of virtue in the past, but as someone to follow in the present. This underpinned his view of an eternal Spain that had a national soul and a destiny, and was not a failed nation. He tried to inject hope and strength into society through writing about his hero during a period when trouble was brewing in Spain. He proposed that the Cid was particularly relevant to the present, because:

> The hero's life is perseverance in the face of the misunderstanding of his fellow citizens, an insistent desire to collaborate with his two most tenacious adversaries, resplendent justice even among his enemies, deference to the people whose enthusiastic adhesion he captured, final victory over the divisive antipathy with which others persecuted him, and the offer of his successes to the king and the people who had banished him.

Yet Menéndez Pidal has been called a 'militant patriot' because he was also a proponent of the cultural and political hegemony of Castile within Spain over the many regions and languages that make up the country, and saw the unification of Spain from the many different kingdoms that once existed in the Iberian peninsula as Castile's historical mission. This made his ideas attractive to Castilian Catholic nationalists.

Because his writings were eventually used by the Francoist dictatorship, he has even been accused of being 'a liberal ideologue of Francoism', at least inadvertently. Yet he certainly did not set out to be one. As the Spanish civil war began in 1936, Menéndez Pidal declared his support for the Republic. In July 1937, the authorities in Segovia sent a report about him and his family to Nationalist headquarters, in which they stated that he was 'a person of great culture, essentially good, weak of character, totally dominated by his wife. At the service of the Government of Valencia as a propagandist in Cuba.' Of his wife María Goyri, the report was even more critical; it said that she was a 'person of great talent, of great culture, of extraordinary energy, who has perverted her husband and her children. She is very persuasive and one of the most dangerous people in Spain.' Clearly, the family was identified as a likely source of threat to, rather than support for, the Nationalist cause. Menéndez Pidal and his wife then spent some time in self-imposed exile; after his return to Franco's Spain in 1939, he was suspect and was deprived of his earlier position, that of the directorship of the Real Academia Española (Royal Spanish Academy). Yet his work ended up as fodder for Franco.

Menéndez Pidal himself found some kind of accommodation with the regime. His return to the country was part of this adaptation; many people, including some of his disciples, chose to leave Spain permanently and live in exile. He also participated in 1943 in the commemoration of the millenary, celebrating the supposed 1,000th anniversary of Castile's existence, where he talked about the 'original character' of Castile, assuming it had a fixed essence, which fitted seamlessly with Francoist ideas. In 1947, he regained his position at the head of the Real Academia, which would have been impossible without the regime's consent. He also published *Los españoles en la historia*, an expansive essay on Spanishness, that in some respects fitted the Francoist agenda of Spanish unity, but also implied criticism of the methods used to achieve it. In the book he meditated on what he saw as the main ills over the course of Spanish history that prevented social cohesion and cultural solidarity, that divided Spain. His belief that Hispanic unity would prevail was fundamental, but the road to that unity, he suggested, was through mutual understanding. He appealed for reconciliation, which required a certain amount of moral courage at the time, as it was contrary to Francoist tenets.

> Will this sinister effort to suppress the adversary cease? . . . It is not one of the half-Spains opposing each other that will have to prevail as the only party, placing an epitaph on the other. There will not be a Spain of the right or of the left; there will be a total Spain, longed for by so many, one that does not amputate one of her arms, one that harnesses all her capabilities . . . A traditional Spain unwavering in its Catholicism . . . and at the same time a new Spain, full of the spirit of modernity.

Characterized as a conservative nationalist who believed in a unique, eternal Spain, Menéndez Pidal proposed an image of the Cid that was immensely powerful and popular, but which does not stand up to scholarly scrutiny. Yet Menéndez Pidal himself continued to adhere to his romanticized and exaggeratedly positive image of the Cid. The experience of Francoism did not deter him from continuing to champion his hero. In his *El Cid Campeador*, published in 1950 and reissued numerous times since, even in the late twentieth century, he repeated his arguments about the Cid's significance, about the negatively distorted testimony and analysis of his medieval and modern detractors, and about the historical value of poetry as a source, which 'had to be truthful . . . founded on the real deeds known by all'. This included not only the *Cantar de Mio Cid* but also later minstrels' songs. He maintained that even the incident at Corpes, where the Cid's daughters were beaten and left for dead by their husbands, could not be completely false because it was based on local tradition. Similarly, he asserted once again that earlier minstrel songs served as the source of the story of the oath of Santa Gadea. He insisted that his hero was 'the incarnation of the highest human qualities', even though he lived in 'one of the most calamitous periods'. The Cid was able to lead not just Castilians, but Asturians, Aragonese, Catalans and so on, therefore, in a sense, unifying Spain under Castilian leadership. It was envy, the Hispanic vice, which led to attacks against the Cid in his lifetime, and continued after his death. Menéndez Pidal always justifies Rodrigo's every deed, even the harshest, for example by arguing that ibn Jahhāf broke the terms of the surrender treaty by hiding al-Qādir's treasure; and even claims his was the 'most benign regime of conquest in Valencia'. The Cid was a restorer of Christianity and Europeanism, established the superiority of Christian over Islamic Spain, and even his enemies recognized his greatness.

The vision of Menéndez Pidal was enormously influential; according to one reminiscence, reading his *España del Cid* revealed the historical hero 'with historical exactitude'. As the British historian Richard Fletcher writes in *The Quest for El Cid*:

> Menéndez Pidal had given the Spaniards the Cid they wanted. And his version was unassailable. The national hero whom he presented so convincingly and so readably in the text of his work was elaborately defended, walled by footnotes, buttressed by appendices of meticulous scholarship, fortified by all the massive intellectual authority of the Director of the Royal Spanish Academy, the editor of the *Poema de Mio Cid* and the *Primera Crónical General*. There could be no criticism of Don Ramón's Cid in his native land.

Menéndez Pidal was one of the key figures of twentieth-century Spanish medieval studies. He gained international recognition in his lifetime; he was the recipient of honorary doctorates from the universities of Oxford, the Sorbonne and Tübingen, as well as France's *Légion d'honneur*. While Menéndez Pidal did not set out to be an apologist for Franco, because of his scholarly reputation many of his dearly held views lent scholarly credibility to ideas that dovetailed with Franco's claims. Although for a while after his return from exile he lived as a semi-recluse and under suspicion, in the end his verdict about the Cid came to refer to himself, offering his successes to the people who had exiled him.

While many no longer idolize either the Cid or Menéndez Pidal, the Cid's historian himself has been turned into something of a legend. Two prestigious scholarly institutions, the Real Academia Española de la Lengua and the Biblioteca Nacional de España organized an exhibition in 2019 entitled 'Two Spaniards in history: el Cid and Ramón Menéndez Pidal', recalling the title of don Ramón's book. Presenting its subjects as the hero and the scholar, connected by the secret affinity of their souls, two people who shared an intimate identity, the organizers 'paid homage to two names that will forever be united'. The exhibition focused on the significance of the Campeador in texts from the Middle Ages onward and Menéndez Pidal's centrality to twentieth-century Spanish culture. The booklet produced for the exhibit, written by Enrique Jerez, credits Menéndez Pidal with doing more than anyone to uncover the life and personality of the flesh and blood Rodrigo. It links the medieval legend and the modern historian as possessing the same temperament.

> The Cidian virtue par excellence, moderation, was perhaps also . . . Menéndez Pidal['s] decisive quality. A declared supporter of the 'neutrality of culture', his conciliatory temperament (suffering from 'the struggle of the two Spains') did not prevent him from expressing himself bluntly, against governments of one persuasion or another . . . Two eloquent examples are two of his articles (both on the front pages of *El Sol*) when he saw two of his 'red lines' crossed (or almost): intellectual freedom and the unity of Spain. The first (published on 2 April 1929), criticizing the repressive measures that Primo de Rivera had undertaken against the public university; the second (on 26 July 1931), against the federalist aspirations of Catalonia, the Basque Country and Galicia.

In the case of the Cid, however, Menéndez Pidal's own infatuation seems to have made him incapable of calling out the Francoist distortions; his Cid was not so very different from Franco's, and was easily bent to serve the Franco regime. Menéndez Pidal's dictum could, indeed, have been written by a flatterer of the dictator: 'The exemplarity of the Cid can continue to animate our collective conscience, and in the future, as in the past, the simple words in which the anonymous poet, patriarch of our literature, formulated the mystical union of the hero with his Spain will retain their elevated meaning "and all gain in honour through the man born in a favoured hour".' His high praise was not unique, and echoes others', such as that of Francisco de Paula Canalejas y Casas (1834–83), a literary scholar who stated '[El Cid] is the soul of our nationality. His memory is our past, and remembrance of him ignites the heart of the young just as much as it revives the shallow breath of the old.' Translated into the context of Francoist Spain, this type of adulation gained an entirely new meaning. It became a prop for a dictatorship. Menéndez Pidal did not envisage such an outcome, but neither did he truly resist it.

9

The Dictator and His Cid

Visitors to Burgos still see the remains of the Francoist cult of the Cid: the bridge of San Pablo adorned with the statues of those closest to the Cid, mostly following the verses of the *Poema de Mio Cid*, and the nearby square with the monumental equestrian statue of the Cid. Franco's Spain engineered the apotheosis of the Cid that ultimately turned into ignominy. In the middle of the brutal Spanish civil war, Francoists chose el Cid, cast as the hero of the medieval Christian Reconquest of the Iberian peninsula from the Muslims, as the emblem of their vision of Spain, which was perpetuated after their victory.

Franco rose to power in the civil war, and the war itself was a culmination of the deep divisions in Spain between modernizers and reactionaries that had built up over more than a century, and of the willingness to find violent solutions to social and political problems. Military dictatorship was very much on the cards, as it was already employed in the 1920s. Yet when the Second Republic was established in 1931, after Republican parties first made major gains at the municipal elections, then won the parliamentary votes, reform seemed to have triumphed. Expectations were high on the left that Spain would be transformed into a modern, democratic country. A new constitution created a democratic framework and gave the vote to women. Full religious freedom and the separation of church and state were also implemented. The army was to be reformed to modernize it (including reducing its size, and changes in organization and military jurisdiction) and make it politically neutral. Various pieces of legislation aimed to help the working classes, and agricultural reform to redistribute land was being prepared. The government also conceded a statute of autonomy to

Catalonia, which became a self-governing autonomous region within the Spanish republic.

The reforms alarmed the political right, which started to organize a broad alliance. At the same time, economic problems meant there was insufficient funding for the desired change and peasants especially started to believe that the government was not serious about agrarian reform. There was no time for the deep social and political reforms on the agenda of the victorious political parties; they ultimately failed to unite society. The political system was under attack from both right and left. An attempted military coup in 1932 and the uprising by the anarcho-syndicalist Confederación Nacional del Trabajo in 1933 were put down by the government. The government itself, however, was disintegrating; it had included socialists who became the majority party in the Cortes, but also Republicans and conservative Catholics. This uneasy coalition fell apart because of the significant underlying differences in ideologies and desired outcomes. In the general election of 1933, the right-wing coalition made significant gains, and a coalition of centre and right-wing parties took power. They undid some of the reforms, and represented the interests of the entrenched landowning elites, industrialists, the Church and the army. In 1934, a general strike and local uprisings were crushed. Tens of thousands of people were arrested, and more of the left-wing reforms were annulled. Left-wing parties were spurred into a new alliance, and won at the 1936 general election. The right refused to accept the result, and when the Popular Front did form a government, right-wingers conspired to overthrow the Republic. While the government tried to revive the reformist programme of 1931, the radical left wanted a revolution to sweep away bourgeois class society. Large swathes of the population no longer believed that parliamentary democracy would bring a discernible difference in their lives and took matters into their own hands: industrial workers went on strike for better wages, while peasants started to occupy some of the lands belonging to large landowners. Street violence erupted. The government was unable to counter right-wing agitation, fostered by speeches in the Cortes, which spread the idea that reconciliation was impossible, 'communism' and 'separatism' were present threats to be confronted and the army alone could restore order.

In 1933, right-wing politicians had already begun to adopt the term 'reconquest' to designate their political goal of creating a unified Spain firmly under right-wing rule. Gil Robles, who was dominant in the right-wing campaign, gave a speech in the run-up to the election, in which he said: 'We must reconquer Spain . . . We must give Spain a true unity, a new spirit, a totalitarian polity . . . It is necessary now to defeat socialism . . . We must proceed to a new state and this imposes duties and sacrifices. What does it matter if we have to shed blood!' In 1936, a military uprising was carefully planned by army generals, which took place on 17–18 July. Repeatedly informed about the plot, the Republican government ignored the warnings. In the preceding days, some pro-Republican army officers had been murdered, and the left-wing revenge killing of the important right-wing politician José Calvo Sotelo provided further justification for military intervention. The coup was led by General Emilio Mola, and the plan was to seize power quickly through coordinated takeovers by military units all over Spain and establish a dictatorship. While the uprising was successful in more conservative areas, in many places working-class resistance blocked the quick seizure of power. The military coup turned into civil war.

The rebels gained the upper hand early on, because arms and military equipment were provided to them by Hitler's Germany, Mussolini's Italy and Salazar's Portugal, in violation of the official policy of non-intervention, which was supposed to prevent external interference. In contrast, fearful of a communist revolution, or the domestic impact of sending help to the Republicans, Western European countries refused meaningful aid to the Spanish government, even though some individual politicians expressed their support of the Republican cause and eventually helped recruit volunteers. The rebels therefore quickly gained control over large areas.

Participants in the uprising called themselves Nationalists; and the massacre of their political opponents, be they communists, anarchists, socialists, or centre-left Republicans, started immediately, not merely in areas where some of the population resisted, but also in the places where the coup was successful. General Mola was a proponent of the use of terror in 'eliminating without scruples or hesitation all those who do not think as we do'. In the words of the historian Paul Preston, 'the rebels made it clear that their objective was not simply to take over the state, but to exterminate an entire liberal and reforming culture'.

In response, Republicans also started to target right-wing sympathizers. Slaughter and cruelty became hallmarks of the civil war. On the Nationalist side, however, murder and torture were not merely actions of the mob, but were deployed consistently and officially sanctioned, not just during the war, but even after its end.

In fact, the two sides did not consist of monolithic blocs; rather, there was a large variety of groups. Among the Nationalists, there were monarchists, fascists and the Catholic Church; while on the Republican side, anarchists, communists, socialists and regional separatists had diverse aims. The Nationalists, however, promoted their war as a crusade against communism, and the main international support for the Republic indeed started to arrive from the Soviet Union. In the face of Nationalist successes with international help, and the inaction of democratic European countries, the Soviet Union decided to send planes, tanks and military equipment from October 1936 in exchange for gold. In addition, volunteers were recruited by the Comintern. These troops who came from all over the world formed the International Brigades, who provided about 40,000 volunteer soldiers by 1937.

Hitler and Mussolini ramped up their support, sending large numbers of trained troops – 20,000 Germans and 80,000 Italians – and a significant air force. Coordinated attacks, including mass bombings – forever memorialized by Picasso's *Guernica* – allowed the Nationalists to wage a war of attrition against the Republicans.

General Francisco Franco was one of the influential anti-Republican figures in the army promoted by the right. He had led the Spanish Moroccan troops that were crucial in quashing the revolt of the Asturian miners in 1934. The Popular Front government removed him from the position of chief of staff and posted him to the Canary Islands in February 1936, to reduce the risk of an army coup. He actually wrote a letter to Prime Minister Santiago Casares Quiroga on 23 June, intimating that the army was hostile to the Republic, but, if treated properly, it would be loyal. Since he was not among the most senior conspirators, this may have been an effort to gain a better position for himself in the Republic by betraying the conspiracy (although later it was represented as a last-ditch gesture of peace-making); his letter was ignored. The strongest base for Franco's rise was the Spanish Moroccan army, which respected him, and which ended up being essential in the military coup; yet Franco's participation in the coup was not certain until quite late. Nobody predicted his quick ascent to prominence; according to the original plans, neither in the coup itself, nor in the planned government after its success was he to play a major role.

A plot was hatched with the help of an English right-wing Catholic, Douglas Francis Jerrold, to enable Franco to join his troops without the knowledge of the Spanish government. On 11 July an aeroplane left England with two female passengers posing as tourists. It picked up Franco from the Canary Islands and took him to Morocco; from there he led the rising of the Moroccan garrisons. After this succeeded, Hitler immediately responded to Franco's appeal and German planes took the Spanish army from Morocco to southern Spain. His control of the 47,000-strong Moroccan army was the basis of Nationalist successes. In September, he was chosen to be commander-in-chief (Generalísimo) of the Nationalist army and the head of the government. Franco's rivals died with uncanny timing, two in plane crashes, some executed by the Republicans. As head of the army and the government, Franco took care to remove any other potential challengers. Among these, José Antonio Primo de Rivera, the charismatic founder and leader of the Falange (a fascist political party), was in a Republican jail in Alicante. Various attempts to free him failed, and when the German consul tried to help, Franco intervened and made various demands that led to the Germans ceasing their efforts. In effect, Franco prevented meaningful negotiations for Primo de Rivera's release. Primo de Rivera was eventually executed by the Republicans.

The Republic was already doomed in 1937, but fighting continued in a few places until 1939 when the last of the Republican army surrendered. During the war, the murder of Republicans continued everywhere in the wake of Nationalist victories; refugees were bombed as they tried to flee. Republican women were particular targets, raped, humiliated in public and killed. Some estimate the number of those killed by Francoists to have been as high as 180,000. All the while, Nationalist propaganda both suppressed the horrors committed by their troops, and gave false accounts of 'Red' atrocities. Franco established a military dictatorship, brutally purging society of all the people who held, or were accused of holding, views incompatible with the traditional values espoused by the Nationalists. He relied on fear not just to establish his regime, but also to stay in power. The Law of Political Responsibilities in 1939 retrospectively criminalized everyone who supported the Republic or trade unions from 1934. Although records were not kept or were even destroyed on purpose, it has been estimated that more than 30,000 people were executed between 1939 and 1945, hundreds of thousands were imprisoned, and extrajudicial killings claimed the lives of many more. They even targeted the dead; for example, hundreds of Republicans and members of the International Brigades who died in the war were buried in Fuencarral cemetery, but in 1941 their remains were dug up and thrown into an unmarked mass grave. The defeated were also economically exploited and used as slave labour for public projects including railways and canals, couched in terms of religious 'redemption'. The last concentration camp for defeated Republicans was closed in 1947. The persecution affected millions of people.

Yet Franco had lacked a real political ideology, and borrowed many of the Falangist ideas propagated by an earlier political movement and then party, which had a strong affinity to fascism. A single-party state was established. Conservative traditionalist views, including Catholicism, the subordination of women, the slogan of 'God, the Fatherland, and family' were upheld. Cultural homogenization was vigorously pursued: Castilian became the only official language for the whole of Spain, while the speaking of Basque, Catalan and Galician was prohibited outside the home. Education, administration and even cultural activities were to be conducted only in Castilian. The Nationalist chant of 'España! Una! Grande! Libre!' (Spain! One! Great! Free!) was to be put brutally into practice.

As the Rector of the University of Salamanca, Miguel de Unamuno, put it in 1936, 'what has to be saved in Spain is Western Christian civilization under threat from Bolshevism, but the methods they are using are not civilized, nor Western, but rather African, and certainly not Christian'. The Catholic Church, however, benefited from and played an important role in legitimizing Francoism.

Many priests had preached against 'the communists', blessed the flags of Nationalist soldiers and some even took up arms and participated in the killing of Republicans. In late August 1936, the archbishops of Zaragoza and Santiago de Compostela declared the Nationalist cause a religious crusade, a pronouncement subsequently repeated by many churchmen.

This identification was coupled to the more specifically Iberian precedent, the 'Reconquest' of the peninsula from 'the Moors', which in its Nationalist recasting was turned into a liberation akin to Franco's endeavours to 'liberate' Spain from Bolsheviks. The Francoist idea of the Reconquista did not merely distort the process through which the power relations in the peninsula changed. It turned the alleged Reconquest into a common past for Spaniards, through which they constructed their identity, the very essence of the Spanish nation. The indiscriminate use of terror, coupled with the lofty rhetoric of crusade and Reconquista made the Cid particularly relevant as a heroic precursor of Franco.

The Cid was thus appropriated by a murderous regime, used to justify both mass killing and foisting a Christian nationalist Castilian identity on Spain. The parallel through military activity is not difficult to find, but Franco, of course, did not go back to medieval sources; he drew on the mythic Cid, and it was the work of Ramón Menéndez Pidal that provided the heroic image of the Cid for Francoist Spain. While Menéndez Pidal did not write with the intention of providing legitimacy for a dictator, it is easy to see how his work segued into Nationalist ideology. He championed the historicity of Castilian epic poetry as well as the collective authorship by 'the people' of the oral poetry before such epics were written down, and espoused romantic ideas of a past age of social harmony. He saw the medieval period as one in which the interest of the community triumphed, with individuals willingly subordinating themselves to the common good. He emphasized the need for social solidarity, based on the idea that all peoples retain a permanent identity throughout history, and have a collective spirit. All this could very easily be reinterpreted as a fascist society, where the individual does not count.

Menéndez Pidal's Cid could also become, with the slightest shifts of emphasis, a representative of loyalty to the fatherland – being faithful even to an unjust king was proof of that. He was an invincible hero, who was morally superior to his king and who took the initiative for a national reconquest, to restore national unity in the face of North African threat. The vision combined all the elements dear to Francoists: obedience to authority as sacred, except when it comes to a military leader, who is extolled for taking supreme power in a social crisis, when government actions deviated from the national interest. The takeover is justified, because it is done in the interest of the nation, rather than for personal gain. Finally, the national unification is carried out under centralizing Castilian leadership. Castilian patriotism in itself was not necessarily Francoist. For example, the famous medieval historian Claudio Sánchez-Albornoz, who spent decades in exile and refused to return to Spain until after Franco's death, celebrated Menéndez Pidal's *La España del Cid* as the rebirth of a dynamic and vital, free and mighty Castile following the path of the Cid. However, Menéndez Pidal's vision ended up justifying a different interpretation of Castilianism, the priority of Castile over the other areas of Spain, one that suppressed the other cultures of the peninsula.

Already in 1935, the Spanish General Staff referenced the work of Menéndez Pidal on the Cid in justifying Spanish action in North Africa: referring to the territory under Spanish rule as a protectorate rather than a colony, this was supposed to be a manifestation of a Spanish style of warfare that differed from the rest of Europe. Then Franco spoke of the civil war as a crusade, a work of national reunification, a new Reconquest, a defence of the fatherland. In his rhetoric, it was a righteous fight against international communism, represented on Spanish soil by the Republicans. The alleged medieval Reconquest and its first hero, the Cid, therefore suited Francoist ideology to a T. The victorious Nationalists appropriated the Cid as a symbol and precursor of their cause. The Cid was chosen as a model for Spaniards, but especially for the military. General Aranda wrote about the military model provided by the Cid, emphasizing loyalty to the chief and love of the troops. Making decisions without consultation, and then simply informing the army – which, according to Menéndez Pidal, was the Cid's modus operandi because he was cautious and did not want plans to be divulged before they were put into motion – was extolled by some of the

Francoist generals as a model for the military high command. One even went so far as to claim that military professionals could learn military techniques from the *Poema*. After the Nationalist victory, Menéndez Pidal's work became compulsory reading at the military academy. Explicit ideological parallels continued to be drawn between his Cid and the Francoist ideals. Menéndez Pidal himself did not contribute in an explicit way to this identification. Indeed, he affirmed in an interview: 'I am no politician, I have never belonged to a political party.' He was sometimes even criticized by the Francoists. Yet he created a hero who now served a monstrous regime.

Moreover, Franco himself soon started to be seen as a new Cid. He did not personally initiate the espousal of such an identity; rather, he was first compared to the Cid by his followers. N. Sanz y Ruiz de la Peña published a poem, the *Romancero de la Reconquista* in 1937, in which he explicitly compared and equated the Cid's epoch with the 'now', the 'third crusade'. Manuel Aznar published an article in 1938 in which he recalled that the Cid's horse galloped over the same lands that the Nationalist troops were marching on. Comparisons were made between military tactics and victories then and now. A work in 1954 on the Cid was dedicated to Franco, 'our invincible Caudillo [leader; the equivalent of Führer], saviour and liberator of Spain, on whose side are all the Spaniards, and we follow him the same way as those who sought Justice and Victory followed the Cid Campeador'.

Franco's Cid was the Castilian leader of the Reconquista, who embodied 'the spirit of Spain', and chose 'a glorious death'. Deeds such as his made Spain great and were to be emulated by Nationalists. A Nationalist legend had it that when the Alcázar of Toledo was being defended by Colonel Moscardó against the Republicans in 1936, the Republican militia leader called him on 23 July and passed the telephone to Moscardó's imprisoned son. Luis Moscardó informed his father that he would be executed unless the colonel surrendered the fortress. Attesting his superhuman dedication to the Nationalist cause, Colonel Moscardó told his son to commend his soul to God and die as a patriot; allegedly he then heard over the phone the shot that killed his son. It was Franco with his Moroccan troops who finally lifted the siege of the Alcázar of Toledo at the end of September. In 1939, in a speech there, Franco extolled Moscardó's deed: 'And here two notable figures are united. The first is the most glorious of medieval times, el Cid Campeador, the most recent is the most symbolic of our times, Colonel Moscardó.' Moscardó, willing to sacrifice his son for Spain, is a modern follower of the Cid who had gloriously fought for the fatherland. The story was turned into a moral lesson for Nationalists. Moreover, because of Toledo's medieval significance as the Visigothic capital and as the site of Alfonso VI's victory for Christendom, it was easy to exploit the symbolism of Toledo to emphasize the identical nature of the medieval and the Francoist crusade.

In fact, the real story of what happened at the Alcázar of Toledo was very different from the myth. The Nationalist garrison had taken about two hundred women and children from the families of left-wing sympathizers hostage and kept them in horrendous conditions in the fortress of Toledo. Moscardó's son was executed a month later than the myth would have it, on 23 August, as part of the reprisal for a Nationalist air raid against Toledo. Foreign journalists, who were only allowed into Toledo the day after Franco's troops had lifted the siege in September, reported on the massacre perpetrated by the Nationalists: the hostages were killed, pregnant women from the maternity hospital were taken to the cemetery and shot, the beheaded corpses of militiamen littered the streets, and grenades were thrown into a Republican hospital on the outskirts of the town, killing those inside. As a Jesuit priest, Alberto Risco, gloated when writing about the events: 'with the encouragement of God's vengeance on the tips of their machetes, they hunted down, destroyed and killed, without giving the fugitives time . . . to take evasive action.'

The Francoist cult of the Cid also benefited Burgos, which could exploit its long association with the hero. Burgos was briefly turned into 'the capital of the crusade'; it was the seat of the first Franco government in 1938–9. After the conquest of Madrid, however, the government moved, and some of the local notables decided that, as a countermeasure, it would be best to recall Burgos's relevance in Spanish history. They found an excuse to organize a large event, announcing the Millenary of Castile (943–1943). The date itself was based on a medieval legend, according to which in 943 Count

Fernán González revolted against the king of León and established the independent county of Castile. Castile's leadership of the Reconquista was a key element of Francoist ideology, which was now to be exploited to underline Burgos's standing. The direction of the celebrations, however, was taken over by the government, turning Fernán González into a medieval Franco, the leader of a people in a national enterprise.

Burgos then focused on its alleged role in the life of the Cid, and in 1947 the city's mayor initiated the creation of a statue of the Cid, which was to be made by the sculptor Juan Cristóbal González Quesada. The dream of honouring the Cid was an old one; a cornerstone for a monument had been placed in 1905 by King Alfonso XIII, although it was never completed. Now there was a new reason to promote this cause; with the Cid's significance to Francoism, it elevated Burgos itself. A competition was announced to create a representative space to celebrate him, combining the bridge of San Pablo and the square that was now renamed after the Cid, which was to be the site of the statue. The winner of that competition proposed the idea of a monumental ensemble. Accordingly, the sculptor Joaquín Lucarini was entrusted with making the statues that still stand on the bridge spanning the River Arlanzón. They were to represent the principal people in the Cid's life according to a selection made at the time; his wife Jimena; Rodrigo's son Diego; Saint Sisebut, abbot of San Pedro de Cardeña (substituting a historical figure for Abbot Sancho of the *Poema* probably because of Sisebut's sanctity); Jerome, bishop of Valencia; Rodrigo's faithful warrior Martín Antolínez, who supposedly received one of the Cid's swords; his nephew Álvar Fáñez; another of his faithful followers, Martín Muñoz; and Ben Galbón, the Cid's Moorish friend and vassal.

The equestrian statue of the Cid by Juan Cristóbal González Quesada was also completed: it shows a heavily bearded Rodrigo in armour, with his mantle flying in the wind, mounted on Babieca, thrusting his sword forward, in the direction of Valencia. The bronze statue towers over the square: the statue itself is 4 m tall and it is set on a high pedestal. The stone pedestal features the coats of arms of the city and of Castile, as well as Spanish inscriptions adapted from medieval texts. One provides a slightly improved version of Ibn Bassām's verdict (without naming him): 'The Campeador, always carrying victory with him, was, because of his clairvoyance that never failed, because of the prudent firmness of his character and his heroic bravery, a miracle of the great miracles of the Creator.'

The other is the announcement of his death from the pen of a monk of Saint-Maixent in France, again without any indication of the source: 'The year 1099: In Spain, at Valencia, Count Rodrigo Díaz died. His death caused the gravest grief in Christendom and great joy among his enemies.' Presumably the choice of texts was based on some idea that it would glorify the Cid more to choose passages from texts not written by those who wanted to exalt him.

The ensemble on the bridge and the square, which was now referred to as the 'Vía sacra Cidiana', was inaugurated in July 1955, with the celebrations lasting for days, and the footage taken was even turned into a propaganda film the following month. On 23 July, Franco himself arrived in Burgos. His speech inaugurating the monument boasted about the parallel between the Cid and the Nationalists: 'El Cid is the spirit of Spain. It is usually in poverty and not in opulence that such great figures emerge . . . A nation once launched down the slope of selfishness and comfort, will perforce fall into debasement . . . Thus it was possible to . . . boast of closing the tomb of the Cid with seven keys. [Here Franco was denigrating the earlier liberal interpretation of the Cid by Joaquín Costa.] The great fear that El Cid would come out of his grave and be incarnated in the new generations! Let the strong and virile people of Santa Gadea rise again and not the docile ones of courtier climbers and merchants! This has been the great service of our Crusade, the virtue of our Movement: having awakened in the new generations the awareness of what we were, of what we are and of what we can be. May this distinguished figure . . . be the symbol of the new Spain. In him is all the mystery of the great epics: serving noble enterprises, . . . fighting in the service of the true God.'

The local daily paper, the *Diario de Burgos*, dedicated its 23 July 1955 issue to the inauguration, as an 'homage to the Cid', with the headline 'Burgos for the Cid Campeador!'. It also commissioned Ramón Menéndez Pidal to contribute an article on the 'human side' of the Cid. The historian begged off, however, citing the pressing need to finish another piece of work, but allowed the paper to print part of his existing writings on the Cid. While any historian, and certainly the one writing these lines now, will sympathize with the predicament of a scholar unable to take on anything new due to existing commitments, was don Ramón being entirely honest, or did he use the excuse to distance himself from a major Francoist celebration? In any case, the newspaper printed the extract prominently on the front page, which also bore photographs of the equestrian statue and the statues on the bridge. By comparison, the effusive and nauseating piece about the arrival of Franco and his wife only appeared on page three. This demonstrates Menéndez Pidal's stature as the scholar who legitimized the Cid. The piece was entitled 'the human profile of the Cid'.

The article admitted that in fact we do not know what the Cid looked like, as no contemporary likenesses remain, and the sources do not describe his physical aspect, apart from his beard. They do, however, tell us about his moral values, 'doubtless an idealized portrait, but nonetheless an authentic one'. Repeating the claim that the epic poetry was a reliable source on the historical personage, Menéndez Pidal affirmed that the Cid was the product of the last heroic age of the western world, but his characteristics differed from those of other epic heroes. These are, first of all, loyalty and the importance of the *patria*, the fatherland. For him the king and the *patria* were synonymous, which is why he retained his loyalty to the king who unjustly exiled him; even though according to the law he no longer owed King Alfonso loyalty, he still continued to honour him and hoped for his pardon. This shows that the Cid's motivations in the conquest of Valencia were not personal ones. The same goes for his suggestion of reconquering the whole of Spain. Secondly, heroic energy, that could be envied by everyone: the Cid does it all personally, from facing the gravest dangers in battle to administering justice in Valencia. Thirdly, the Cid refrained from courtly adulation to curry favour and exercised caution, taking the gravest decisions on his own. Fourthly, justice. He always acted according to the law, whether fighting judicial duels, exacting the oath of Santa Gadea, or during his exile. Moreover, he was just in his dealings with the Muslims 'of the Spanish race'; he always scrupulously respected their religion, laws, customs and property, and this much was acknowledged by even his greatest Muslim enemies. Fifth, invincible valour. While epic poetry always confers such a status on heroes, in the Cid's case reality was no different from poetry. Even his Muslim detractors acknowledged that, and while all other Christian rulers fighting against the Almoravids at the time suffered defeats, the Cid alone was victorious. Finally, tenderness towards his wife and daughters; Menéndez Pidal cites the lines of the *Poema* about the Cid taking tearful leave of them on the eve of his departure for exile.

Given the identification of Franco with the Cid, did Menéndez Pidal not see that this description was easily interpreted as a justification of Franco, pretending that his atrocious cruelty was only against real enemies who threatened the fatherland, that his injustice was justice, that his coup was the salvation of the nation? Did he not understand this, or did he choose to ignore it?

The rest of the newspaper included many other articles on the celebrations and the Cid. It detailed the affectionate reception of Franco in the city, and the honour to Burgos deriving from his presence. It also urged the readers always to remain worthy of the example of the Cid. As well as many notables, an army corps from Valencia named after the Cid attended the celebrations, and the role of Burgos during Franco's glorious crusade was recalled. The closing ceremony of a Francoist youth-group camp was also scheduled to take place that day. Franco made another speech for the participants of that camp, recommending that they steep themselves in the spirit of the Cid: nobility, courage, generosity. An address by the mayor of Burgos emphasized that the Cid had forged the unity of Spain, and was a symbol of the defence of the eternal values of the Spanish race. His indomitable spirit in the face of adversity, consubstantial with the Spanish spirit, lived on in the Falangist youth who had attended the camp.

So many officials were eager to add to the adulation, either of the Cid alone – although surely aware that it would be taken as an allusion to Franco – or outright comparing the two. The mayor contributed a piece, explaining why the citizens of Burgos could be doubly proud: to have been the cradle of a major hero of Christendom, and because this hero of Spanish birth was of universal influence. Others rejoiced in the paying of a sacred debt to the Cid. All agreed that he was an exemplar for all times. The dean of the Faculty of Law at the University of Valladolid extolled the Cid as an exemplary jurist; others did the same for his military qualities and human values. He was a historical figure and a legend, and 'both, the historical and legendary Cid are equally true . . . The hero who represents the soul of Spain.' Yet he was most especially relevant for the present: a Caudillo of Castile, leader of a crusade. A parish priest, using the attack in Corpes as a metaphor for the state of Spanish lands, enslaved, prostituted and desecrated by the Republicans, wrote: 'until one day, the happy day of redemption, the Spanish Cid of the twentieth century, Franco, the Caudillo of Spain, leading his hosts, rescued them from the shame and slavery'; so the 'glorious soul' of the Cid 'communes with the heroic soul of the Caudillo of Spain in an intimate and redeeming communion of Castilian greatness, Spanish exaltation and ecumenical Christendom and Catholicism'.

An article waxed lyrical on the conjunction of one figure, the Cid, who was the 'incarnation of all the virtues of our race' with another, Franco, with his hand providentially on the rudder, steering the country towards greatness. 'The Spain of the Cid has been definitively resuscitated and now there will be no locks that can bury him again.' Further disputing Joaquín Costa, yet another author defended the values of the Cid, which he defined as: Christian religious unity under 'the social sovereignty of Christ', justice, which is necessary to keep power, national unity, the imperial idea, advocating expansion, crusade, generous peace with the defeated, loyalty, juridical security and respecting the law, legislative and executive power held in one hand, and a sense of responsibility. He could not have been more transparent: the adulation lavished on the Cid was clearly meant for Franco. The same author also claimed that by the time of the 'universal Hispanic shipwreck' of 1898, Spanish hearts were already imploring Rodrigo for a new victory after death, because he retained a position as patron and helper of the population in times of danger. The author clearly projected this idea back to 1898, the pre-Francoist period when the Cid did not enjoy such universal worship in Spain.

Readers perhaps found some light amusement as a counterpoint to so much cloying adulation in the little doggerel advertising aniseed pastilles, that begins with:

There is no doubt, who shines
Who is imposing in Castile
The Knight in the battle
Who sweetens the palate
To whom nothing compares
Is the only aniseed of the Cid.

In Franco's Spain the Cid became an inescapable part of everyday life. Statues in honour of him were erected in some other towns, such as Vivar in 1963. He was on a mould to make chocolate bars in the 1940s, on matchboxes, playing cards and postage stamps. As with every other aspect of life, theatre was brought under central control, and had to express the values of patriotism, civilian heroism and respect for and compliance with the authority of the state. Guillén de Castro's *Las Mocedades del Cid* was performed to celebrate the second anniversary of the victory of Franco's troops, with Franco himself present. The Cid was not only exalted at the military academy as an example but was turned into a fundamental figure of the Francoist educational system. The Cid became the paradigm of the Spanish nobility of race and patriotic values; he was also the perfect family man. His status as a warrior was linked to the just cause he supposedly represented, even as violence itself was reframed to emphasize the positive outcome of war, rather than its actual course. Francoist education tried to inculcate loyalty to the regime by presenting it as a culmination of centuries of striving and the embodiment of all that was good in Spanish history. In the prescriptive school syllabus of 1939, the teaching of history became the story of the struggle of the *patria* to achieve and maintain its identity and universal mission.

High school textbooks between 1938 and 1953, during the consolidation of the regime, taught the history of Spain in order to indoctrinate. Their message was simple. The Spanish *patria* was formed through its religious spirit; a Spaniard is a Catholic, a defender of Catholicism, and the creator of an empire based on faith. The universal Catholic mission of Spain was given her by God; therefore all those inside and outside Spain who oppose this mission are enemies, and the fight against them is a fight of good versus evil. It was the influence of evil that had led to the loss of the Spanish empire, and it was the achievements of the charismatic leader Franco that had brought about a return to the essence of Spain, a recreation of Catholicism and Spanish grandeur. In this scheme, the period up to the end of the fifteenth century laid the groundwork for the unification of Spain. Muslims were the common enemy of the Spanish Christians, the reconquest against them led to the complete equivalence of being a Spaniard and being a Catholic. In this heroic story, the Cid had a foundational role as a first leader of the Reconquest. The Cid contributed to the triumphs of the fatherland, and students were to be taught to identify with a series of Christian knights from the Cid to Franco.

A history textbook for students in upper elementary school in 1941, María del Pilar Ibáñez de Opacua's *El Libro de España*, extolled the Cid thus: 'Castile, scene of the heroic deeds of the race, when the Cid rode and battles freed the Christian princes in the . . . Reconquest! When was Castile born? In the first centuries of the Reconquest. It is the . . . heart of Spain . . . the Castile of today, palpitating with emotion, that joined the glorious national movement from the first moments.' The glorious national movement itself was a crusade that was victorious against the Republicans who were anti-Catholic revolutionaries in league with the Soviet Union. As late as 1967, Antonio Álvarez Pérez's *Enciclopedia*, used in schools, declared that 'A long time ago, some people who were not Christians entered Spain. They were called Arabs and they took almost all our land. The Spanish Christians fought against them for eight hundred years, and finally they kicked them out from our fatherland. Among the Christian warriors, one called the Cid excelled. This famous warrior was victorious over the Arabs in many battles, and took from them the city of Valencia. El Cid is considered to be a model knight, because he was very good and because he did everything well.'

In this way, Menéndez Pidal's Cid was central to the school curriculum's attempt to indoctrinate children, although he was not the sole accidental contributor to the Francoist propaganda machine. The story of the Cid was not only disseminated through the teaching of history but also in literature courses. Manuel Machado's poem *Castilla*, originally published in 1900, became just as much part of the shaping of young minds. Focusing on the episode from the *Poema* of Rodrigo's departure for exile, when a young girl in Burgos pleads with him and his men not to demand food, because the king would retaliate, the poem depicts a hard yet compassionate warrior. After hearing the girl's plea and sobs, 'an uncompromising voice shouts: "March!" / The blind sun, thirst and fatigue, / through the terrible Castilian plains, / into exile, with twelve of his own / – dust, sweat and iron –, the Cid rides.'

In the educational programme of the Francoist period, ideological propaganda was not distinguished from teaching. An unquestioning obligation to adhere to prescribed views was labelled patriotism; compulsory loyalty to the Francoist regime was the cornerstone of patriotism and of education. Menéndez Pidal's patriotic Cid buttressed Francoist ideology; that is why he has been called an 'inadvertent ideologist' of the regime, who was the more efficient because of his political independence and scholarly stature.

For the Franco regime, the Cid not only rode again, he truly trampled on everyone else. Franco's identification as a new embodiment of the Cid, the military leader, Caudillo of Spain, expressed in many texts, was most strikingly demonstrated on a mural, commissioned for the Valle de los Caídos (Valley of the Fallen, in 2022 renamed Valley of Cuelgamuros). This is the gigantic monument to 'those who fell in the Crusade of Liberation', where ultimately Franco himself was buried, and which has been at the centre of controversy for decades. A huge monastery and basilica were built by the slave labour of about 20,000 Republican prisoners between 1940 and 1959. The mural (1948–9) was an allegory of Franco and the crusade, with diverse groups of soldiers, including a representative of the Moroccan Guardia Mora, and clergy, as well as a lone intellectual holding a book, surrounding Franco who stands in the centre. Franco is the Cid, in medieval armour, with a white mantle and holding a sword that doubles as a cross. Above him, on a white horse, with sword drawn, rides the heavenly vision of St James. In the end, the mural was never installed, ironically because the artist Arturo Reque Meruvia was Bolivian, and therefore not considered 'national' enough to produce work for such a prominent centrepiece of Franco's Spain. Other representations drew visual parallels to the Cid, for example depicting Franco on horseback, against a backdrop of the Castilian countryside in Agustín Serrano de Jaro's textbook for schools *Yo soy español*, 'I am Spanish', from 1957. Under the image, the text reads: 'Franco, Franco, Franco! Who is Franco? Franco is the Caudillo of Spain, he commands and we obey.' Children are also told that Franco works very hard, he is very religious and a very good family man. He loves Spain very much, and to defend Spain he was wounded in war several times.

Francoist propaganda painted an image of a monolithic Spain, liberated by Franco's glorious 'crusade', and embracing a Catholic nationalism. Now often seen as an opportunist military dictatorship without an ideology that borrowed its tenets from the Falange, Franco's regime made the Cid sacred as a prefiguration of the glorious Caudillo.

10

The Cid Conquers the Big Screen

Ramón Menéndez Pidal also played another key role as the historical adviser for *El Cid*, the well-known film starring Charlton Heston and Sophia Loren, made in Franco's Spain in 1961. As the Spanish writer José María Pemán said, 'The Cid went from life to the *Poema*, from the *Poema* to romance, from romance to the theatre. But then he became Charlton Heston.' The film was directed by Anthony Mann and produced by Samuel Bronston, who was trying to create a film studio to rival Hollywood, based in Spain. While the actors were not Spanish, the film was a way of legitimizing Franco's regime internationally, and putting Spain on the map for tourism.

After the Second World War, Spain was internationally ostracized, but with the advent of the Cold War the United States increasingly saw Spain as a valuable strategic ally. In the 1950s, diplomatic relations were reestablished, the US gained airbases in Spain, a concordat with the Vatican was signed, and by the middle of the decade Spain was admitted as a member of the United Nations. Economic problems, however, necessitated significant reforms; these began to be implemented from the very end of the decade. Consequently, the film was made at a pivotal moment.

The setting itself reveals the true correlation between film and historical reality. Touted as being filmed in original locations (with an eye on the tourist industry), the film indeed had medieval towns as its backdrop, yet they had nothing to do with Rodrigo or even the period he lived in. The fifteenth-century castle of Belmonte, Cuenca, stands in for Calahorra; Valencia is represented by Peñiscola in the film – its castle was built between 1294 and 1307 by the Knights Templar and modified for use as a papal palace under Pope Benedict XIII (1417–23). The city walls that are so prominent in the film, serving as the backdrop for the dramatic final battle, were mostly constructed during the Renaissance, in the sixteenth century. There is thus nothing associated with the historical Rodrigo that features in the film. That, of course, was not because the director chose to avoid the real places: nothing survived from the late eleventh century in the original locations. Visitors to Valencia today need every ounce of their imagination to try to conjure up Rodrigo's realm. Yet the subterfuge of 'selling' a mixture of much later historical places as original is an apt symbol for the entire film.

It conveyed Menéndez Pidal's vision of the Cid as a perfect knight, loyal to his king and unifying Spain, and added some of the film-makers' own distortions. Most egregiously, Charlton Heston's Cid uses violence only as a last resort. He only fights when he has to. Indeed, audiences first see him sheathing his sword, and throughout, while he is a superior warrior, he prefers peace. He pardons and releases the Muslim captives he takes when he defends a town against their raid, on condition they never attack the lands of the king of Castile, earning Moutamin's admiration and loyal friendship. El Cid wins the hearts of the citizens of Valencia when he catapults bread to the starving Valencians he is besieging, so they decide to open the city gates to him. He forgives García Ordóñez who tries to kill him in an ambush and, as a result, gains another loyal follower. Akin to the Miss America contestants, he wants world peace, a presentation bizarre on more than one level. It is a curious misrepresentation not merely of the original Rodrigo Díaz, but also ironic in light of the later role Charlton Heston would play, as the gun-toting five-term president of the National Rifle Association (although, to be fair, at the time he was still in favour of gun control). Finally, but most significantly, it is a grotesque distortion of Franco's bloody rise to power.

The film's Cid also incorporates elements of St James, Santiago Matamoros, who appeared as a white knight and fought with Christian armies against Muslims in medieval stories. This is particularly striking in the final battle, when the sun shines on him, blinding the Almoravid troops dressed in black, and Babieca, carrying the dead Cid, crushes the leader of the Almoravids, Ben Yussuf, under his hoofs.

Finally, the film's Cid is turned into a saintly and even Christ-like figure. The Cid carries a cross on his shoulder he had just rescued from a pillaged church, clearly evoking the road to the crucifixion. (The Almoravids indeed crucify, as a sort of proxy, his ally García Ordóñez.) When he is going into exile, at around the mid-point of the film, he encounters a leper at a place with three crosses, who hails him, asking for water to quench his thirst: 'I thirst, lord knight. There is no spring nearby from which a leper is allowed to drink.' Rodrigo is moved by pity despite his horror, and pours him some water, then gives him his entire pouch. The leper thanks him, calling him 'my Cid'. When Rodrigo, amazed, asks him how he knows his name, he answers that 'there is only one man in Spain who could humble a king and give a leper to drink from his own pouch'. Asked his name, the leper says he is called Lazarus and blesses the Cid. This figure is evocative of the leper of medieval legends. As a lowly outcast he doubles for the figure of Christ who appears to the virtuous, for example in the hagiographical lives of St Francis of Assisi. St Francis overcame a natural repulsion towards lepers and took pity on him, whereupon the leper miraculously disappeared, signalling that he was an otherworldly apparition. In this way, the film intimates the Cid's elevated role, although instead of a miraculously disappearing leper it is Chimène who suddenly appears, having chosen to follow Rodrigo and professing her love.

Another scene that reinforces Rodrigo's superhuman status later in the film is linked to García Ordóñez. García is willing to die for the Cid. He is captured by the Almoravids after Valencia is conquered by Rodrigo and tortured by Ben Yussuf while tied to an X-shaped cross. He says that since all men die, why not die for a good cause. Asked what cause could possibly be worth such torture, he responds 'the Cid'. Ben Yussuf retorts: 'He is a man like other men. He'll die; I'll kill him.' García denies this, and to Ben Yussuf's question 'you dare think of him as we think of our prophet?' says that he does. As he plunges his knife into García's breast, Ben Yussuf replies: 'Then this will be more than a battle. It will be our God against yours.'

Ultimately, Rodrigo's self-sacrifice, one of the most dramatic scenes of the film, means he willingly dies for the common good. After being wounded by an arrow in battle, he is told that doctors could save his life, but removing the arrow would incapacitate him for a while, and he would not be able to continue fighting against the invading Almoravids. Therefore, he chooses not to have the arrow removed, exacting Chimene's promise to let him return to battle. He can only do so in death. His seemingly miraculous return completely terrifies the invaders and his corpse, mounted on horseback, leads the Spanish troops to victory. The film's Cid as embodied by Charlton Heston thus bears almost no relationship to the historical figure; it is also a whitewashing of Franco's brutality.

With Menéndez Pidal as its adviser, the film was based on the medieval sources to a large extent. But, again true to the historian's devotion to his hero, later legends are amalgamated into the storyline, and the 'historical' figure is already distorted. The film in this way incorporates the oath Rodrigo imposes on Alfonso, Corneille's drama when it comes to the relationship between Rodrigo and Chimène and the legend from San Pedro de Cardeña of the Cid winning his last battle as a corpse, riding out on Babieca. Moreover, many allusions are incomprehensible to audiences without a good knowledge of the medieval sources. For example, the Cid's beard grows long during the film; this seems to be a mere signal of the passage of time, or perhaps of difficult conditions, whereas it is an oblique rendering of Rodrigo's oath in the *Poema*:

> Now his beard grew long and flowing.
> These words were on My Cid's lips:
> 'For love of King Alfonso, who has exiled me,
> I would not take shears to it or cut a single hair'

References from the sources were also taken out of context and reused, giving them a different meaning. For example, the *Poema*'s popular outcry at Rodrigo being exiled – 'The same words were in the mouths of all: / Lord God, what a good vassal! If only he had a good lord!' – is put in the mouth of the emir Moutamin at the capture of Valencia. 'What a noble subject! If he had only a noble lord!' This accentuates Rodrigo's loyalty to Alfonso and the king's unreasonable rejection of him, that can be recognized even by a Muslim, and also reinforces the possibility of cooperation by right-thinking people of both religions.

Historical characters are given legendary roles. In the film García Ordóñez is initially Rodrigo's enemy, accusing him of treason for releasing the emirs of Zaragoza and Valencia, whom Rodrigo had captured in battle. García Ordóñez then ambushes Rodrigo so as to kill him, after Chimène promises to marry him if he succeeds, in order to revenge her father. After that fails and he experiences Rodrigo's magnanimity, however, he eventually sides with the Cid, rescuing his wife and daughters from the unjust King Alfonso's prison, reuniting the family. He joins the Cid in defending Spain against the troops of Ben Yussuf. In the end, he willingly dies for the Cid, after he is captured reconnoitring the enemy troops. The historical Count García Ordóñez was one of the leading magnates and a cousin of Alfonso VI, and tutor to Alfonso's son. In 1079, he was one of the nobles defeated and captured by Rodrigo, and they remained enemies. García died many years after the Cid, in 1108 at the Battle of Uclés.

Another such misappropriated figure is Álvar Fáñez, Rodrigo's faithful nephew, who was a commander and warrior in his own right, rather than a faithful sidekick. He did not accompany Rodrigo into exile. He led the Castilian troops sent by Alfonso VI to install al-Qādir as puppet ruler of Valencia in 1086, he participated in the Battle of Sagrajas, and on the order of Alfonso led the punitive campaign against the taifa of Granada for having helped the Almoravids. He controlled the south-eastern frontier zone of the taifa of Toledo, and from 1098 was in charge of the defence of Toledo against the Almoravids. He died in 1114. Álvar's contemporary fame was such that the author of the anonymous Latin poem composed in celebration of the conquest of Almería by Alfonso VII of León-Castile in 1147 felt it might overshadow the Cid's and was compelled to declaim Rodrigo's priority. 'Rodrigo, often called "My Cid", of whom it is sung that he was never defeated by his enemies . . . himself used to praise this man [Álvar Fáñez], and used to say that he himself was of lesser reputation: but I proclaim the truth, . . . my Cid was the first, and Álvar the second.'

Finally, and most deviously, al-Muʾtamin, ruler of Zaragoza, who employed Rodrigo during his exile as a mercenary in his service, is merged in the film with the *Poema de Mio Cid*'s Avengalvón (Ibn Ghalbun), Muslim governor of Molina, 'friend' of the Cid; a tributary, who, as Fletcher put it, was 'nobly submissive to the Cid.' The film's Moutamin is captured and freed by the Cid, recognizes him as superior – calling him al-Sidi, my lord – and swears allegiance to him. He protects the Cid from the ambush of García Ordóñez, fights with him against the Almoravids and rides, together with King Alfonso, alongside the dead Cid in the final battle. He is wise, sharing the vision of a peaceful coexistence with the Cid, but aware of the many opponents of that vision, as attested by their conversation after combining their forces to take Valencia:

> Cid: How can anyone say this is wrong?
> Moutamin: They will say so, on both sides.
> Cid: We have so much to give to each other, and to Spain.

At the same time, his is clearly the subordinate role, voluntarily acknowledging the Cid's superiority.

Whether or not it was intentional on the part of the filmmakers, one can see an implied parallel between the film's Cid and Franco, suggesting that the latter was a heroic figure fighting for the common good, both to unify Spain and to protect it (and Europe) from invaders. A pamphlet published for Spanish youth after the film's release featured the Cid on the front cover, and the Francoist coat of arms and the symbol of the Falange on the back, suggesting their equivalence. As John Aberth remarked, the 'Cid! Cid! Cid!' acclamations in the film are a hallmark of populist dictatorship. Indeed, the newspaper *Diario de Burgos*, when reporting the arrival of Franco in the town for the inauguration of the Cid monument on 23 July 1955, described the applause and the cries of 'Franco! Franco! Franco!'. The film easily accommodates both Francoist and Cold War ideology. The invading Almoravids are communists, allied with the 'bad' Muslims of the Iberian peninsula, the Republicans. Spain is the bastion of the free world, with Cid/Franco bringing peace to the country, which could only be united by a single visionary leader. At the same time, he is also defending Europe against the Almoravids (communists) who want world domination.

It jibes well with Franco's ideas of a new crusade against communists. Yet Franco's relationship to Muslims certainly complicated their portrayal in the film and accounts for the dual representation of Muslims. While the Almoravids stand in for communists – brutal and devoid of humanity, intent on conquering the world – the peninsula's Muslim leaders are split. Some ally with the evil horde, but others, most notably Moutamin, cooperate with the Cid, acknowledging his leadership. While superficially this looks like an attempt to stay close to historical sources on alliances across the confessional divide, in fact it isn't that, for the black and white division between evil local leaders and noble ones precludes the temporary and ever-changing alliances that were characteristic of the medieval period. Instead, the Almoravids' Iberian allies stand in for the Republicans, while the 'good' Iberian Muslims represent the Muslims fighting for the Francoist cause – who, ironically, in reality were Moroccans. The film's battle cries in the Cidian camp are carefully crafted to cover this; any explicit Christian exclamation, such as 'Santiago!', as mentioned in the medieval sources, would undermine possible unity. Instead, the film's Cid buoys the troops with 'for God, for Alfonso, and Spain!'. In turn, at the side of the dead Cid, Alfonso spurs the army on 'for God, for Cid, and Spain!' The appeal to God could be one shared by Christians and Muslims alike. The explicitly Christian element is added by a monk bearing a cross blessing the troops prior to the final battle, and so an uneasy manoeuvre tries to show a manifestly Christian cause, while bridging the gap between the different contingents.

For all his rhetoric about a new crusade, and identification with the Cid, Franco relied, in part, on Muslim soldiers. This affinity originated from his time in the Spanish foreign legion in Morocco, where he was made commander in 1923. In 1936, he took command of the Spanish Army of Africa. It was with troops from this army that he was airlifted to Spain. By 1936, he had a Moroccan guard, the Guardia Mora: at his inauguration as head of state, he was accompanied by them. They rode on horseback and wore hooded cloaks as part of their uniform. They were dissolved in 1956 as Morocco gained independence. While Franco idolized the Cid as a Christian warrior who defeated Muslims, he also actively recruited Muslims for the Nationalist army. About 80,000 Muslims fought on the Nationalist side, committing terrible massacres. Nationalists represented them as devout Muslims making common cause with devout Christians against atheist communists. Nationalist recruitment in Morocco represented the war as a religious cause. The Moroccan Khalifa designated the war a jihad, a holy war. In this way the civil war was both a crusade and a jihad. Showing respect for Islamic religious precepts was thus important, and Nationalists organized halal food, a hospital and a Muslim cemetery for the Moroccan soldiers. Franco was hailed as a 'protector of Islam' and he sponsored the hajj, the pilgrimage to Mecca, in 1937. The Spanish navy and air force accompanied the ship transporting pilgrims, affording it protection. Yet there was a controversy even among Nationalists about the alliance with the 'Moros', who had been represented for centuries as traditional enemies of Spain. The justifications for such an alliance ranged from mere political expediency to a common reverence for religious ideals. The portrayal of Moroccans, previously depicted as fanatical and irrational, was also transformed, to suggest their innocent, childlike piety. The Francoist defence for employing North African Muslims for a national, Catholic cause that was also presented as the cause of Europe, fell to Federico García Sanchiz, who called the troops 'mudéjar militia' and recalled that 'Mahometans and Christians became allies on various occasions, even under the leadership of the Cid . . . If the Son of Thunder fought against the Arabs, Berbers and mestizos . . . that is Moors, this was because they represented heresy, which currently is linked to Marxists.'

The dual depiction of Muslims in the film therefore served political needs. Yet as any 'text', the film can also be interpreted in multiple ways, and opens up the possibility of alternative readings. It has been taken up by advocates of multiculturalism, who credit the Cid with a desire to live peacefully with Christians and Muslims alike. Further, the Republicans called the Francoists *Moros*, 'Moors', as the lines of the famous Republican song, 'Viva la Quinta Brigada' or '¡Ay Carmela!' show:

> Luchamos contra los moros,
> rumba la rumba la rumba la
> mercenarios y fascistas,
> ¡Ay Carmela! ¡Ay Carmela!

'We fight against the moors, mercenaries and fascists'; Ben Yussuf's Moors can even be seen as Franco and his troops. There is one more, prophetic, if definitely unintentional, parallel between the end of the film and the end of the Franco era: a king who at first seems a mere figurehead, but grows into his role to bring about real change. In the film Alfonso VI is an initially weak figure, who is finally shaken by the Cid's gift of the crown of Valencia. At first asking what the Cid's conditions are, only to find out there are none, although Rodrigo knew that his wife and children had been kept in a dungeon, he exclaims: 'What kind of man is this?' While drawing on the medieval sources depicting Alfonso as unjust and a possible conspirator concerning his brother's death, the film's character development was also underpinned by the guiding principle of the Francoist regime: there could be only one leader, and that was Franco.

By the end of the film, however, Alfonso VI grows into his responsibilities, and assumes leadership. Álvar Fáñez tells him that while the Cid asked for nothing in return for sending him the crown, he does need help to defend Valencia against Ben Yussuf. Urraca sends Álvar away, telling him that they do not expect anything from the Cid, nor are they willing to give him anything. She then crows to Alfonso: 'You are king of Valencia!' Alfonso, however, responds, 'I am king of nothing, no king at all', and rushes out of the palace. He then leads his troops to Valencia and arrives as the Cid lies dying. He asks for the Cid's forgiveness and tries to kneel before him, but the Cid prevents him: 'My king kneels to no man.' Rodrigo then expresses his regret that he will not live long enough to see Spain at peace, but asserts: 'I have not failed; Spain has a king.' He promises Alfonso they will ride out together against the enemy the next day: 'I'll be at your side.' Alfonso then leads the troops out together with the Cid's corpse for the final victory.

There is an uncanny resemblance to events in Spain after Franco's death. Franco himself chose as his successor Prince Juan Carlos in 1969. In his political testament, Franco warned Juan Carlos, 'the enemies of Spain and of Christian civilization are on the alert'. Despite having been trained by the regime, after Franco's death in 1975 King Juan Carlos restored democracy in Spain. He facilitated the reconciliation of progressive elements of the Francoist elite and the moderate democratic opposition. He appointed a prime minister, Adolfo Suárez, who introduced political reforms that established a democratic political system in Spain. Francoist institutions were abolished, political prisoners were freed, and political parties were legalized in 1977. This eventually paved the way for the electoral victory of a socialist government in 1982.

The film whitewashed Franco's deeds and pretended that his cause was just and noble. It did this so effectively, however, that later audiences ended up believing the Cid truly advocated peaceful coexistence and tolerance. The film's Cid, if he was conceived to justify Franco and transform him into a sympathetic character acceptable to people in democratic countries, in the end wreaked his revenge by becoming a multicultural hero, the opposite of Franco's Christian national unifier.

11

The Two Cids: Into the Twenty-First Century

With the democratization of Spain following Franco's death, the Cid, an important emblem of the past regime, fell out of favour in official circles, becoming an embarrassment to many Spaniards because of his prominent association with the murderous Franco dictatorship. Many now baulk at the whitewashed image of the peace-loving humanitarian who feeds the inhabitants of the very city he is besieging. Yet the Cid is far from being dead and buried, and indeed, after a hiatus in the late twentieth century following Franco's death in 1975, he is back in fashion.

Some of that has to do with local pride in places that have been associated with him, tourism, or an unreflective recourse to a traditional heroic figure. Others, however, are once again using him as a paragon. Unsurprisingly, this is most prominent in the far right, where he features as the medieval precursor to white supremacists, leading vital warfare against Muslims and 'migrants'. Yet, more astonishingly, attempts to reclaim him for a nobler cause have multiplied as well.

The Cid's legend has been picked up and made use of in a variety of contexts, without necessarily embracing any particular political orientation: computer games, rock bands and TV films now either use him unthinkingly or grapple with the myth and the historical truth beneath the legend. 'Blood and sweat / its liberator rides to Castile / to expel the infidel' starts the song 'Legendario' about el Cid by the heavy metal band Tierra Santa (1999). It demonstrates how difficult it is to shift the image of mythic heroes after centuries. They cannot be forgotten; they cannot be slain. Nor is this the only band to refer to the Cid; in the same year, another heavy metal band,

Avalanch, produced a song that depicts a weeping hero lamenting his sacrifices for God, when fighting for the cross only brought exile.

The monastery of San Pedro de Cardeña now produces a liqueur named Tizona; the lure of modern tourism is perhaps not entirely dissimilar to the appeal of medieval pilgrimage. After the dissolution of the Spanish monasteries, San Pedro was abandoned, but in the late nineteenth century there were efforts to revive it. Between about 1880 and 1921, a variety of monastic communities tried to settle there, but all soon gave up. From the end of 1936 to November 1939, the monastery was used as a Francoist concentration camp for captured members of the International Brigades; it housed over 4,000 prisoners. Monastic life was re-established in 1942, by Trappist monks. In the 1970s they tried to reclaim the remains of the Cid; and in 1999 the abbot declared the inextricable identification of the monastery with the Cid, and made a claim for the authenticity of the Cidian tradition.

In Burgos, of course, the Cid is present at every turn. In 2015, the three strategic priorities for the municipality's tourism policy were gastronomy, conferences – and the Cid. A 'medieval festival' in the autumn of 2022 offered the experience of stepping into the supposed past and recreating eleventh-century life for a few days, from tournaments to workshops. Even without the festival, the name of a pastry shop, images of the Cid – and even humorous advertisements, such as the Burgos equestrian Cid statue spearing potato crisps on its sword – are constant reminders of the city's ties to the Campeador. In the small nearby village of Cardeñajimeno, a statue erected in 2019 by the local council reminds visitors that they are on the Camino del Cid. The Camino itself fosters the idea of an extraordinary individual in whose footsteps one should walk. Although its website features excellent analysis of the historical context by leading historians, the sources, and the distinctions between history and legend, and despite the fact that certainly many who walk, cycle or drive part or all of the route experience it as nothing more than a nice vacation, the Camino del Cid continues to elevate the legendary Cid.

Cid statues are springing up along the Camino, the earlier ones representing Rodrigo as a warrior, clad in armour, but this time on foot, perhaps as a way of distancing the present from the Francoist imagery of the past. In 1999, for the 900th anniversary of his death, just such a statue was erected in el Poyo del Cid, which according to the *Poema* was an important place for him during his exile. It is two and a half metres high, and it seems there was rivalry as to who could possess the most towering representation: in 2008, a Cid statue was installed in Mecerreyes, which, from the bottom of the base to the tip of the Cid's lance, measures 7 m. In 2017, it was the turn of Caleruega to pay homage, in this case with a new equestrian statue of the Cid. As an added bonus, there is also a tile with the image of a crow, which is supposed to bring luck to those who touch it.

Films continue to be made, to entertain and to bring in profit, but some also claim to demystify the protagonist and to represent reality more closely than the Charlton Heston movie. *Ruy, el pequeño Cid* was an animated TV film series made in 1980 about the imaginary adventures of the Cid during his childhood. Another animated film, *El Cid: La leyenda*, hit the screen in 2003. It concentrates on the period of the Almoravid invasion. A cruel Ben Yusuf leads the Moroccans, while Urraca is made arch-villainess, secretly scheming. Rodrigo is even more blameless than in the *Poema*, and is granted Valencia as a reward.

Most recently, a live action Spanish series on Prime Video (2020–22) recreated the story of the Cid. As analysed by the literary scholar Anita Savo, it depicts a fragmented world, where the Cid is not Anthony Mann's great reunifier; yet that world speaks just as much to the current political climate as to historically accurate recreation. Disintegration works in another way as well, clearly evoking our problems, rather than the historical Rodrigo Díaz's: the film's Ruy is pulled in different directions by conflicting demands of politics, kinship, religion and self-interest.

Although various historical errors have been enumerated by critics, such as its use of heraldic images, jousts and a sword type from the fifteenth century, as Savo perceptively argued the orientalized image of 'magic Arabs' playing second fiddle to the Christian hero, and the depiction of Muslim women as freely available to Christian men, are much more problematic than slight inaccuracies. Moreover, 'If literature and other forms of fiction have the potential to transmit an ideology to their audience, then the series' embrace of actions based on pragmatism, compromise, and economic profit is troubling.' Seen by some as a series intended to humanize and democratize the Cid, it, like all the others, continues to depict the Cid as a hero. Blood-soaked battles and military valour continue to be part of that heroization.

The Cid also became a topic for children's books in the twentieth century. In the Spanish-language Walt Disney comic book *El Cid Campeador* of the 1980s, Donald Duck returns to the age of the Cid in a time machine. Once again, though, the Cid has been turned into a warrior for peace and understanding between people, supposedly an exemplar for our times. Violeta Monreal's 2006 *Las espadas del Cid*, or 'The swords of the Cid', subtitled 'A thrilling tale of loyalty and nobility', is an illustrated children's book in which Rodrigo recounts his own story. The tale and its protagonist are made appealing through a series of distortions in addition to borrowing the medieval legends. According to this book, Rodrigo dreamed about becoming the most famous knight in the whole world as a child. His loyalty to his friends, and to the ruling king, is exemplary, fighting alongside Kings Fernando, Sancho and Alfonso VI. His fame earns him two titles: Cid, 'my lord' in Arabic, bestowed upon him by his enemies, and Campeador, conferred by the king in appreciation. His fall is explained by the jealousy of people at court, especially the *infantes* of Carrión, who are suddenly promoted into his long-standing enemies, and the king's pride, who cannot forgive Rodrigo for making him swear he had no part in the death of King Sancho.

His exile is also misrepresented: three of his nephews, as well as many of his faithful men, join him; there is no mention of his service to Muslim rulers. Above all, the Cid is presented in the most favourable light not only through an emphasis on war as a necessity but also by drastically changing his own role in it. The Cid and his men had to engage in war in enemy territory to survive, but Rodrigo always first tried to negotiate with towns so they would surrender, and only if they refused did he attack, winning one victory after another. After these conquests they did not kill or take prisoners but allowed people to continue their lives as before, provided they paid tribute. All this makes the Cid's military enterprises appear palatable, but at the expense of completely recasting the reality of war.

The book emphasizes Rodrigo's conviction that he could regain the king's confidence; his attempts to placate the king; and the length of time it took to obtain the longed-for royal pardon. Rodrigo sent a gift of sixty horses to Alfonso VI, and another hundred after the conquest of Valencia; having promised not to cut his beard for love of Alfonso when he left Castile, Rodrigo's beard grew longer and longer.

The storyline follows the *Poema*, with the Cid's daughters marrying the *infantes* of Carrión who beat them severely and leave them to be torn apart by wild beasts before they are rescued. The author also repeats the story that the Cid presented the *infantes* with his swords Colada and Tizona. Subsequently, he demanded not only justice from the royal court but also that his swords and the riches he gave the *infantes* be returned to him. After the *infantes'* defeat in judicial duels, the Cid gave his Tizona to his nephew Pedro Bermúdez and Colada to his good friend Martín Antolínez. The same day, the *infantes* of Navarra and Aragón asked for the hand of the Cid's daughters in marriage, so Elvira and Sol became the future queens of these realms. The Cid finally expresses his hope of peace, and reaffirms that the only way for him as a knight to live is to be strong, loyal, just, brave, prudent, temperate, cultured and a warrior.

The book offers the sanitized image of a just warrior and at the same time simplifies the story by assuming an enemy group; there is nothing about Rodrigo's service to Muslim rulers, and while the author does not use the word, Muslims are the enemies Rodrigo fights. Giving his swords a more central place in the story presumably serves the purpose of attracting the attention of children. The book avoids depicting the true horrors of war, and suggests the Cid represents the highest human ideal. At the end of the text, certain facts are provided, for example that the daughters of the Cid did not marry the *infantes* of Carrión. Yet, by implication, various other mythical events recounted in the book are presented as true, since they are not debunked in the appendix.

In this way, even while the explicit politicization of the Cid was dormant, or independently of it, his heroization in films and books continued. Such entertainment in itself may seem harmless, but because figures like the Cid do not lose the layers of association that have built up over time, it is nonetheless dangerous, for it keeps alive

Cid the hero. By necessity, however nuanced, the protagonist will come across as a positive figure. This, then, is mirrored in political exploitation. While it may be strange that the same figure can be seen as a hero by opposing political camps, there are elements of the Cid story that, with a little tweaking, can be made to fit either vision.

The strong association of the Cid with Francoism has not been forgotten, and so he can serve as a dog whistle for nationalist ideas. Thus the Cid continues to find a natural home in right-wing worldviews. José María Aznar, leader of the Partido Popular between 1990 and 2004 and president of Spain between 1996 and 2004, created a storm when, in 1987, as president of the Junta of Castilla y León, he dressed up as the Cid for a photograph in the paper *El País*, although this was for publication in a section called 'crazy passions'. Subsequently, however, the need to distance themselves from Francoism made conservatives more cautious about openly embracing the Francoist legacy of the Cid, even though Aznar himself propagated a neoconservative ideology, where the conquest and colonization of the Americas was a positive aspect of the Spanish past.

Such apprehension has not held back the resurgent far right in the twenty-first century. The relatively recent political party Vox, which split from the People's Party and positioned itself as a more right-wing alternative to it, used various images of el Cid to launch its electoral campaign in 2019, calling for the unity of Spain. During that electoral campaign, Vox's president, Santiago Abascal, declared, 'We are not very much with the CIS [a reference to the institution that organizes electoral polling, implying it is pro-government], we are more with El Cid. We like reconquests.' Abascal spoke out repeatedly against what Vox sees as the two great dangers in Spain today: independence movements and immigration. Abascal also believes in the right to bear arms in self-defence.

A Cid of the 'Reconquista', fighting for Spanish unity and a foe of Muslims, easily fits the agenda of Vox; echoes of Francoism do not matter, as the Catholic nationalist orientation appeals to a similar part of the electorate. In January 2022, Javier Ortega Smith, the general secretary of Vox, promised in Burgos that an electoral victory for his party would 'end the exile and el Cid would return to ride for Castile and León'. The association between the Cid and a united Spain on the one hand, and the defence of Christianity on the other, thus seamlessly fits modern-day 'defenders' of Christianity. More broadly the Reconquista, and the Cid as its important early leader, feature prominently in xenophobic anti-immigrant discourse. The rise of populist right-wing nationalism has once again opened the door to embracing the rhetoric of violence and therefore the violent aspect of the Cid. It is with good reason, therefore, that Joaquín Reyes, a Spanish actor and comedian, parodied a Vox politician as the Cid: 'Tremble Muslims, blacks, communists, separatists, fags – now called the gay lobby – the gender fluid, abortionists, women in general . . .' he warned, defining himself as a 'valiant icon of the right, without complexes or hair on the bal . . ., on the tongue'.

It may, then, come as a surprise that some people tenaciously try to recover the Cid for a humane, multicultural Spain. This is partly due to the desire to prevent the political right from monopolizing a figure traditionally identified as a key character in the national pantheon. It is, however, also inherent in the legends surrounding the Cid. Despite his Francoist prominence, there is also another storyline surrounding the Cid that can be resurrected and channelled into such endeavours. The key elements of the liberal, leftist image of the Cid are the oath of Santa Gadea that he purportedly forced Alfonso to take to clear himself of any part in the murder of his brother Sancho before accepting him as king; more broadly his relationship to his king; and his interactions with Muslims.

The oath of Santa Gadea has been variously seen as a story of personal valour, or a service to society, preventing a potential tyrant from succeeding to the throne through a deed unworthy of a king. Consequently, the Cid can represent social conscience; he can be seen as the guardian of the common good. Stretching it even further, he can be seen as an anti-monarchist, a republican. Not only is he innocent of any wrongdoing, but he acts in the public interest, to exercise control over unbounded royal power, at considerable cost to himself. As the only one who dared administer the necessary oath to Alfonso, he provoked the king's hostility. Based on the *Cantar de Mio Cid*'s rendering of his unjust exile, where the Cid's jealous enemies and an unreasonable king are to blame, while the protagonist remains loyal and tries to placate the ruler, the Cid can easily be transformed into a victim of excesses of power, who nonetheless holds on to honour and fidelity. He is fully justified and reintegrated at the end, and becomes a model after death. Therefore, the Cid can be, and has been, used in reflections on the legitimacy of power and on the question of social control over the exercise of power.

In such discourses he is a symbol of the restraint on tyrannical power, representing a superior moral position. This was more in vogue in the late nineteenth and early twentieth centuries, but can still inform more positive representations of the Cid. Coupled with this, the myth of his humble origins and phenomenal rise to power can be used to depict a figure whose merits led to his advancement, therefore as some kind of forerunner of self-made men in democratic societies, rather forgetting that those merits consisted mainly of killing many people. In the post-Francoist revival of regionalism in the peninsula, the Cid has even been harnessed to the attendant local patriotism: in one work printed locally in the Basque Country, the Cid gains good Basque allies who are noble savages and who teach him sword fighting. More attractive for today's well-meaning champions of the Cid, his interaction with Muslims, which included alliances, his exposure to and presumed adoption of Muslim customs, and accounts that he allowed Muslim inhabitants of Valencia to keep their own laws, can easily be distorted as multiculturalism, a prototype of interfaith relations based on mutual respect. Indeed, such misrepresentations are not confined to contemporary Spain; Charlton Heston's Cid, according to an article on HuffPost in 2017, teaches us an important lesson today on how to live in a pluralistic culture where Christians, Muslims and Jews can coexist. 'By incorporating the tale of El Cid into our shared cultural lexicon we can better . . . take on the seemingly impossible task of establishing a peaceful co-existence between the three Monotheistic religions.'

It is as well to remember that the original stories did not portray a tolerant Cid, respectful of another religion. Opportunistic cooperation and service and self-serving deeds, exploiting those who paid tribute, and bringing swift retribution against those who refused to, are closer to the mark, as shown by several episodes in the *Historia Roderici*. 'He went into the land round Albarracín, whose people had defaulted on the payment of tribute to him. He laid waste all that land and . . . returned . . . with immense plunder.' In the *Poema*, the Cid is anything but an emblem of multiculturalism. The poet exults over the bloodbath that proves the Cid's military valour. Even when he is merciful, it is not exactly for humanitarian reasons. For example, after his victory over the town of Alcocer, his troops killed most of the Moors, but then the Cid intervened: 'we should gain nothing by beheading them / Let us bring them in, for we are the lords; / we shall stay in their homes and use them as our servants.' Hardly a model for proponents of peaceful coexistence. Yet in various ways it is coexistence with Muslims that has been picked up in a number of works to offer an alternative Cid.

María Teresa León Goyri – whose mother was, coincidentally, a relative of Ramón Menéndez Pidal's wife – a feminist, writer and secretary of the Alliance of Antifascist Intellectuals for the Defence of Culture created in 1936, went into exile in Buenos Aires after Franco's victory. She returned to Spain in 1977. In exile, she published *El Cid Campeador* (1954), a mix of biography and novel for young readers, and then, in 1960, another book entitled *Doña Jimena Díaz de Vivar, gran señora de todos los deberes*. In this book, Jimena, the great lady of all duties, is primarily a mother and spouse, living much of her life in solitude, but always equal to the occasion. Jimena's fate conjures up the civil war and Republican exile; women who suffer war and exile because of the choices men make. María Teresa León was praised after the end of Francoism for returning the Cid to the Spanish people, and a 2010 edition included an illustration representing mourning after the Cid's death with black flags on poles, some decorated with a cross, others with a crescent. This suggests a multicultural Cid, a benevolent leader of all, who is equally mourned by all.

Dolores Oliver Pérez's monograph implicitly offers a Cid who was idolized by at least some Muslims. Arguing for the Arabic authorship of the *Poema* in her *El Cantar de Mío Cid: génesis y autoría árabe*, she claims that generosity, courage, intelligence and moderation are the four virtues of the Cid in the *Poema*, which correspond with those of a *sayyid*, chief, which was also the title given to taifa rulers. Finding parallels with Arabic customs and models, Oliver Pérez draws the conclusion that such knowledge of Arabic customs can only be accounted for by a Muslim author. These conventions are, according to her, pervasive in the *Poema*: they include tricking Jews by lying (giving them two chests filled with sand pretending they contain treasures, in exchange for gold and silver coins); oaths to renounce something that gives one pleasure; augury; women watching their husbands fight; giving thanks to God after military victories; a particular type of warfare using light cavalry practised by Muslims; and what she calls the bedouin concept of honour. This ignores the fact that such customs also existed in Christian Iberia at the time. The final proof is purported respect for Muslims, and never being offensive to Muhammad.

She claimed the author of the *Poema* was the jurist al-Waqqašī (1017/8–1096) at the end of the eleventh century in Valencia, whom the Cid allegedly appointed qāḍī (judge) of Valencia at the request of the Muslim citizens. He features in the *Estoria de España* under the name Alhuacaxi. According to her, authorship by a Muslim legal expert would explain the strong presence of Christian legal terminology in the *Poema*. Such an attribution of authorship is quite impossible and has been discounted by Cid scholars, including Alberto Montaner, who prepared the critical edition of the *Poema*. Moreover, contrary to the legends, al-Waqqašī ultimately fled to Denia and composed a lament on the fall of Valencia to Rodrigo. The suggestion of an Arabic author paying homage to the Cid, however, is symptomatic of the myth of *convivencia*, the idea of a much more harmonious coexistence of Muslims and Christians than the texts on Rodrigo would warrant.

Arturo Pérez-Reverte's *Sidi*, a novel about life on the frontier, sums up the author's verdict on the Cid and his followers: 'they were not bad people . . . nor alien to compassion. Only hard people in a hard world.' Set in the dangerous frontier zone of the Duero, a world without laws where desperate communities live in hardship, under the constant threat of Christian and Muslim raids, the novel tries to reconstruct the eleventh-century world that gave birth to the Cid. Yet the readers' first glimpse of that world is the immediate aftermath of a Moorish attack on a monastery, where they went to kill and pillage. Ruy Díaz first appears with his troops chasing Moors who had taken Christian captives. He is a good warrior and strategist; he also knows the minds of his men. He is introduced as already a legend during the time of his exile, from humble origins, yet able to impel a king to take an oath; having fought numerous battles over fifteen years, he has never been defeated.

He is depicted as a human being with whom the reader can empathize. He is merciful to the girl and her family who cannot help him and his troops at the outset of his exile for fear of the king's revenge; moreover, she reminds him of his own daughters, causing a curious prickling in his throat. The myth of his marriage to Jimena is included, too, updated, and once more making him a sympathetic character. Her father refused her hand in marriage because of Ruy's lower social status, and even struck Ruy's father when he sought the marriage of their children; a duel necessitated by the rules of honour followed, with its fatal outcome. Jimena refused to consummate the marriage out of loyalty to her father, until, finally, Ruy cries in front of her and she pardons him.

King Alfonso VI is squarely to blame for Ruy's exile, vengeful because of the oath of Santa Gadea, finding an excuse when Ruy defends the taifa of Sevilla, where he was sent by the king to collect tribute, from the attack of García Ordóñez and the troops of Granada. Ruy can be brutal, but for a reason: verbally tormenting a captive Moor, he threatens him with a particularly dishonourable death, in order to find out the details of the enemy's strength and movements. He and his men also kill, even captives if they are North Africans, but he does not employ 'unnecessary' cruelty.

He is a Christian who prays and asks for absolution before battle, while also being loyal to those Muslims who are in alliance with his king or himself. Mutamán, ruler of Zaragoza, is a wise and experienced man who sees the injustice and folly of Alfonso in exiling Ruy. Cultured and fearful of the North African fanatics, he envisages a world where Christians and Muslims can live in peace. In turn, Ruy is open to learning from Muslim ideas. He enters Mutamán's service, but refuses ever to fight against Alfonso VI, his lord, and even reserves part of the booty he would take in Mutamán's service for Alfonso. Mutamán and Ruy discover their common humanity; in the end, not much separates them. Ruy and Raxida, Mutamán's sister, even develop a platonic relationship.

In interviews, Pérez-Reverte explained his motivation clearly: Francoism contaminated history, presenting the Cid as a forerunner of Franco; subsequent left-wing governments, instead of cleansing the symbols used by Franco discarded them and never wanted to refer to them. Francoists polluted all the symbols, the entire epic tradition, filling them with cheap jingoism, stupidity and imperial rhetoric. It is this ideological problem that impels people to frown upon heroes and upon epic poetry. Therefore, Pérez-Reverte wanted to show a decontaminated past. The resurgence of right-wing appropriation, he maintained, was only possible because the left had relinquished all claims to the Cid and effectively gifted him to the political right.

While Pérez-Reverte's empathetic reconstruction is immeasurably closer to the medieval world than were Franco's chimeras, the Cid still ends up on a kind of pedestal, allowing and inviting sympathy. While, as he had wanted to, Pérez-Reverte masterfully shows that the Cid was neither a Spanish patriot nor a forerunner of the crusaders, he does not divest him of his almost superhuman fame. It is hard to escape the conclusion that, despite attention to historical realities in so far as the background is concerned, it is not the historical Rodrigo himself, but a figure swathed in the layers of legend that appears. And as long as the Cid continues to be a figure to excite, rouse and elicit sympathy, can we truly escape his lure? I doubt many on the left would sympathize with the historical Rodrigo; the moral frame of reference we use is very different from the one in the eleventh century. We may understand the times and the people such times gave birth to; but would we feel the pull of a man of those times?

The transformation of the Cid in the name of well-meaning ideologies is not the real antidote to Francoist claims and their right-wing revival. However well-intentioned, it is perhaps even more dangerous to try to reshape the Cid as a multicultural hero. The myth of *convivencia*, a more or less harmonious coexistence of Christians and Muslims in the peninsula, may be opposed to that of the *Reconquista*, but it is just as much a myth. While teaching the real history of the eleventh century, and Rodrigo Díaz's place in it, would surely be beneficial, left-wing attempts to cleanse him and thus make him an inappropriate symbol for the right and the far right won't work. Not only because myth cannot be sanitized this way; not only because many attempts to redress the balance end up portraying him in a sympathetic light after all; but because such a strategy has been tried and failed.

Trying to recuperate the Cid for a left-wing agenda is not a new phenomenon, but, rather, has deep roots going back to the nineteenth century. Therefore, in order to understand twenty-first-century attempts to do this, we must first make a detour to the nineteenth century. There was a liberal and republican Cid in the nineteenth and early twentieth centuries. This Cid confronted the powerful, while remaining free and true to himself; alternatively, he rendered loyalty due to the office, while confronting an unworthy person filling that office. His advance was based on his own merits rather than birth, so he could embody the democratic ideal. He rose to significance in early Republicanism, as he was linked to the origins of the Spanish nation, an opponent of absolutism and arbitrary royal power and a defender of liberty. He demonstrated the liberal ideal that personal valour should be a precondition for the exercise of power. He continued to be a reference point for Republicans during the civil war. It did not prevent Franco from laying claim to the Cid.

This liberal and republican heroization of the Cid built on foundations from the early nineteenth century. The 'Anthem of Riego', which became the Republican national anthem, called the liberals, soon seen as all Republicans, 'sons of the Cid'. It was written in 1820 by Evaristo Fernández de San Miguel for the unit of Colonel Rafael de Riego, who helped restore the liberal constitution. (This constitution was written in 1812, but King Ferdinand VII rejected it in favour of absolutist rule in 1814; it was reinstated by the military coup Riego led in 1820.) It briefly became the national anthem in 1822, until the government was overthrown. While never regaining that status, it was used during the first and second Spanish Republics and continued in use under the Republican government in exile.

Serenos, alegres, valientes y osados,
cantemos, soldados, el himno a la lid.
De nuestros acentos el orbe se admire
y en nosotros mire los hijos del Cid.

Serene, happy, valiant and daring
Let us sing, soldiers, the battle hymn.
The world admires our accents
And in us it beholds the sons of the Cid.

The link between the Cid and freedom was so strong that the Cuban painter Armando Menocal, who studied art for some time in Spain, and later took part in the Cuban war of independence against Spain, made a painting in 1889 representing the oath of Santa Gadea, with the Cid towering over a kneeling Alfonso who is touching the gospels on the altar.

The nineteenth- and early twentieth-century battle for the Cid between liberals and nationalists played out in textbooks as well. While Catholic and nationalist history books represented the Cid Campeador as a man of ardent faith, and a glory of the *patria*, which is allegedly exactly why Protestants and freethinkers criticized him or doubted his existence – as in the textbook by Manuel Merry y Colón and Antonio Merry y Villalba, in 1889 – liberals such as Joaquín Costa Martínez and Fernando José de Larra reinterpreted the Cid as the embodiment of constitutionalism or of honour. The strong, romanticized Cid of the nineteenth century was certainly no prototype for the Francoist one; indeed it was one of the culminations of this Romantic vision, José Zorrilla's *Cid* (1882), that inspired the child Pérez-Reverte.

The Cid continued to be evoked by the Republicans in the twentieth century. The poet Antonio Machado, who finally fled to France from Franco's troops, said at the 1937 International Congress of Writers for the Defence of Culture, which was organized to declare solidarity with the people of Spain and express a rejection of fascism: 'There will be no shortage of those who think that today the shades of the Cid's sons-in-law accompany the factious armies and advise them to do deeds as lamentable as that of the Corpes oak grove . . . But I believe, with all my soul, that Rodrigo's shade accompanies our heroic militiamen and that in the Judgment of God that today, as then, takes place on the banks of the Tagus, the best will triumph again. Or it will be necessary to disrespect the divinity itself.'

As the civil war raged, so a war of words also erupted over the Cid. He became a point of direct controversy, with both sides claiming him as their own. Republicans now played up the Cid, slayer of Muslims, against Franco's reliance on Moroccan troops. The parallel was too perfect: a fight against invaders from North Africa, called in by locals.

Although with Franco's victory the Catholic national vision triumphed in Spain, the left-wing interpretation of the Cid was kept alive by Republicans in exile, but now focusing on his suffering in exile and the injustice of the king who had banished him. This tradition of a liberal and Republican Cid was no obstacle to the Francoist annexation of the hero. Equally, to return, even in modified form, to the pre-Francoist Cid, will not eliminate right-wing appropriations today. A champion of democracy and opponent of a Catholic monolithic nation; peacefully coexisting with and learning from Muslims, rather than a rabid supremacist intent on exterminating Muslims; a sympathetic person who did his best in rough times – these portrayals simply keep the legend alive. And because, at the root of all the stories, there is the historical epoch of bloody wars, it will not be possible to divorce the Cid from violence. What Spain, and our world, needs is not another blood-spattered hero, but rational, consensual government.

Does this mean that the Cid must be abandoned to the political right? It is his heroization that must be abandoned. He did not stand for the control of tyrannical monarchical power; rather, he wanted power. He was not a victim of irrational vengeful ire, nor of a tragic accident that kept his beloved from him for a long period. Instead of turning him into a sympathetic figure fit for a democratic or multicultural age, we need to see him as a man who killed and plundered for a living. Of course, he was conditioned by his times, as we are by ours. That does not make him a model, or even someone with whom we should sympathize.

Epilogue: Fascination and Repugnance

What term would best encapsulate the essential characteristics of the historical Rodrigo? After the first historical works, and especially the nineteenth-century research of Reinhart Dozy, which deprived him of his legendary fame, he was branded a 'mercenary' as a counterpoint to the legendary Christian hero. This designation insisted on his service, for pay, for the Muslim rulers of Zaragoza, because it was exactly this aspect of the historical Rodrigo that was first erased and distorted by later legends, which turned him into an untarnished hero. For Dozy, the point of this terminology was to signal that the Cid was fighting without faith and law, for either Muslims or Christians. Menéndez Pidal's angry criticism of the word 'mercenary', which he believed belittled and maligned the Cid, included the claims that the Cid did not change lords, that unlike mercenaries he was loyal to King Alfonso and that he had a Castilian fatherland. Menéndez Pidal's assertions, however, did not stand up to rigorous textual analysis.

There have been gentler tugs of war between scholars on the choicest word. Some modern scholars have returned to the 'mercenary' label, notably Richard Fletcher. Peter Linehan called el Cid 'an entrepreneur by conviction – an entrepreneur of substance . . . Clearly, there are problems about regarding the Cid as a "Christian hero". Evidently, he was a freebooter who offered what he had to offer wherever he could secure the best price for it.' Brian Catlos cautiously modified this a little, writing, 'it is extremely doubtful that he saw himself in anything but the vaguest of terms as a participant in a teleologically driven mission to restore Hispania to Christendom'. Simon Barton claimed that the donation charter to the bishopric of Valencia from 1098 'can help us to steer a path between . . . seemingly implacably opposed positions'. These are on the one hand the revisionist claim that 'El Cid's operations were altogether devoid of the heroic, pious, patriotic content which later generations would ascribe to them; Rodrigo Díaz was his own man, no more, no less, . . . the hard-nosed, pragmatic Rodrigo Díaz, the ruthless soldier of fortune', and, on the other hand, 'the patriotic, Christian El Cid, champion of the *Reconquista*'. Yet, since the representation of Rodrigo in the charter was already the first step on the way to the legend, it cannot counterbalance the other evidence; we do not discover a more balanced image of Rodrigo, but rather, the nascent myth, through the charter.

More recently, the use of the word 'mercenary' has been criticized from a different angle. David Porrinas González pointed out that, at most, Rodrigo could only be called a mercenary during his years of service in the taifa of Zaragoza, while his actions before and after those years were not those of a mercenary: before that, he served the Christian kings as so many other vassals did, and afterwards he carved out his own principality. Thus, the argument goes, he should be called a warlord rather than a mercenary. While it is true that, in its technical sense as a soldier hired for service, 'mercenary' does not describe Rodrigo's entire career, and that, unlike him, there were indeed later mercenaries who spent their entire lives as paid soldiers of fortune, in its meaning as someone motivated by a desire for gain the term does characterize him rather well. He was indeed, in Simon Barton's words, a 'pragmatic opportunist, who skilfully exploited the fluid political conditions of his time'. Above all, the 'mercenary' label deprives him of the halo that even the term warlord does not undermine. The French scholar Ernest Renan (1823–92) was right to point out that no hero lost more than the Cid when he passed from legend to history. Yet so many people, even some historians, cannot quite resist elevating the Cid to something more than a successful, opportunistic warrior. He was a man of his times, and men of those times attached honour to victories and booty, but in the twenty-first century we need not accept that perspective and continue to lionize him.

It is important to emphasize that Rodrigo was far from the only one operating across the supposed Christian–Muslim divide. Tenth-century Umayyad caliphs had the support of some Christian lords in frontier regions in their incursions against the northern Christians. In the twelfth century, Tello Fernández and Reverter, lord of La Guardia de Montserrat, were in the service of the Almoravid ruler in the Maghreb. Even in the late twelfth century, Christians were in the service of Almohads, the next rigorist Moroccan regime. Fernando Rodríguez de Castro first gained fame in the service of Fernando II of León, but then transferred his loyalty to the Almohads and in 1174 attacked Leonese territory. Even the multiple switching of loyalties back and forth is attested in some high-profile cases. Fernando Rodríguez de Castro's son Pedro Fernández participated in the Battle of Alarcos in 1195 on the Almohad side, defeating Alfonso VIII of Castile; he was then instrumental in bringing about an alliance between the Almohad caliph Yaʿqūb al-Manṣūr and Alfonso IX of León. He was excommunicated by Pope Celestine III in 1196, yet managed to return to León-Castile, only to finally seek refuge in the Maghreb.

Some Christians entered Muslim service because they were exiled, such as Lorenzo Suárez Gallinato, banished by Fernando III before 1236, who entered the service of the Muslim ruler of Ecija. Others just sought greater opportunities and wealth. One of the best-known figures in that respect is Geraldo Sem Pavor ('without fear'). According to one account: 'The dog [Gerald] marched on rainy and very dark nights, with strong wind and snow, towards the cities and, having prepared very large wooden ladders for scaling [walls], so that they could pass over the wall of the city, . . . when the group had completed scaling the highest wall in the city, they shouted in their language with an abominable screech, and they entered the city and fought whomever they found and robbed them and took captive and prisoner all who were there.' His conquests included Évora, and Beja during a period when the Portuguese and Leonese on the one hand and the Almohads on the other were locked in warfare, creating opportunities for freelancing (1172). When things got tight in Portugal, he offered his services to the caliph and ended up in Morocco. He became the governor of southern areas, but he entered into a secret correspondence with the Portuguese ruler to prepare an invasion of Morocco. When the plot was discovered, he was put to death.

As late as the thirteenth century, Almohad rulers of Morocco employed numerous Christian mercenaries; some of them broadcast their intentions prior to leaving the Iberian peninsula, and even recruited others to accompany them. Some settled with their families in the Maghreb. Nor were these mercenaries, who were seeking gain or escaping from their enemies, the only ones to cross the supposed religious divide; magnates and rulers also sought help against co-religionists from religious enemies, even after the Battle of Las Navas de Tolosa that briefly united Christian Iberian rulers against Muslims. Such figures included Fernando Núñez de Lara who died at the Almohad court, and Sancho VII of Navarre who sought Almohad help in self-defence against Castile and Aragón. Disaffected noblemen left the court of Alfonso X in 1272 and became vassals of the ruler of Granada; it seems this was a way to put pressure on Alfonso, since these exiles regained royal favour the following year.

Why are the others relatively unknown even among scholars, and certainly among the wider public, when the Cid is internationally famous? It is so tempting to see it as a result of some inherent quality of Rodrigo Díaz himself. Yet, however he excelled as a warrior, the only historical kernel for his fame consists of his successes against the Almoravids and his descendants' reasons for both whitewashing and lionizing him. Indeed, in the medieval period some other warriors were similarly exalted, with poems written about them; retrospectively they were also turned into patrons of monasteries. But the Cid's fame took off in a way the others' renown did not. The story of the Cid's fame is a story of many protagonists, and not of one hero; for heroes are made through the agency of many people. Jimena, the monks of San Pedro de Cardeña, the royal court, the citizens of Burgos, novelists, historians and politicians – all participated in transforming him. In each retelling, his story was tailored to the expectations of the period and to the needs of those who extolled him. That is how he could adopt so many different guises, and have so many, even completely contradictory, faces. The man who was celebrated as a warrior and successful plunderer could be exalted for the bloody killing of enemies in one retelling, while in another, later one, he could be portrayed as a perfect peace-loving gentleman. The story of his exile appealed to those themselves exiled for political reasons centuries later. The legend of the oath of Santa Gadea spoke to those who wanted the powerful to be accountable to the people. The Cid could be turned into the perfect patriot or the multicultural hero. He could be cast as the embodiment of Spanish national identity, and as an international figure.

As he passed into legend, it was increasingly easy to select the part of the story, choose those facts or those elements of the myth that suited the aims of the person or group wishing to make use of the Cid. He became a hero for all who wanted a hero, easily customizable in myriad different directions.

He was none of the things later generations claimed him to be. He was a successful warrior at a time when fighting was endemic and violence, military victory and looting made men famous. Those conflicts were not part of a clash of civilizations, nor was a society protecting itself from murderous conquerors. In fact, should we wish to formulate the conflict in terms of civilizations, the world of Islam at the time was both far more advanced and more tolerant than that of Christianity. Eleventh-century warfare did not consist of the 'good' fighting against the 'bad'; it was part of a messy process of conquest and counter-conquest, brutality and death, which coexisted with one of learning. Europeans gained more advanced scientific knowledge from Muslims, and fruitful hybridity developed in Spain through the cross-fertilization of multiple languages and cultures.

Why do we create heroes from the likes of the Cid? It may be straightforward why a military dictator was fascinated by such a figure, but Franco was far from alone, and even those who abhorred murder and wished for reconciliation were drawn to the Cid. Some Spaniards today say Franco besmirched the Cid, and the left is partly to blame for allowing the right to capitalize on el Cid. Part of the problem, however, is why those who do not believe in warfare and murder as the highest endeavour for mankind insist on seeing the Cid as a hero. Military success dressed up in providential garb was a sufficient basis initially to celebrate a mythologized Rodrigo. His transformation continued until he became the ideal man, strong, brave, invincible, who prefers peace to war, but will fight successfully when forced to do so, who fights for values we can all embrace, for a more humane society. We thus imagine a perfect hero. We need perfect heroes in our fantasy; in times of peace and plenty we still want the comfort of believing that there are people out there who uphold and would defend concord and our way of life. In times of man-made disasters, amid economic catastrophe and war, we desperately need to hope that good ultimately triumphs over bad. We put our faith in mythologized historical figures and fictional heroes, such as el Cid and Tolkien's Lord Aragorn.

The historical Rodrigo was no Francoist; he was no Lord Aragorn either. As we understand him in his own context and understand the circumstances and reasons for his transformation, it becomes clear that in our illusionary comfort is our danger; Lord Aragorns don't walk this earth, but Francos do. When we make heroes of historical figures, the lines between reality and our dreams become blurred, but the former, however obscured, has a far-reaching legacy. The Cid's fame is ultimately founded on glorified killing; this can always be reclaimed as the baseline for the adoration of new audiences.

In his 2010 article 'In Search of the Eternal Nation', Simon Barton wrote:

> True, the figure of the Cid continues to keep numerous academics in gainful employment and is the subject of umpteen publications and conferences, as well as a children's cartoon and even a rock song, but he is no longer invoked by politicians and intellectuals as a role model for twenty-first century Spaniards to follow and emulate . . . Who is to say that at some point in the future, in the renewed search for *cohesión social* or *solidaridad nacional*, the collective memory of the Cid and the *Reconquista*, so lovingly and passionately articulated by Menéndez Pidal, will not be dusted down by his fellow Spaniards and pressed into service once more?

Barton's words proved to be chillingly prophetic, but just how quickly they would come true, with the new rise of the political right, nobody would have imagined in 2010. The Cid can be recast as a tolerant multicultural figure just as easily as a forerunner of bloody, faith-based war. His story lends itself to such appropriation through the selective choice of episodes and warped interpretations. Yet we should beware of even the best-intentioned multicultural reconfiguration. We can build our own society to live and let live; do we need to justify this through the use of distorted historical figures? For the historical Rodrigo does not fit this mould; indeed, he does not fit any of the modern moulds. He did not fight for the faith and he was not tolerant. We need to understand him in the context of his own age, where it was acceptable both to kill in the name of religion, but also to plunder and fight people regardless of their religion. It was equally possible to ally with those of another faith, but this was not multiculturalism, it obeyed the opportunistic dictates of a warrior society.

Of course, literary epic heroes are never true depictions of flesh and blood people; their role is to entertain, or to strengthen some social group's solidarity. Neither of those depends on historicity and a truthful mirroring of reality. Yet the problem is that audiences do start to mix up the literary image with truth. Ramón Menéndez Pidal is an excellent example; despite his erudition, despite his profession, he, too, fell for the lure of literary fiction. That is why purely fictional heroes serve us better. We are better off creating fantasy figures who embody perfection, rather than misleading ourselves that we can find them in reality.

Would Rodrigo Díaz have enjoyed such posthumous attention? He certainly yearned for fame and immortality, as warriors of his status at the time did. Yet he may have been bemused to find himself the centre of so much attention, in so many guises. Nothing remains of the Cid's Valencia, not even the Turia river. Visitors today can walk in a park in the old riverbed. They can also take the metro to the beach; there is no fortified wall there, only palm trees, cafés and restaurants line the shore. The peaceful murmur of the sea fills the air. We cannot resuscitate the past; we attempt to do so at our peril.

Acknowledgements

I am grateful to Carlos Reglero de la Fuente and Pascual Martínez Sopena, as well as the University of Valladolid for hosting me and facilitating my research. I thank Fernando Gutierrez Baños, who gave me advice on the Cristo de las Batallas, and Rodrigo García-Velasco, who drew my attention to an article on Franco and Muslims. Very many thanks to Juliet Brooke, Charlotte Humphery, Nico Parfitt and Richard Collins for their enthusiastic work on the book.

Sources and Studies

ʿAbd Allāh ibn Buluggīn, *The Tibyān: Memoirs of ʿAbd Allāh b. Buluggīn, the last Zīrid Amīr of Granada*, trans. Amin T. Tibi (Leiden: Brill, 1986).

Aberth, John, *A Knight at the Movies: Medieval History on Film* (New York: Routledge, 2003).

Al Tuma, Ali, 'Moros y Cristianos: Religious Aspects of the Participation of Moroccan Soldiers in the Spanish Civil War', in *Muslims in Interwar Europe: A Transcultural Historical Perspective*, ed. Bekim Agai, et al. (Leiden and Boston: Brill, 2016): 151–177.

Alvar, Carlos, Martin Gómez Redondo and Georges Martin, *El Cid: de la materia épica a las crónicas caballerescas: actas del congreso internacional 'IX centenario de la muerte del Cid', celebrado en la Univ. de Alcalá de Henares los días 19 y 20 de noviembre de 1999* (Alcalá de Henares, Madrid: Servicio de Publicaciones de La Universidad de Alcalá, 2002).

Ayala Martínez, Carlos de, 'Podemos seguir hablando de "reconquista"? Nacimiento y desarrollo de una ideología', *Al-Andalus y la Historia* 10 September 2018, https://www.alandalusylahistoria.com/?p=474

Bailey, Matthew, ed. and trans., *Las Mocedades de Rodrigo. The Youthful Deeds of Rodrigo, the Cid* (Toronto: University of Toronto Press, 2007).

Balfour, Sebastian, *The End of the Spanish Empire, 1898–1923* (Oxford: Oxford University Press, 1997).

Barton, Simon, *The Aristocracy in Twelfth-Century León and Castile* (Cambridge: Cambridge University Press, 1997).

Barton, Simon, 'Traitors to the Faith? Christian Mercenaries in al-Andalus and the Maghreb, *c.*1100–1300', in *Medieval Spain: Culture, Conflict, and Coexistence: Studies in Honour of Angus MacKay*, ed. Roger Collins and Anthony Goodman (London: Palgrave Macmillan, 2002): 23–45.

Barton, Simon, *A History of Spain*, 2nd edn (Basingstoke and New York: Palgrave Macmillan, 2009).

Barton, Simon, 'In Search of the Eternal Nation: Ramón Menéndez Pidal and the History of Spain', in *Ramón Menéndez Pidal after Forty Years: A Reassessment*, ed. Juan-Carlos Conde (London: Department of Hispanic Studies, Queen Mary University of London, 2010): 95–110.

Barton, Simon, 'El Cid, Cluny and the Medieval Spanish Reconquista', *English Historical Review* 126 (2011): 517–543.

Barton, Simon, *Conquerors, Brides and Concubines: Interfaith Relations and Social Power in Medieval Iberia* (Philadelphia: University of Pennsylvania Press, 2015).

Barton, Simon, and Richard Fletcher, trans., *The World of el Cid: Chronicles of the Spanish Reconquest* (Manchester and New York: Manchester University Press, 2000).

Basilio, Miriam M., *Visual Propaganda, Exhibitions, and the Spanish Civil War* (London and New York: Routledge, 2017).

Bautista, Francisco, 'Sancho II y Rodrigo Campeador en la Chronica naierensis', *e-Spania* 7 June 2009, https://doi.org/10.4000/e-spania.18101

Beck, Lauren, *Illustrating El Cid, 1498 to Today* (Montreal and Kingston: McGill-Queen's University Press, 2019).

Beevor, Antony, *The Spanish Civil War* (London: Cassell, 1982).

Berganza, Francisco de, *Antigüedades de España propugnadas en las noticias de sus reyes, en la corónica del Real Monasterio de San Pedro de Cardeña, en historias, cronicones y otros instrumentos manuscritos que hasta ahora no han visto la luz pública*, 2 vols (Madrid: Francisco del Hierro, 1719–1721).

Bolorinos Allard, Elisabeth, 'The Crescent and the Dagger: Representations of the Moorish Other during the Spanish Civil War', *Bulletin of Spanish Studies* (2015): 96588. DOI: 10.1080/14753820.2015.1082811

Boyd, Carolyn P., *Historia Patria: Politics, History and National Identity in Spain 1875–1975* (Princeton: Princeton University Press, 1997).

Camino del Cid: https://www.caminodelcid.org/

Casanova, Julián, *The Spanish Republic and Civil War* (Cambridge: Cambridge University Press, 2010).

Castillo Robles, María José, 'María Teresa León y doña Jimena, mujeres de España', *Philologica Urcitana: Revista Semestral de Iniciación a la Investigación en Filología* 9 (September 2013): 17–41.

Corneille, Pierre, *Le Cid, Tragi-Comédie 1637*, ed. Jean Serroy (Paris: Gallimard, 1993).

Costa, Joaquín, *Crisis política de España: doble llave al sepulcro del Cid*, 5th edn (Madrid: Biblioteca Costa, 1914).

Crónica del famoso cavallero Cid Ruy Díez Campeador (Burgos, 1512, reprint New York: De Vinne Press, 1903).

Dávila, Gil González, *Historia del origen del Cristo de las Batallas (Una devoción popular salmantina)* (Salamanca: Instituto de las Identidades, 2018).

Deyermond, A. D., *Epic Poetry and the Clergy: Studies on the 'Mocedades de Rodrigo'* (London: Tamesis Books, 1968).

Domke, Joan, *Education, Fascism, and the Catholic Church in Franco's Spain, 1936–1975* (Saarbrücken: VDM Verlag Dr Müller, 2011).

Dozy, Reinhart Pieter Anne, *Le Cid d'après de nouveaux documents* (Leiden: Brill, 1860).

El Cid en el teatro de los siglos de Oro, exhibition catalogue (Burgos: Instituto Castellano y Leonés de la Lengua, 2007).

Escobar, Ángel and Alberto Montaner, eds, *Carmen Campidoctoris o Poema latino del Campeador* (Madrid: Sociedad Estatal España Nuevo Milenio, 2001).

Fletcher, Richard, *The Quest for El Cid* (New York and Oxford: Oxford University Press, 1989).

Flores, Javier, 'Entrevista a Arturo Pérez-Reverte', *Historia National Geographic*, 23 August 2021, https://historia.nationalgeographic.com.es/a/arturo-perez-reverte-eso-que-cid-era-patriota-espanol-es-mentira_14733

Funes, Leonardo and Felipe Tenenbaum, *Mocedades de Rodrigo: Estudio y Edición de Los Tres Estados Del Texto* (Woodbridge, Suffolk: Tamesis Books, 2004).

García-Sanjuán, Alejandro, 'Rejecting al-Andalus, exalting the Reconquista: Historical memory in contemporary Spain', *Journal of Medieval Iberian Studies* (2016): 127–145.

González de Santiago, Ignacio, 'El Arco de Santa María de Burgos', *Boletín del Seminario de Estudios de Arte y Arqueología* 55 (1989): 289–306.

Hernández Alonso, César, ed., *El Cid, Poema e Historia: Actas del Congreso Internacional (12–16 de julio, 1999)* (Burgos: Ayuntamiento de Burgos, 2000).

Hook, David, 'A marginal sketch in BL, Additional MS. 25690, the Cronica del Cid Campeador, and the legend of the "Jura de Santa Gadea"', *The British Library Journal* 22, No. 2 (1996): 186–192.

Jaspert, Nikolas, 'Christian expatriates in Muslim lands: The many roles of Aragonese mercenaries in medieval North Africa', in *Military Diasporas: Building of Empire in the Middle East and Europe (500 BCE–1500 CE)*, ed. Georg Christ, Patrick Sänger, Mike Carr (London: Routledge, 2022): 194–233.

Jerez, Enrique, *Dos españoles en la historia: el Cid y Ramón Menéndez Pidal* (Madrid: Biblioteca Nacional de España, 2019).

Lacarra, María Eugenia, 'La utilización del Cid de Menéndez Pidal en la ideologia militar franquista', *Ideologies and Literature: A Journal of Hispanic and Luso-Brazilian Literatures* 3 (1980): 95–127.

Lacombe, Claude, 'De la Iglesia Santa María hasta la Catedral Nueva con Jerónimo de Périgueux, primer obispo de Salamanca desde la Reconquista y el Cristo de las Batallas', in *La catedral de Salamanca. De 'Fortis' a 'Magna'*, ed. Mariano Casas Hernández (Salamanca: Diputación Provincial de Salamanca, 2014): 1141–1190.

Lázaro, Margarita, 'Por qué a la derecha le pone tanto el Cid', 18 December 2020 *Huffingtonpost.es*, https://www.huffingtonpost.es/entry/derecha-ultraderecha-cid-campeador-relacion_es_5fd9f553c5b62f31c201f623.html

Lévi-Provençal, Évariste, 'La prise de Valence par le Cid, d'après les sources musulmanes et l'original arabe de la "Crónica General de España"', *Islam d'Occident: Études d'histoire médiévale* (Paris: Maisonneuve, 1948): 187–238.

Linehan, Peter, *History and the Historians of Medieval Spain* (Oxford: Oxford University Press, 1993).

Marrodán Ezquerro, Jesús, *San Pedro de Cardeña, historia y arte* (Burgos: Aldecoa, 1985).

Martin, Georges, 'Le premier témoignage chrétien sur la prise de Valence (1098)', *e-Spania* 10 December 2010, https://doi.org/10.4000/e-spania.21583

Martín, Óscar, 'Sobre héroes, tumbas y reyes: Cardeña, 1512 y la publicación de la Crónica particular', *Boletín de la Biblioteca de Menéndez Pelayo* 83 (2007): 49–64.

Martínez Díez, Gonzalo, *El Cid histórico* (Barcelona: Planeta, 1999).

Martínez Frías, José, 'La nueva imagen visual de Cristo de las Batallas de la Catedral de Salamanca', in *Alma Ars: Estudios de Arte e Historia en homenaje al Dr Salvador Andrés Ordax*, ed. Miguel Ángel Zalama and Pilar Mogollón Cano-Cortés (Valladolid: Ediciones Universidad de Valladolid, 2013): 329–334.

Menéndez Pidal, Ramón, 'Autógrafos inéditos del Cid y de Jimena en dos diplomas de 1098 y 1101', *Revista de Filología Española* 5 (1918): 1–20.

Menéndez Pidal, Ramón, *El Cid en la historia* (Madrid: Jiménez y Molina, 1921).

Menéndez Pidal, Ramón, *La España del Cid* (Madrid: Espasa-Calpe, 1929).

Menéndez Pidal, Ramón, *El Cid Campeador* (Buenos Aires: Espasa-Calpe, S.A., 1950).

Menéndez Pidal, Ramón, ed., *Primera Crónica General de España* (Madrid: Gredos, 1977).

Molina, Luis and Alberto Montaner, 'Nota bibliográfica: El Cantar de mio Cid y su supuesta autoría árabe. El Cantar de mio Cid and its supposed Arabic author', *Al-Qantara* XXXI 1 (2010): 311–323 https://digital.csic.es/bitstream/10261/27822/1/Molina_Resena_Oliver.pdf

Monreal, Violeta, *Las espadas del Cid* (Madrid: Bruño, 2006).

Montaner Frutos, Alberto, 'Ficción y falsificación en el cartulario cidiano', *Cahiers d'Études Hispaniques Médiévales* (2006): 327–357.

Montaner Frutos, Alberto, 'La "carta de arras" del Cid: Algunas precisiones diplomáticas, filológias y jurídicas', *E-legal history review* 4 (2007).

Montaner Frutos, Alberto, 'Rodrigo el Campeador como princeps en los siglos XI y XII', *e-Spania* 10 December 2010, https://journals.openedition.org/e-spania/20201

Montaner Frutos, Alberto, ed., *Cantar de Mio Cid* (Galaxia Gutenberg; Real Academia Española, 2011).

Montaner Frutos, Alberto, 'El corpus cidiano: de los primeros textos al Cantar de mio Cid', *Cahiers d'études hispaniques médiévales* (2017, no. 1): 131–136.

Montaner Frutos, Alberto, 'Las reliquias cidianas', in *El culto a las reliquias: Interpretación, difusión y ritos*, ed. Francisco J. Alfaro and Carolina Naya, (Zaragoza: Servicio de Publicaciones, Universidad de Zaragoza, 2018): 99–106.

Moreno Martín, Francisco J., ed. *El franquismo y la apropriación del pasado: el uso de la historia, de la arqueología y de la historia del arte para la legitimación de la dictadura* (Madrid: Pablo Iglesias, 2017).

Oliver Pérez, Dolores, *El Cantar de Mío Cid: génesis y autoría árabe* (Almería: Fundación Ibn Tufayl de Estudios Árabes, 2008).

Peña Pérez, Francisco Javier, *El Cid Campeador: Historia, leyenda y mito* (Burgos: Dossoles, 2000).

Peña Pérez, Francisco Javier, 'Los monjes de san Pedro de Cardeña y el mito del Cid', in *Memoria, mito y realidad en la historia medieval: XIII Semana de*

Estudios Medievales, Nájera, del 29 de julio al 2 de agosto de 2002, ed. José Ignacio de la Iglesia Duarte and José Luis Martín Rodríguez (Logroño: Instituto de Estudios Riojanos, 2003): 331–344.

Peña Pérez, F. Javier, *El surgimiento de una nación: Castilla en su historia y en su mitos* (Barcelona: Crítica, 2005).

Pérez-Reverte, Arturo, *Sidi: un relato de frontera* (Miami: Penguin Random House, 2019).

https://www.perezreverte.com/articulo/perez-reverte/1108/sidi-un-relato-de-frontera/

Peterson, David, 'The Castilian Origins of the Epithet *Mio Cid*', *Bulletin of Hispanic Studies* 98, No. 3 (2021): 213–229.

Piechocki, Julia Magdalena, *El Cristo de las Batallas en la Catedral Nueva y el Cristo pectoral del Cid en la torre medieval de la Catedral vieja de Salamanca*, MPhil dissertation, Vienna 2012.

Poema de Mio Cid. The Poem of my Cid, trans. Peter Such and John Hodgkinson, 2nd edn (Warminster: Aris & Phillips, 1991).

Porrinas González, David, *El Cid: Historia y mito de un señor de la guerra*, 6th edn (Madrid: Desperta Ferro Ediciones, 2021).

Preston, Paul, *Franco* (London: HarperCollins, 1993).

Preston, Paul, *The Spanish Civil War: Reaction, Revolution & Revenge* (London and New York: Harper Perennial, 2006).

Ratcliffe, Marjorie, 'Diego, hijo del Cid y la fecha de composición del Cantar del Mio Cid', *Dicenda: Cuadernos de Filología Hispánica* 9 (1990): 163–169.

Reilly, Bernard F., *The Kingdom of León-Castilla under King Alfonso VI, 1065–1109* (Princeton: Princeton University Press, 1988).

Riquer, Martín de, 'Babieca, caballo del Cid Campeadro y Bauçan, caballo de Guillaume d'Orange', *Boletín de la Real Academia de Buenas Letras de Barcelona* XXV (1953): 127–144.

Rodiek, Christoph, *Die internationale Cid-Reception: Sujet – Kontext – Gattung* (Berlin and New York: Walter de Gruyter, 1990).

Romero Salvadó, Francisco J., *Twentieth-Century Spain: Politics and Society in Spain, 1898–1998* (Basingstoke and New York: Palgrave Macmillan, 1999).

Salustiano Moreta Velayos, *El Monasterio de San Pedro de Cardeña: Historia de un dominio monástico castellano (902–1338)* (Salamanca: Ediciones Universidad de Salamanca, 1971).

Santos, Francisco, *La verdad en el potro y el Cid resucitado* (Madrid: L. A. de Bedmar, 1686).

Savo, Anita, 'History and Story in Amazon's El Cid (2020)',

https://www.europenowjournal.org/2021/05/10/history-and-story-in-amazons-el-cid-2020/

Shasha, David, 'Charlton Heston's "El Cid": A Hero for Our Time', 15 August 2010 https://www.huffpost.com/entry/charlton-hestons-el-cid-a_b_679711

Smith, Colin, 'The Cid as Charlemagne in the Leyenda de Cardeña', *Romania* 97 (1976): 509–531.

Smith, Colin, 'The diffusion of the Cid cult: A survey and a little-known document', *Journal of Medieval History* (1980): 37–60.

Smith, Colin, *The Making of the Poema de Mio Cid* (Cambridge: Cambridge University Press, 1983).

Southey, Robert, *The Chronicle of the Cid* (New York: Dodd, Mead & Company, 1883).

Thiébault, Paul-Charles-François, *Mémoires du Général Baron Thiébault* (Paris: E. Plon, 1893).

Ticknor, George, *History of Spanish Literature*, vol. 1, 4th edn (Boston: Houghton Mifflin, 1863).

Zadarenko, Irene, *El monasterio de Cardeña y el inicio de la épica cidiana* (Alcalá de Henares: Universidad de Alcalá de Henares, 2013).

Index

Nora Berend is Professor of European History in the Faculty of History at the University of Cambridge. She has worked on medieval social and religious history, including minorities and state building. Her publishing on medieval history includes *At the Gate of Christendom: Jews, Muslims and Pagans in Medieval Hungary c. 1000–c. 1300*, which won the Royal Historical Society's Gladstone Prize. Her fascination with modern uses of medieval history and love of Spain lead her to the Cid.